MUGHAL CULTURE

Encyclopaedic History of India Series

MUGHAL CULTURE

Dr. Mahesh Vikram Singh
Professor, Deptt. of History
Mahatma Gandhi Kashi Vidyapeeth
Varanasi (UP)

Dr. Brij Bhushan Shrivastava
Head of Deptt., Ancient History, Archeology & Culture
SMMTPG College, Ballia (UP)

CENTRUM PRESS
NEW DELHI-110002 (INDIA)

CENTRUM PRESS
H.O.: 4360/4, Ansari Road, Daryaganj,
New Delhi-110002 (India)
Tel: 23278000, 23261597, 23255577, 23286875
B.O.: No. 1015, Ist Main Road, BSK IIIrd Stage,
IIIrd Phase, IIIrd Block, Bangalore-560085 (INDIA)
Tel: 080-41723429
Email: centrumpress@gmail.com
Visit us at: www.centrumpress.com

Mughal Culture

First Edition, 2011

ISBN 978-93-80836-77-5

PRINTED IN INDIA

Printed at Mehra Offset Press, Delhi

प्रो. विपिन चंद्रा
अध्यक्ष
Prof. Bipan Chandra
Chairman

नेशनल बुक ट्रस्ट, इंडिया
नेहरू भवन
5 इंस्टीट्यूशनल एरिया, फेज़-II, वसंत कुंज, नई दिल्ली-110 070
फोन/ Phone: 011-26121880 फैक्स/ Fax: 011-26121883
NATIONAL BOOK TRUST, INDIA
Nehru Bhawan
5 Institutional Area, Phase II, Vasant Kunj, New Delhi-110 070
ई-मेल / E-mail. chairman@nbtindia.org.in
वेबसाइट / Website: www.nbtindia.org.in

FOREWORD

The term 'history' is derived from the Greek word 'historia' that means knowledge acquired through investigation. Obviously, this knowledge can be correct if the method of investigation is objective and not vitiated by any kind of bias. In other words, if the study of human past is comprehensive and obtained through scientific inquiry, it can provide perspective on the present day problems and help one plan for the future.

A true historian has to identify the sources that can be most useful in a given context. Documents, coins, archaeology, anthropology, geography, travel accounts, oral traditions, mythology and so on can be useful but they can be used only after their veracity is tested and they are critically examined. They should be checked and counter-checked.

Over the centuries, one finds the study and writing of history vitiated by biases. There are numerous instances in which historical data have been distorted to support or oppose certain preconceived ideas and purposes. Strictly speaking such history is just like fiction to accord with preconceived notions and serve some ulterior purposes.

The study of the past has never been static. Conclusions go on changing because of the discovery of new materials and tools of investigation. To give a concrete example, the carbon 14 or radiocarbon dating test has revolutionized the study of civilizations and settlements, especially of prehistoric times, for which written documents, coins, etc. are seldom available. This method has enabled historians to determine more accurately than before the time period of a particular civilization or settlement. This method was discovered only 70 years ago by American scientists.

In our country, excavations brought to light the Indus Valley Civilization and its various features, hitherto unknown. Similarly, no complete text of Kautilya's Arthashastra was available before it was discovered by Shamasastry, the chief of the Mysore Government Oriental Library in the first decade of the last century. Likewise, people's knowledge of the history of the Buddhist period got extended after excavations at Sarnath and the ruins of the Asokan period at Patna. In the future, if the Harappan inscriptions are deciphered, our knowledge of the Indus Valley Civilization will increase enormously. All these instances underline the fact that our knowledge of history is never static and its frontiers go on extending.

In the light of what has been said above the encyclopedic history is going to be of great help to students interested in Indian history. It is comprehensive and as far as possible free from biases. It includes the latest materials, and objective conclusions.

Prof . Bipan Chandra

Professor Emeritus, JNU

Chairman, National Book Trust, India

Contents

Preface

The people of India have had a continuous civilization since 2500 B.C., when the inhabitants of the Indus River valley developed an urban culture based on commerce and sustained by agricultural trade. This civilization declined around 1500 B.C., probably due to ecological changes. During the second millennium B.C., pastoral, Aryan-speaking tribes migrated from the northwest into the subcontinent. As they settled in the middle Ganges River valley, they adapted to antecedent cultures.

The political map of ancient and medieval India was made up of myriad kingdoms with fluctuating boundaries. In the 4th and 5th centuries A.D., northern India was unified under the Gupta Dynasty. During this period, known as India's Golden Age, Hindu culture and political administration reached new heights. Islam spread across the Indian subcontinent over a period of 500 years. In the 10th and 11th centuries, Turks and Afghans invaded India and established sultanates in Delhi. In the early 16th century, descendants of Genghis Khan swept across the Khyber Pass and established the Mughal (Mogul) Dynasty, which lasted for 200 years. From the 11th to the 15th centuries, southern India was dominated by Hindu Chola and Vijayanagar Dynasties. During this time, the two systems—the prevailing Hindu and Muslim—mingled, leaving lasting cultural influences on each other.

The first British outpost in South Asia was established in 1619 at Surat on the northwestern coast. Later in the century, the East India Company opened permanent trading stations at Madras, Bombay, and Calcutta, each under the protection of native rulers. The British expanded their influence from these footholds until, by the 1850s, they controlled most of present-day India, Pakistan, and Bangladesh. In 1857, a rebellion in north India led by mutinous Indian soldiers caused the British Parliament to transfer all political power from the East India Company to the Crown. Great Britain began administering most of India directly while controlling the rest through treaties with local rulers.

In the late 1800s, the first steps were taken toward self-government in British India with the appointment of Indian councillors to advise the British viceroy and the establishment of provincial councils with Indian members; the British subsequently widened participation in legislative councils. Beginning in 1920, Indian leader Mohandas K. Gandhi transformed the Indian National Congress political party into a mass movement to campaign against British colonial rule.

—Authors

1

Mughal Architecture

Mughal architecture, an amalgam of Islamic, Persian and Indian architecture, is the distinctive style developed by the Mughals in the 16th and 17th centuries in what is now India, Pakistan, and Bangladesh.

Some of the first and most characteristic examples that remain of early Mughal architecture were built in the short reign (1540–1545) of emperor Sher Shah Suri, who was not a Mughal; they include a mosque known as the Qila i Kuhna (1541) near Delhi, and the military architecture of the Old Fort in Delhi, Lal Bagh (Dhaka) in Bangladesh, and Rohtas Fort, near Jhelum in present-day Pakistan. His mausoleum, octagonal in plan and set upon a plinth in the middle of an artificial lake, is in Sasaram, and was completed by his son and successor Islam Shah Suri (1545AD-1553AD).

Akbar

The emperor Akbar (1556–1605) built largely, and the style developed vigorously during his reign. As in the Gujarat and other styles, there is a combination of Muslim and Hindu features in his works. Akbar constructed the royal city of Fatehpur Sikri, located 26 miles (42 km) west of Agra, in the late 1500s. The numerous structures at Fatehpur Sikri best illustrate the style of his works, and the great mosque there is scarcely matched in elegance and architectural effect; the south gateway is well known, and from its size and structure excels any similar entrance in India. The Mughals built impressive tombs, which include the fine tomb of Akbar's father Humayun, and Akbar's tomb at Sikandra, near Agra, which is a unique structure of the kind and of great merit.

Humayun's Tomb

Humayun's tomb is a complex of buildings built as the Mughal Emperor Humayun's tomb, commissioned by Humayun's wife Hamida Banu Begum in 1562 CE, and designed by Mirak Mirza Ghiyath, a Persian architect. It was the first garden-tomb on the Indian subcontinent, and is located in Nizamuddin East, Delhi, India, close to the *Dina-panah* nothing also known as *Purana Qila,* that Humayun founded in 1533. It was also the first structure to use red sandstone at such a scale The complex was declared a UNESCO World Heritage Site in 1993, and since then has undergone extensive restoration work, which is still undergoing.

The complex encompasses the main tomb of the Emperor Humayun, which houses the graves of his wife, Hamida Begum, and also Dara Shikoh, son of the later Emperor Shah Jahan, as well as numerous other subsequent Mughals, including Emperor Jahandar Shah, Farrukhsiyar, Rafi Ul-Darjat, Rafi Ud-Daulat and Alamgir II. It represented a leap in Mughal architecture, and together with its accomplished Charbagh garden, typical of Persian gardens, but never seen before in India, it set a precedent for subsequent Mughal architecture. It is seen as a clear departure from the fairly modest mausoleum of his father, the first Mughal Emperor, Babur, called *Bagh-e Babur* (Gardens of Babur) in Kabul (Afghanistan). Though the latter was the first Emperor to start the tradition of being buried in a paradise garden. Modelled on *Gur-e Amir,* the tomb of his ancestor and Asia's conqueror Timur in Samarkand, it created a precedent for future Mughal architecture of royal mausolea, which reached its zenith with the Taj Mahal, at Agra.

The site was chosen on the banks of Yamuna river, due to its proximity to Nizamuddin Dargah, the mausoleum of the celebrated Sufi saint of Delhi, Nizamuddin Auliya, who was much revered by the rulers of Delhi, and whose residence, *Chilla Nizamuddin Auliya* lies just north-east of the tomb. In later Mughal history, the last Mughal Emperor, Bahadur Shah Zafar took refuge here, during the Indian Rebellion of 1857, along with three princes, and was captured by Captain Hodson before being exiled to Rangoon. At the time of the Slave Dynasty this land was under the 'KiloKheri Fort' which was capital of Sultan Kequbad, son of Nasiruddin (1268-1287).

History

After his death on January 20, 1556, Humayun's body was first buried in his palace in Delhi, thereafter it was taken to Sirhind, in Punjab by Khanjar Beg, there in 1558, it was seen by his son, then Mughal Emperor, Akbar, who also visited the final resting place of his father, when it was about to be completed in 1571.

The tomb of Humayun was built by the orders of Hamida Banu Begum, Humayun's widow starting in 1562, nine years after his death, at a cost of 15 lakh rupees (1.5 million) at the time. At many places she is confused with another royal, Haji Begum, the first wife of Humayun, though according to *Ain-i-Akbari,* a 16th century detailed document written during the reign of Akbar, there is another Haji Begum, who was the daughter of brother of Humayun's mother, and was later in life was put in charge of the tomb.

According to 'Abd al-Qadir Bada'uni, one of the few contemporary historians to mention its construction, the architect of the edifice was the Persian architect, Mirak Mirza Ghiyas as who was brought in from Herat (northwest Afghanistan), and had previously designed several buildings in Herat, Bukhara (now Uzbekistan), and elsewhere in India. Unfortunately, before the structure's completion, he died and his son *Sayyed Muhammad ibn Mirak Ghiyathuddin* took his father's vision to completion in 1571.

An English merchant, William Finch, who visited the tomb in 1611, describes the interior furnishing of central chamber, compared with its barren look today. He mentioned the presence of rich carpets, and a *shamiana,* a small tent above the cenotaph, which was covered with pure white sheet and with Holy books in front along with his sword, turban and shoes.

Fortunes for once famous Charbagh (Foursquare) gardens, spread over 13 hectares, surrounding the monument changed rapidly over the coming years. The capital had already shifted to Agra in 1556, the decline of Mughals soon aggradized the decay of the monument and its features, as upkeep of the garden, naturally a costly affair proved impossible. By early 18th century, the once lush gardens were replaced by vegetable garden of people who had settled within the walled area. However, the capture of the last Mughal emperor, Bahadur Shah Zafar during Indian Rebellion of 1857 with the premises, and his subsequent sentencing to exile, along with execution of his three sons, meant that the monument's worse days lay ahead, as the British took over Delhi completely.

In 1860, the Mughal design of the garden changed to a more English garden-style, with roundabouts replacing the fours central water tanks on the axial pathways, and trees were profusely planted in flowerbeds, lining them. This fault was corrected in early 20th century, when on Viceroy, Lord Curzon's orders the original garden were restored in the major restoration project between 1903-1909, which also included add lining the plaster channels with sandstone; a 1915 planting scheme, added emphasis to the central and diagonal axis by lining it with trees, though some trees were also planted on the platform originally reserved for tents.

During the Partition of India, in August 1947 the Purana Qila along with Humayun's Tomb, major refugee camps for Muslims migrating to newly founded Pakistan, and were later managed by government of India, these camps stayed on for about five years, and caused considerable damaged to not only the extensive gardens, but also to the water channels and the chief structures, eventually to avoid vandalism the cenotaphs within the mausoleum were encased in bricks; though in the coming years, the Archeological Survey of India, took up the cause of heritage monuments of India, and gradually the building and its gardens were restored; however till 1985, four attempts had been made to activate the original water features, and all remained unsuccessful.

Architecture

The high rubble built enclosure is entered through two lofty double-storeyed gateways on the west and south, 16 m. high with rooms on either side of the passage and a small courtyards on the upper floors. Six-sided stars that adorn the main gateway, are also seen on the iwan of the main tomb structure, though it has been used as ornamental cosmic symbol. The tomb built of rubble masonry and red sandstone, uses white marble as a cladding material and also for the flooring, lattice screens (jaalis), door frames, eaves (chhajja) and for the main dome.

It stands on a vaulted terrace eight-metre high and spread over 12000 sq. mt. It is essentially square in design, though chamferred on the edges to appear octagonal, to prepare ground for the design of the interior structure. The plinth made with rubble core has fifty-six cells all around, and houses over 100 gravestones. Plus, the entire base structure is on a raised platform, a few steps high.

Inspired by Persian architecture; the tomb reaches a height of 47 mt. and is 300 feet wide, and uses the Persian Bulbous double dome-seen 1st in the tomb of Sikander Lodhi-on a high neck drum, and measures 42.5 m, and is topped by 6 mt high brass finial ending in a crescent, common in Timurid tombs. The double or 'double-layered' dome, has its the outer layer which supports the white marble exterior, while the inner part gives shape to the cavernous interior volume. As a contrast to the pure white exterior dome, rest of the building is made up of red sandstone, with white and black marble and yellow sandstone detailing, to relieve the monotony.

The symmetrical and simple designed on the exterior is in sharp contrast with the complex interior floor plan, of inner chambers, which is a square 'ninefold plan', where eight two-storyed vaulted chambers radiate from the central, double-height domed chamber. Underneath this white dome in a domed chamber (hujra), lies the central octagonal sepulcher, the burial chamber containing a single cenotaph, that of the second Mughal Emperor, Humayun. It can be entered through an imposing entrance *iwan* (high arc) on the south, which is slightly recessed, while others sides are covered with intricate *jaalis,* stone lattice work.

The real burial chamber of the Emperor, however lies further away in an underground chamber, exactly beneath the upper cenotaph, and is accessible through a separate passage outside the main structure, which remains mostly closed to visiting public. This technique along with *pietra dura,* a marble inlay ornamentation, seen all around the facade is an important legacy of the Indo-Islamic architecture, and flourished in many later mausolea of the Mughal Empire, like the Taj Mahal, where again we twin cenotaphs and exquisite 'pietra dura' craftsmanship.

The main chamber also carries the symbolic element, a *mihrab* design over the central marble lattice or *jaali,* facing Mecca in the West, here instead of the traditional Surah 24, An-Noor of Quran which is inscribed on the mihrabs, this one is just an outline allowing light to enter directly into the chamber, from *Qibla* or the direction of Mecca, thus elevating the status of the Emperor, above his rivals and closer to divinity.

This chamber with high ceiling is then encompassed by four main octagonal chambers on two floors, set at the diagonals with arched lobbies leading to them also connecting them, plus there are four auxiliary chambers in between suggesting that the tomb was built as a dynastic mausoleum. Collectively the concept of eight side chambers not only offers passage for circumambulation of the main cenotaph, a practice common in Sufism and also visible in many Mughal imperial mausoleums, it also the reflect the concept of Paradise in Islamic cosmology.

Each of the main chambers has in turn eight more, smaller chambers radiating from them, and thus the symmetrical ground plan reveals itself to contain 124 vaulted chambers in all. Many smaller chambers too, contain cenotaphs of other members of the Mughal royal family and nobility, all within main walls of the tomb. Prominent among them cenotaphs of Hamida Begum herself, alongside Dara Shikoh. In all there are over 100 graves within the entire complex, including many on the first level terrace, earning it the name "Dormitory of the Mughals", since the graves are not inscribed their identification remains uncertain.

The building was first to use its unique combination of red sandstone and white marble, and includes several elements of Indian architectural, like the small canopies, or *chhatris* surrounding the central dome, popular in Rajasthani architecture and which were originally covered with blue tiles.

Char Bagh Garden

While the main tomb took over eight years to build, it was also placed in centre of a 30-acre Char Bagh Garden (Four Gardens), a Persian-style garden with quadrilateral layout and was the first of its kind in the South Asia region in such a scale. The highly geometrical and enclosed Paradise garden is divided into four squares by paved walkways (khiyabans) and two bisecting central water channels, reflecting the four rivers that flow in *jannat*, the Islamic concept of paradise.

Each of the four square is further divided into smaller squares with pathways, creating into 36 squares in all, a design typical of later Mughal gardens. The central water channels appear to be disappearing beneath the tomb structure and reappearing on the other side in a straight line, suggesting the Quranic verse, which talks of rivers flowing beneath the 'Garden of Paradise'.

The entire tomb and the garden is enclosed within high rubble walls on three sides, the fourth side was meant to be the river Yamuna, which has since shifted course away from the structure. The central walkways, terminate at two gates: a main one in the southern wall, and a smaller one in the western wall. It has two double-storey entrances, the West gate which used now, while the South gate, which was used during Mughal era, now remains closed. Aligned at the centre on the eastern wall lies a *baradari,* literally a pavilion with twelve doors, which is a building or room with twelve doors designed to allow the free draught of air through it, finally on the northern wall lies a *hammam,* a bath chamber.

Towards the south-east corner, within the 'char bagh' garden, lies a tomb known as *Nai-ka-Gumbad,* or Barber's Tomb (c.1590). Its very presence within the royal enclosure speaks of the importance of person, who was but a the royal barber. The tomb stands on a raised platform, reached by seven steps from the south, it has a square plan and consists of a single compartment covered with a double-dome. Inside lie two graves each inscribed with verses from the Quran. Also, one of the graves is inscribed with the figure 999 which may stand for the Hijra year 1590-91.

Other Monuments

Several monuments dot the pathway leading up to the Humayun's tomb from the main entrance in the West, prominent among them is one that predates the main tomb itself, by twenty years, built in 1547 CE, it is the tomb of Isa Khan Niyazi, a Afghan noble in Sher Shah Suri's court of Sur dynasty, who fought against the Mughals. The tomb which was built during his own lifetime, later served as burial place for the entire family of Isa Khan. On the western side of the tomb lies a three-bay wide mosque, in red sandstone.

Built within its own enclosed garden, the octagonal tomb bears striking resemblance to other tombs of the Sur dynasty monuments in the Lodhi Gardens, in Delhi, showing a marked progression in the development of the architectural style which the main tomb displays in its full splendour as several of the early architectural nuances that can be seen again seen later tombs.

Other monuments within complex, though outside the main enclosed area are: Bu Halima's Tomb, and its surrounding Garden, though little is known about her, and since the tomb or the raised platform where it once stood is not at the centre, so seems like a later addition. Next comes the *Arab Sarai* (Arab Rest house), built by Hamida Begum, ostensibly built for the craftsmen who came for the construction work. Inside this last complex lies the *Afsarwala* tomb belonging to a nobleman in Akbar's court and also his mosque.

Standing outside the entire complex is the tomb known as *Nila Burj* (now known as *Nila Gumbad*) or 'Blue Dome', called so as it bears striking blue glazed tiles. It was built by Abdul Rahim Khan-I-Khana, son of Bairam Khan also a courtier in Mughal Emperor, Akbar's court, for his servant Miyan Fahim, who not only grew up with his son, but later also died along side one of Rahim's own son, Feroze khan, while fighting against the rebellion of Mughal general Mahabat Khan in 1625/26, during the reign of Jahangir.

This structure is known for its unique architecture, as it is octagonal on the outside while square within; its ceiling is decorated with painted and incised plaster, plus it has a high neck dome and shows a conspicuous absence of a double dome feature, common to tombs of the period. Yet further away from the tomb complex, lie Mughal-period monuments, Bada Bateshewala Mahal, Chote Bateshewala Mahal, and *Barapula*, a bridge with 12 piers and 11 arched openings, built in 1621 by Mihr Banu Agha, the chief eunuch of Jahangir's court.

Agra Fort

Agra Fort is a UNESCO World Heritage site located in Agra, India. The fort is also known as Lal Qila, Fort Rouge and Red Fort of Agra. It is about 2.5 km northwest of its much more famous sister monument, the Taj Mahal. The fort can be more accurately described as a walled palatial city.

It is the most important fort in India. The great Mughals Babur, Humayun, Akbar, Jehangir, Shah Jahan and Aurangzeb lived here, and the country was governed from here. It contained the largest state treasury and mint. It was visited by foreign ambassadors, travelers and the highest dignitaries who participated in the making of history in India.

History

This was originally a brick fort and the Sikarwar Rajputs held it. It was mentioned for the first time in 1080 AD when a Ghaznavide force captured it. Sikandar Lodi (1487-1517) was the first Sultan of Delhi who shifted to Agra and lived in the fort. He governed the country from here and Agra assumed the importance of the 2nd capital. He died in the fort in 1517 and his son, Ibrahim Lodi, held it for nine years until he was defeated and killed at Panipat in 1526. Several palaces, wells and a mosque were built by him in the fort during his period.

After Panipat, Mughals captured the fort and a vast treasure-which included a diamond that was later named as the Koh-i-Noor diamond-was seized. Babur stayed in the fort in the palace of Ibrahim. He built a baoli (step well) in it. Humayun was crowned here in 1530. Humayun was defeated in Bilgram in 1530. Sher Shah held the fort for five years. The Mughals defeated the Afghans finally at Panipat in 1556. Realizing the importance of its central situation, Akbar decided to make it his capital and arrived in Agra in 1558. His historian, Abdul Fazal, recorded that this was a brick fort known as 'Badalgarh'. It was in a ruined condition and Akbar had it rebuilt with red sandstone. Architects laid the foundation and it was built with bricks in the inner core with sandstone on external surfaces. Some 1,444,000 builders worked on it for eight years, completing it in 1573.

It was only during the reign of Akbar's grandson, Shah Jahan, that the site finally took on its current state. The legend is that Shah Jahan built the beautiful Taj Mahal for his wife, Mumtaz Mahal. Unlike his grandfather, Shah Jahan tended to have buildings made from white marble, often inlaid with gold or semi-precious gems. He destroyed some of the earlier buildings inside the fort in order to make his own.

At the end of his life, Shah Jahan was imprisoned by his son, Aurangzeb, in the fort, a punishment which might not seem so harsh, considering the luxury of the fort. It is rumored that Shah Jahan died in Muasamman Burj, a tower with a marble balcony with an excellent view of the Taj Mahal.

This was also a site of one of the battles during the Indian rebellion of 1857, which caused the end of the British East India Company's rule in India, and led to a century of direct rule of India by Britain.

Layout

The fort has a semi-circular plan, its chord lying parallel to the river. Its walls are seventy feet high. Double ramparts have massive circular bastions are regular intervals as also battlements, embrasures, machicolations and string courses. Four gates were provided on its four sides, one Khizri gate opening on to the river.

Two of the fort's gates are notable: the "Delhi Gate" and the "Lahore Gate." The Lahore Gate is also popularly also known as the Amar Singh Gate, for Amar Singh Rathore.

The monumental Delhi Gate, which faces the city on the western side of the fort, is considered the grandest of the four gates and a masterpiece of Akbar's time. It was built circa 1568 both to enhance security and as the king's formal gate, and includes features related to both. It is embellished with inlay work in white marble, proof to the richness and power of the Great Mughals.

A wooden drawbridge was used to cross the moat and reach the gate from the mainland; inside, an inner gateway called Hathi Pol ("Elephant Gate")-guarded by two life sized stone elephants with their riders-added another layer of security. The drawbridge, slight ascent, and 90 degree turn between the outer and inner gates, make the entrance impregnable. During a siege, attackers would employ elephants to crush a fort's gates. Without a level, straight run-up to gather speed, however, something prevented by this layout, elephants are ineffective.

Because the Indian military (the Parachute Brigade in particular) is still using the northern portion of the Agra Fort, the Delhi Gate cannot be used by the public. Tourists enter via the Lahore Gate, so named because it faces Lahore, now in Pakistan.

The site is very important in terms of architectural history. Abul Fazal recorded that five hundred buildings in the beautiful designs of Bengal and Gujarat were built in the fort. Some of them were demolished to make way for his white marble palaces. Most of the others were destroyed by the British between 1803 and 1862 for raising barracks. Hardly thirty Mughal buildings have survived on the south-eastern side, facing the river. Of these, the Delhi Gate and Akbar Gate and one palace-"Bengali Mahal"-are representative Akbari buildings.

Akbar Darwazza (Akbar Gate) was renamed Amar Singh Gate by the British. The gate is similar in design to the Delhi Gate. Both are built of red sandstone.

The Bengali Mahal is also built of red sandstone and is now split into Akbari Mahal and Jahangiri mahal.

Some of the most historically interesting mixing of Hindu and Islamic architecture are found here. In fact, some of the Islamic decorations feature haraam (forbidden) images of living creatures-dragons, elephants and birds, instead of the usual patterns and calligraphy seen in Islamic surface decoration.

Sites and Structures within Agra Fort

Jahangiri Mahal

Jahangiri Mahal is perhaps the most noteworthy building inside the Agra Fort of India. The Mahal was the principal zenana palace.

Architecture

A splendid gateway leads to an interior courtyard surrounded by grand halls covered with profuse carvings on stone, heavily fashioned brackets, piers, and crossbeams. One can still spot remnants of decoration in gold and blue done in the prevalent Indo-Persian style. Jahangiri Mahal mixes Transoxanian (Central Asian) features, such as the verandah on the east front with its high slender columns (a translation into stone of the timber iwan of vernacular Transoxanian architecture), with courtyard halls styled in the broader Gujarat-Malwa-Rajasthan tradition as it had been passed onto the Mughals by the early 16th-century architecture of Raja Man Singh of Gwalior. This exotic medley and adventurous eclecticism suggests a daring approach in architecture. The typically Gujarati brackets-fabulously carved animal and floral motifs-register a dominating effect on the few Islamic features such as the verandah on the eastern front with exquisitely slender pillars facing the riverfront. Jahangiri Mahal is the most important building of the Akbari period in the Agra Fort.

Mina Masjid

Mina Masjid or the Heavenly Mosque was built by Shah Jahan between 1631-40 near Diwan-i-Khas in Agra Fort. This is a small mosque was built, entirely of white marble, by the Mughal king Shah Jahan for his personal use.

Architecture

It has a small open court in front of the three-arched prayer-chamber. There is no ornamentation and it is simple. It is enclosed and secured on all sides by high walls and, it appears that, Shah Jahan used this mosque during his imprisonment in the adjoining apartment of Musamman Burj, also called shah-burj, from 1658 to 1666 A.D.

Moti Masjid, Agra

The Moti Masjid in Agra was built by Shah Jahan. During the rule of Shah Jahan the Mughal emperor, numerous architectural wonders were built. Most famous of them being the Taj Mahal. Moti Masjid earned the epithet Pearl Mosque for it shined like a pearl. It is held that this mosque was constructed by Shah Jahan for his members of royal court.

Architecture

Moti Masjid's architectural features are quite similar to that of the Saint Basil's Cathedral in Moscow.Moti Masjid stands on the ground that slopes from east to west to the north of Diwan-i-Am complex in Agra Fort. The courtyard of the Moti Masjid has side arcades and arched recessions and the main sanctuary facade beyond. The sanctuary is roofed with three bulbous domes built of light white marble and stand on the red sandstone walls. There are a series of Hindu-style domed kiosks along the parapet. There are seven bays that are divided into a number of aisles which are supported by piers and lobed arches. The Moti Masjid boasts of extensive white marble facing, a typical stylistic feature of architecture during the reign of Shah Jahan.

Musamman Burj

Musamman Burj also known as the Saman Burj or the Shah-burj, is a beautiful octagonal tower standing close to the Shah Jahan's private hall Diwan-e-Khas in Agra Fort.

History

Musamman Burj was built by Shah Jahan for his beloved wife Mumtaz Mahal. It is said that at first a small marble palace built by Akbar was situated at this site, which was later demolished by Jehangir to erect new buildings. Shah Jahan in his turn chose this site to erect the multi-storied marble tower inlaid with precious stones for Mumtaz Mahal. It was built between 1631-40 and offers exotic views of the famous Taj Mahal.

Architecture

The Musamman Burj is made of delicate marble lattices with ornamental niches so that the ladies of the court could gaze out unseen. The decoration of the walls is pietra dura. The chamber has a marble dome on top and is surrounded by a verandah with a beautiful carved fountain in the centre.

The tower looks out over the River Yamuna and is traditionally considered to have one of the most poignant views of the Taj Mahal. It is here that Shah Jahan along with his favourite daughter Jahanara Begum had spent his last few years as a captive of his son Aurangzeb. He lay here on his death bed while gazing at the Taj Mahal in Agra.

Nagina Masjid

The Nagina Masjid is a masjid in Agra Fort built by Shah Jahan. It is also known as the Gem Mosque or the Jewel Mosque.

Architecture

Nagina Masjid is an architectural beauty in Agra Fort. It is located nearby another eye catching Masjid known as Moti Masjid. This mosque is constructed with pure white attractive marble and encloses the prayer chamber exquisitely designed.

The Nagina Masjid bears a very simple architecture and a descent decoration. The mosque is separated into three bays by simple pillars underneath the keen arches above. The arch in the centre is bigger and has nine cusps, once on either face has seven cusps only. The mosque is 10.21 meter broad and 7.39 meter deep, facing a lined patio. There is a balcony presenting the panoramic views of the road that runs towards the Hathi Pol lies on the northern side of the Masjid

This beautiful structure was built for the ladies of the Royal family. This private mosque has special features of three majestic domes and wonderful arches. A luxurious bazaar, known as Mina Bazar, was functioning down the road from where royal ladies could purchase items standing in the balcony of Nagina Masjid.

Shah Jahani Mahal

It is situated between the white marble Khas-Mahal and the red stone Jahangiri mahal and is set, transitionally, in between these two major residential complexes of two different ages. It is the earliest attempt of the Mughal Emperor Shah Jehan to convert an existing redstone building in accordance with his taste. It is his earliest palace in Agra Fort and has a large hall and side rooms, and an octagonal tower on the river side.

The skeletal construction of the brick masonry and red stone were all white, stuccoed with a thick plaster and colourfully painted with floral designs. The whole palace once glistened white, like white marble.

On its face towards the khas-mahal is a white marble dalan, composed of five nine-cusped arches supported on double pillars and protected externally by a Chhajja. Its western bay was closed to house the Ghaznin gate. Babur's baoli and well are situated beneath it. The subterranean apartments in several stories are also situated under this palace.

- Anguri Bagh (Grape Garden)- 85 square, geometrically arranged gardens
- Diwan-i-Am (Hall of Public Audience)-was used to speak to the people and listen to petitioners and once housed the Peacock Throne
- Diwan-i-Khas (Hall of Private Audience)-was used to receive kings and dignitary, features black throne of Jehangir
- Golden Pavilions-beautiful pavilions with roofs shaped like the roofs of Bengali huts
- Khas Mahal-white marble palace, one of the best examples of painting on marble
- Macchi Bhawan (Fish Enclosure)-grand enclosure for harem functions, once had pools and fountains
- Naubat Khana (Drum House)-a place where the king's musicians played
- Rang Mahal-where the king's wives and mistresses lived
- Shahi Burj-Shah Jahan's private work area
- Sheesh Mahal or Shish Mahal (Mirror Palace)-royal dressing room featuring tiny mirror-like glass-mosaic decorations on the walls
- Zenana Mina Bazaar (Ladies Bazaar)-right next to the balcony, where only female merchants sold wares.

Lahore Fort

The Lahore Fort, locally referred to as *Shahi Qila* is citadel of the city of Lahore, Punjab, Pakistan. It is located in the northwestern corner of the Walled City of Lahore. The trapezoidal composition is spread over 20 hectares. Origins of the fort go as far back as antiquity, however, the existing base structure was built during the reign of Mughal emperor Akbar (1556-1605), and was regularly upgraded by subsequent rulers, having thirteen gates in all..

Thus the fort manifests the rich traditions of the entire Mughal architecture. Some of the famous sites inside the fort include: Sheesh Mahal, Alamgiri Gate, Naulakha pavilion, and Moti Masjid. In 1981, the fort was inscribed as a UNESCO World Heritage Site along with the Shalimar Gardens (Lahore).

Origins

The origins of Lahore Fort are obscure and are traditionally based on various myths. However, during the excavation carried out in 1959 by the Department of Archaeology, in front of *Diwan-e-Aam*, a gold coin of Mahmood of Ghazni dated A.H. 416 (1025 A.D.) was found at a depth of 7.62 metres from the level of the lawns. Cultural layers continued to a further depth of 5 metres, giving strong indications that people had lived here, long before the conquest of Lahore by Mahmood in 1021 A.D. Further mention of the fort is traceable to Shahab-ud-din Muhammad Ghuri's successive invasions of Lahore from 1180 to 1186 A.D.

Timeline

- It cannot be said with certainty when the Lahore Fort was originally constructed or by whom, since this information is lost to history, possibly forever. However, evidence found in archaeological digs gives strong indications that it was built long before 1025 A.D
- 1241 A.D.-Destroyed by Mongols.
- 1267 A.D.-Rebuilt by Sultan Ghiyas ud din Balban.
- 1398 A.D.-Destroyed again, by Amir Tamir's army.
- 1421 A.D.-Rebuilt in mud by Sultan Mubark Shah Syed.
- 1432 A.D.-The fort is occupied by Shaikh Ali of Kabul who makes repairs to the damages inflicted on it by Shaikha Khokhar.

- 1566 A.D.-Rebuilt by Mughal emperor Akbar, in solid brick masonry on its earlier foundations. Also perhaps, its area was extended towards the river Ravi, which then and up to about 1849 A.D., used to flow along its fortification on the north. Akbar also built *Doulat Khana-e-Khas-o-Am*, the famous *Jharoka-e-Darshan* (Balcony for Royal Appearance), Masjidi Gate etc.
- 1618 A.D.-Jehangir adds *Doulat Khana-e-Jehangir*
- 1631 A.D.-Shahjahan builds *Shish Mahal* (Mirror Palace).
- 1633 A.D.-Shahjahan builds *Khawabgah* (a dream place or sleeping area), *Hamam* (bath), *Khilwat Khana* (retiring room), and *Moti Masjid* (Pearl Mosque).
- 1645 A.D.-Shahjahan builds *Diwan-e-Khas (Hall of Special Audience)*.
- 1674 A.D.-Aurangzeb adds the massively fluted *Alamgiri Gate.*
- (Sometime during) 1799-1839 A.D.-The outer fortification wall on the north with the moat, the marble *athdera, Havaeli Mai Jindan* and *Bara Dari Raja Dhiyan Singh* were constructed by Ranjit Singh, Sikh ruler from 1799-1839 A.D.
- 1846 A.D.-Occupied by the British.
- 1927 A.D.-The British hand over the Fort to the *Department of Archaeology* after demolishing a portion of the fortification wall on the south and converting it into a stepped form thus *defortifying* the fort.

Structure

The strategic location of Lahore city between the Mughal territories and the strongholds of Kabul, Multan, and Kashmir required the dismantling of the old mud-fort and fortification with solid brick masonry. The strcucture is dominated by Persian influence that deepened with the successive refurbishments by subsequent emperors. The fort is clearly divided into two sections: first the administrative section, which is well connected with main entrances, and comprises larger garden areas and *Diwan-e-Aam* for royal audiences.

The second-a private and concealed residential section-is divided into courts in the northern part, accessible through 'elephant gate'. It also contains *Shish Mahal* (Hall of Mirrors of Mirror Palace), and spacious bedrooms and smaller gardens. On the outside, the walls are decorated with blue Persian kashi tiles. The original entrance faces the Maryam Zamani Mosque, whereas the larger Alamgiri Gate opens to the Hazuri Bagh through to the majestic Badshahi Mosque.

Allahabad Fort

Allahabad Fort at Allahabad, Uttar Pradesh, India was built by Emperor Akbar in 1583. The fort stands on the banks of the Yamuna near the confluence site. It is the largest fort built by Akbar. In its prime, the fort was unrivaled for its design, construction and craftsmanship. This huge fort has three galleries flanked by high towers.

At present is used by the army and only a limited area is open to visitors. The outer wall is intact and rises above the water's edge. Inside the fort there is the Zenana, Palace of Mariam-uz-Zamani and the 3rd century BC Ashoka pillar and *Saraswati Koop* as well, said to be the source of the Saraswati river. The Patalpuri temple is also here.

Allahabad Fort is the location of the much revered Akshaya Vat which mean *immortal tree*. Legends say that if anyone jumped from this centuries old banyan tree he would attain immortality. Civilians are not allowed to see this tree. It is near the southern wall and is one among the many trees seen from outside the southern wall of the fort.

Fatehpur Sikri

Fatehpur Sikri is a city and a municipal board in Agra district in the state of Uttar Pradesh, India. The historical city was constructed by Mughal emperor Akbar beginning in 1570 and served as the empire's capital from 1571 until 1585, when it was abandoned for reasons that remain unclear. The surviving palace and mosque are a tourist attraction and a UNESCO World Heritage Site.

History

Akbar had inherited the Mughal Empire from his father Humayun and grandfather Babur. During the 1560s he rebuilt the Agra Fort and established it as his capital. With his wife Mariam-uz-Zamani he had a son and then twins, but the twins died. He then consulted the Sufi Saint Salim Chishti from the Chishti Order who lived as a recluse in the small town Sikri near Agra. Salim predicted that Akbar would have another son, and indeed one was born in 1569 in Sikri.

He was named Salim to honor the saint and would later rule the empire as Emperor Jahangir. The following year, Akbar, then 28 years old, determined to build a palace and royal city in Sikri, to honor his pir Salim Chishti. The tomb of Salim Chishti, "Salim Chisti Ka Mazar" was built there within the grounds of the Jama mosque.

The name, Fateh is of Arabic origin and means "victory", also in Urdu and Persian; Mughal Emperor Babur defeated Rana Sanga in a battle at a place called Khanwa (about 40 KM from Agra).

Fatehpur Sikri shared its imperial duties as a capital city with Agra, where a bulk of the arsenal, treasure hoards, and other reserves were kept at Agra Fort for security. During a crisis, the court, harem, and treasury could be removed to Agra, only 26 miles away, less than a day's march..

It is at Fatehpur Sikri that the legends of Akbar and his famed courtiers, the *nine jewels* or Navaratnas, were born. The legendary musician Tansen is said to have performed on an island in the middle of the pool Anup Talao (lit. *anup*= without metaphor, unmatched). A strong belief comes across from generations that a tunnel from here stretches to Delhi and from there to Lahore and on the other end to Agra. Due to nonmaintenance, the tunnel had been closed in 1952 at approx 500m. Innovations in land revenue, coinage, military organisation, and provincial administration emerged during the Fatehpur Sikri years.

Fatehpur Sikri was abandoned in 1585 and the capital moved to Lahore. The reasons for this remain obscure; it is possible that water sources dried up or that Akbar needed to be closer to invading Persian and Afghan armies.

Significance

Fatehpur Sikri is regarded as Emperor Akbar's crowning architectural legacy. Indeed, its numerous palaces, halls, and masjids satisfy his creative and aesthetic impulses, typical of Mughals.

Fatehpur Sikri is a World Heritage Site. Some contemporary Indian architects, notably B. V. Doshi, have cited it as an important source of inspiration. Architect or layperson, this city generally captures the imagination and wonder of all who experience its urban spaces and see its buildings. Charles and Ray Eames cited Fatehpur Sikri in the landmark 'India Report' that led to the conception of the National Institute of Design, India's premiere design school.

Description

The layout of the city shows a conscious attempt to produce rich spatial effects by the organization of built forms around open spaces in interesting ways. Of particular note is the way in which shifts in axes occur as one moves along the city and the location of squares in important places with buildings forming a backdrop or envelope. It was here, in Fatehpur-sikri, Akbar tried to propagate a new religion:' Deen-e-Ilahee' after he got sincerely interested in scholarly discourses on comparative religion-especially those relating to Sufism.

For that matter a separate place Diwan-e-khas was earmarked, where scholars, saints and noblemen all congregated. Although historically speaking, the new religion propounded by Akbar never saw the light of the day yet Fatehpur-Sikri is a great example of (officially less-literate) Akbar's unblemished desire for learning!

Unlike other important Mughal cities (such as Shahjahanabad, which has a very formal planning), Fatehpur Sikri has aspects of informality and improvisation. Indeed, the newly constructed city bore a similarity to the movable imperial encampment also designed by Akbar.

Important Buildings

The buildings of Fatehpur Sikri show a synthesis of various regional schools of architectural craftsmanship such as Gujarati and Bengali. This was because indigenous craftsmen from various regions were used for the construction of the buildings. Influences from Hindu and Jain architecture are seen hand in hand with Islamic elements. The building material predominantly used is red sandstone, quarried from the same rocky outcrop on which it is situated.

Buland Darwaza

Buland Darwaza meaning 'high' or 'great' gate in Persian, is the largest of gateways in the world. It is located in Fatehpur Sikri which is located 43 km away from Agra, India. It is also known as the "Gate of Magnificence".

History

It was built by Mughal Emperor Akbar in 1572 to commemorate his conquest of Gujarat. A Persian inscription on the eastern archway of the gateway records Akbar's conquest of the Deccan in 1601.

Architecture

The gateway is approached by 42 steps. The Buland Darwaza is 53.63m high and 35 meters wide. Buland Darwaza is the highest gateway of 172ft tall entrance in the world and an astounding example of the Mughal architecture. It is built of red sandstone and inlaying of white marble.

The Buland Darwaza towers above the courtyard of the mosque. The Buland Darwaza is semi octagonal in plan and is topped by pillars and chhatris. Buland Darwaza echoes early Mughal design with simple ornamentation, carved verses from the Koran and towering arches. There are thirteen smaller domed kiosks on the roof, stylized battlement and small turrets and inlay work of white and black marble. On the outside a long flight of steps sweeps down the hill giving the gateway additional height. A Persian inscription on eastern archway of the Buland Darwaza records Akbar's conquest over Deccan in 1601 A.D.

Buland Darwaza has a very famous inscription written on it. This inscription is actually a quote attributed to Jesus Christ, who is revered equally by both Christians as well as Muslims. It says, *"The World is but a bridge, pass over but build no houses on it."*

- Diwan-i-Am (Hall of Public Audience): A building typology found in many Mughal cities where the ruler meets the general public. In this case, it is a pavilion-like multi-bayed rectangular structure fronting a large open space.
- Diwan-i-Khas (Hall of Private Audience): Famous for its central pillar with thirty-six voluted brackets supporting a circular platform for Akbar. It is here that Akbar had representatives of different religions discuss their faiths.

- Hujra-i-Anup Talao (Small Chamber of Anup Talao): Said to be the residence of Akbar's Muslim wife, although this is disputed due to its small size.
- Jama Masjid (Grand Mosque): The mosque, built in the manner of Indian mosques, with liwans (aisles) around a central courtyard. A distinguishing feature is the row of chhatris (small domed pavilions) over the sanctuary.
- Mariam-uz-Zamani's Palace: The building of Akbar's wife shows *Gujarati* influence and is built around a courtyard, with special care being taken to ensure privacy.

Mariam-uz-Zamani

Mariam uz-Zamani Begum Sahiba (often shortened to Mariam-uz-Zamani), nee Rajkumari Hira Kunwari Sahiba, alias Harkha Bai,, (October 1, 1542-1622), was a Rajput princess who became the Mughal Empress, and the eldest daughter of Kacchwaha Rajput, Raja Bharmal, Raja of Amber, the older name of the Rajput State of Jaipur.

Her notability arises from her marriage to the Mughal emperor Jalaluddin Muhammad Akbar. She was also the mother of emperor Nuruddin Salim Jahangir, her husband's heir.

Her name as recorded in Mughal chronicles was Mariam-uz-Zamani. This is why the mosque of Mariyam Zamani Begum was constructed in Lahore, Pakistan, in her honour. She has been also referred to as Jodha Bai or Jodhabai in modern times, although she was never known as such during her lifetime. Hira Kunwar, Akbar's first Rajput wife, was the eldest daughter of Raja Bhar Mal of Amer. She was also the sister of Bhagwandas and the aunt of Man Singh I of Amber, who later became one the nine jewels (Navaratnas) in the court of Akbar..

Mosque of Mariyam Zamani Begum built by her son Nuruddin Salim Jahangir, is situated in the Walled City of Lahore, Pakistan, while Mariam's Tomb is situated one km away from Tomb of Akbar the Great, at Sikandra, near Agra.

Life

Hira Kunwari (her maiden name) was married to Akbar on January 20, 1562, at Sambhar, near Jaipur. She was Akbar's third wife and one of his three chief queens. She was 22 days older than her husband. Akbar's first queen was the childless Ruqaiyya Begum, and his second wife was Salima Sultan, the widow of his most trusted general, Bairam Khan. After her marriage, Hira Kunwari was given the title Mariam-ul-Zamani ("Mary of the Age").

She is said to have been politically involved in the court until Nur Jahan became empress.

Like few other women at the Mughal court, Maryam-uz-Zamani could issue official documents (singularly called *farman*), which was usually the exclusive privilege of the emperor. Maryam Zamani used her wealth and influence to build gardens, wells, and mosques around the country.

In 1586, she arranged a marriage of her son, Prince Salim (later Jahangir), to her niece, Princess Manmati (Manbhawati Bai), who was the mother of Prince Khusrau Mirza.

Maryam Zamani owned and oversaw the ships that carried pilgrims to and from the Islamic holy city Mecca. In 1613, her ship, the *Rahimi* was seized by Portuguese pirates along with the 600-700 passengers and the cargo. When the Portuguese officially refused to return the ship and the passengers, the outcry at the Moghul court was quite severe. Zamani's son, the Indian emperor Jahangir ordered the seizure of the Portuguese town Daman. This episode is considered to be an example of the struggle for wealth that would later ensue and lead to colonization of India.

Maryam Zamani died in 1622. As per her last wishes, a *vav* or step well was constructed by Jahangir. Her tomb, built in 1611, is on the Tantpur road now known as in Jyoti Nagar. Her tomb is now known as "Jodhabai ki chhatri". She was buried according to Islamic custom.

- Naubat Khana (Drum House): Near the entry, where important arrivals are announced.
- Pachisi Court: A square marked out as a large sized board game (the precursor to modern day Ludo and Parcheesi) where people served as the playing pieces.

Panch Mahal

Panch Mahal is a five-storey also known as "*Badgir*", which means windcatcher/tower. Panch Mahal stands close to the Zeenana quarters or Harem and that supports the fact that it acted as a pleasure palace. This is an extraordinary structure, entirely columnar, consisting of four storeys of decreasing size disposed asymmetrically upon a ground floor, which contains 84 columns. The pillars, that originally had jaali between them, support the whole structure. Once these screens provided purdah (cover) to queens and princess on the top terraces enjoying the cool breezes and watching splendid views of Sikri fortifications and the town nestling at the foot of the ridge.

The pavilion gives a majestic view of the fort that lays on its left. It is built by *Akbar* and only took 10 years to build the whole country

- Raja Birbal's House: The house of Akbar's favourite minister, who was a Hindu. Notable features of the building are the horizontal sloping sunshades or chajjas and the brackets which support them.
- Sunahra Maken: The residence of Akbar's Christian wife.

Tomb of Salim Chisti

The Tomb of Sheikh Salim Chishti is famed as one of the finest examples of Mughal architecture in India. Situated near Zenana Rauza and facing south towards Buland Darwaza, it enshrines the burial place of the Sufi saint who lived a religious life here. The mausoleum, constructed by Akbar as a mark of his respect for the Sufi saint, was built during the years 1580 and 1581.

Architecture

The tomb has been constructed on a platform which is about 1 m. high, a flight of five steps leading to the entrance portico. The main tomb building is enclosed by delicate marble screens on all sides, and the tomb is located in the centre of the main hall, which has a single semi-circular dome. The marble building is beautifully carved, and has an ivory-like appearance.

The plinth is ornamented with mosaics of black and yellow marble arranged in geometric patterns. An ebony "chhhaparkhat" enclosure surrounds the marble cenotaph, which is usually covered by a green cloth. The door to the main chamber is intricately carved with arabesque patterns and bears inscriptions from the Koran. Brown marble borders the interior bays while the relief panels-with the Koranic verses-have a blue background. The carved and painted tomb chamber has a white marble floor, which is inlaid with multicolored stones.

Tomb of Akbar the Great

The Tomb of Akbar the Great is an important Mughal architectural masterpiece, built 1605-1613, set in 48 Ha (119 acres) of grounds in Sikandra, a suburb of Agra, Uttar Pradesh, India.

History

The third Mughal Emperor Akbar the Great (1542 – 1605), himself commenced its construction in around 1600, according to Tartary tradition to commence the construction of one's tomb during one's lifetime. Akbar himself planned his own tomb and selected a suitable site for it, after his death, Akbar's son Jahangir completed the construction in 1605-1613.

Location

It is located at Sikandra, in the suburbs of Agra, on the Mathura road (NH2), 8 km WNW of the city center.About 1 km away from the tomb, lies Mariam's Tomb, the tomb of Mariam-uz-Zamani, wife of the Mughal Emperor Akbar and the mother of Jehangir.

Architecture

The grounds are a precise 690 m square, aligned with the points of the compass, surrounded by walls, and laid out as a classic charbagh garden style. A gatehouse stands at the centre of each wall, and broad paved avenues, laid out in Mughal style with central running water channels representing the four rivers of Paradise, lead from these to the tomb at the centre of the square.

The south gate is the largest, with four white marble chhatri-topped minarets which are similar to (and predate) those of the Taj Mahal, and is the normal point of entry to the tomb. The tomb itself is surrounded by a walled enclosure 105 m square. The tomb building is a four-tiered pyramid, surmounted by a marble pavilion containing the false tomb. The true tomb, as in other mausoleums, is in the basement. The buildings are constructed mainly from a deep red sandstone, enriched with features in white marble. Decorated inlaid panels of these materials and a black slate adorn the tomb and the main gatehouse. Panel designs are geometric, floral and calligraphic, and prefigure the more complex and subtle designs later incorporated in Itmad-ud-Daulah's Tomb.

Under Jahangir (1605–1627) the Hindu features vanished from the style; his great mosque at Lahore is in the Persian style, covered with enamelled tiles. At Agra, the tomb of Itmad-ud-Daula completed in 1628, built entirely of white marble and covered wholly by pietra dura mosaic, is one of the most splendid examples of that class of ornamentation anywhere to be found. Jahangir also built the Shalimar Gardens and its accompanying pavilions on the shore of Dal Lake in Kashmir. He also built a monument to his pet antelope, Hiran Minar in Sheikhupura, Pakistan and due to his great love for his wife, after his death she went on to build his mausoleum in Lahore.

Itimad-ud-Daulah's Tomb

Itmad-ud-Daula's Tomb is a Mughal mausoleum in the city of Agra in the Indian state of Uttar Pradesh. Often described as 'jewel box', sometimes called the 'Baby Taj', the tomb of Itimad-ud-Daulah is often regarded as a draft of the Taj Mahal.

Along with the main building, the structure consists of numerous outbuildings and gardens. The tomb, built between 1622 and 1628 represents a transition between the first phase of monumental Mughal architecture-primarily built from red sandstone with marble decorations, as in Humayun's Tomb in Delhi and Akbar's tomb in Sikandra-to its second phase, based on white marble and pietra dura inlay, most elegantly realized in the Taj Mahal.

The mausoleum was commissioned by Nur Jahan, the wife of Jahangir, for her father Mirza Ghiyas Beg, who had been given the title of *Itimad-ud-Daulah* (pillar of the state). Mirza Ghiyas Beg was also the grandfather of Mumtaz Mahal (originally named Arjumand Bano, daughter of Asaf Khan), the wife of the emperor Shah Jahan, responsible for the building of the Taj Mahal.

The Tomb

Located on the left bank of the Yamuna river, the mausoleum is set in a large cruciform garden criss-crossed by water courses and walkways. The mausoleum itself covers about twenty-three square meters, and is built on a base about fifty meters square and about one meter high. On each corner are hexagonal towers, about thirteen meters tall.

The walls are white marble from Rajasthan encrusted with semi-precious stone decorations-cornelian, jasper, lapis lazuli, onyx, and topaz formed into images of cypress trees and wine bottles, or more elaborate decorations like cut fruit or vases containing bouquets. Light penetrates to the interior through delicate jali screens of intricately carved white marble.

Many of Nur Jahan's relatives are interred in the mausoleum. The only asymmetrical element of the entire complex is that the cenotaphs of her father and mother have been set side-by-side, a formation replicated in the Taj Mahal

Pietra Dura

Pietra dura or *pietre dure,* called 'Parchin kari in South Asia, is an art-historical term for the technique of using exquisitely cut and fitted, highly-polished coloured stones to create what amounts to a painting in stone. It is considered a decorative art. The stonework, after the work is assembled loosely, is glued stone-by-stone to a substrate after having previously been "sliced and cut in different shape sections; and then assembled together so precisely that the contact between each section was practically invisible".

Stability was achieved by grooving the undersides of the stones so that they interlocked, rather like a jigsaw puzzle, with everything held tautly in place by an encircling 'frame'. Many different colored stones, particularly marbles, were used, along with semiprecious, and even precious stones. It first appeared in Rome in the 16th century, reaching its full maturity in Florence. Pietra dura items are generally crafted on green, white and black marble colour base stones. Typically the resulting panel is completely flat, but some examples where the image is in low relief were made, taking the work more into the area of hardstone carving.

Related arts and Terms

Pietre dure is an Italian plural meaning "hard rocks"; the singular *pietra dura* is also encountered in Italian. In Italian, but not in English, the term embraces all gem engraving and hardstone carving, which is the artistic carving of three-dimensional objects in semi-precious stone, normally from a single piece, for example in Chinese jade. The traditional usage in English has been to use the singular *pietra dura* just to denote multi-colored inlay work.

However in recent years there has been a trend to use *pietre dure* as a term for the same thing, but not for all the techniques it covers in Italian. But the title of a 2008 exhibition at the Metropolitan Museum of Art, New York *Art of the Royal Court:*

Treasures in Pietre Dure from the Palaces of Europe used the full Italian sense of the term, probably because they thought it had greater brand recognition. The material on the website speaks of objects such as a vase in lapis lazuli as being examples of "hardstone carving (*pietre düre*)"

The Victoria & Albert Museum in London uses both versions on its website, but pietra dura ("A method of inlaying coloured marbles or semi-precious stones into a stone base, often in geometric or flower patterns....") in its "Glossary", which was evidently not consulted by the author of another page, where the reader is told: "Pietre dure (from the Italian 'hard stone') is made from finely sliced coloured stones, precisely matched, to create a pictorial scene or regular design". The English term "Florentine mosaic" is sometimes also encountered, probably developed by the tourist industry.

It is distinct from mosaic in that the component stones are mostly much larger and cut to a shape suiting their place in the image, not all of roughly equal size and shape as in mosaic. In pietra dura the stones are not cemented together with grout, and works in pietra dura are often portable. Nor should it be confused with micromosaics, a form of mosaic using very small tesserae of the same size to create images rather than decorative patterns, for Byzantine icons, and later for panels for setting into furniture and the like.

For fixed inlay work on walls, ceilings and pavements that do not meet the definition for mosaic, the terms intarsia or cosmati work/cosmatesque are better used. Similarly, for works that use larger pieces of stone (or tile), opus sectile may be used. Pietre dure is essentially stone marquetry. As a high expression of lapidary art, it is closely related to the jewelers art. It can also be seen as a branch of sculpture as three-dimensionality can be achieved, as with a bas relief.

History

Pietra dura developed from the Ancient Roman opus sectile, which at least in terms of surviving examples, was architectural, used on floors and walls, with both geometric and figurative designs. In the Middle Ages cosmatesque floors and small columns etc on tombs and altars continued to use inlays of different colours in geometric patterns. Byzantine art continued with inlaid floors, but also produced some small religious figures in hardstone inlays, for example in the Pala d'Oro in San Marco, Venice (though this mainly uses enamel). In the Italian Renaissance this technique again was used for images. The Florentines, who most fully developed the form, however, regarded it as 'painting in stone'. It is stated that Domenico Ghirlandaio *"dubbed the medium 'Pittura per l'eternità' — that is, painting for eternity"*.

As it developed in Florence, the technique was initially called *opere di commessi* (approximately, "Works of the commissariat"). Medici Grand Duke Ferdinando I of Tuscany founded the *Galleria di'Lavori* in 1588, now the Opificio delle pietre dure, for the purpose of developing this and other decorative forms.

A multitude of varied objects were created. Table tops were particularly prized, and these tend to be the largest specimens. Smaller items in the form of medallions, cameos, wall plaques, panels inserted into doors or onto cabinets, bowls, jardinieres, garden ornaments, fountains, benches, etc. are all found. A popular form was to copy an existing painting, often of a human figure, as illustrated by the image of Pope Clement VIII, above. Examples are found in many museums.

The medium was transported to other European centres of court art and remained popular into the 19th century. In particular, Naples became a noted centre of the craft. By the 20th century, the medium was in decline, in part by the assault of modernism, and the craft had been reduced to mainly restoration work. In recent decades, however, the form has been revived, and receives state-funded sponsorship. Modern examples range from tourist-oriented kitsch including syrupy reproductions of 19th century style religious subjects (especially in Florence and Naples), to works copying or based on older designs used for luxurious decorative contexts, to works in a genuinely contemporary artistic idiom.

Parchin Kari

By the early part of the 1600s, smaller objects produced by the Opificio were widely diffused throughout Europe, and as far East to the court of the Mughals in India, where the form was imitated and reinterpreted in a native style; its most sumptuous expression is found in the Taj Mahal.

Due to the Taj Mahal being one of the major tourist attractions, there is a flourishing industry of Pietra Dura artifacts in Agra ranging from tabletops, medallions, elephants and other animal forms, jewellery boxes and other decorative items. This art form is fully alive and thriving in Agra, India though the patterns in the designs are more Persian than Roman or Medician.

Hiran Minar

Hiran Minar is set in peaceful environs near Lahore in Sheikhupura, Pakistan. It was constructed by Emperor Jahangir as a monument to Mansraj, one of his pet deer.

The structure consists of a large, almost-square water tank with an octagonal pavilion in its centre, built during the reign of Mughal emperor Shah Jahan; a causeway with its own gateway connects the pavilion with the mainland and a 100-foot (30 m)-high minar, or minaret.

At the centre of each side of the tank, a brick ramp slopes down to the water, providing access for royal animals and wild game. The minar itself was built by Emperor Jahangir in 1606 to honor the memory of a pet hunting antelope named Mansraj.

Unique features of this particular complex are the antelope's grave and the distinctive water collection system. At each corner of the tank (approximately 750 by 895 feet (273 m) in size), is a small, square building and a subsurface water collection system which supplied the tank; only one of these water systems is extensively exposed today.

Another special feature of Hiran Minar is its location and environment: the top of the minar is perhaps the best place in the province of Punjab to get a feel for the broader landscape and its relationship to a Mughal site.

Looking north from the top of the minar, one can see a patch of forest which is similar to the scrub forest vegetation of Mughal times, while to the west are extensively-irrigated fields, a product of the late nineteenth and early twentieth centuries, but similar in size and appearance to the well-irrigated fields of the Mughal period.

Shah Jahan

The force and originality of the style gave way under Shah Jahan (1627–1658) to a delicate elegance and refinement of detail, illustrated in the magnificent palaces erected in his reign at Agra and Delhi, the latter one the most exquisitely beautiful in India. The most splendid of the Mogul tombs, and the most renowned building in India, is the Taj Mahal at Agra, the tomb of Mumtaz Mahal, the wife of Shah Jahan.

The Moti Masjid (Pearl Mosque) in the Agra Fort and The Jama Masjid at Delhi are an imposing building, and their position and architecture have been carefully considered so as to produce a pleasing effect and feeling of spacious elegance and well-balanced proportion of parts. In his works Shah Jahan presents himself as the most magnificent builder of Indian sovereigns.

He also built the mausoleum and sections of the huge Lahore Fort that include the impressive Moti Masjid, Sheesh Mahal, and Naulakha pavilion which are all enclosed in the fort. He also built a mosque after himself in Thatta called Shahjahan Mosque. Another mosque was built during his tenture in Lahore called Wazir Khan Mosque, by Shaikh Ilm-ud-din Ansari who was the court physician to the emperor.

The Taj Mahal is a mausoleum located in Agra, India, built by Mughal Emperor Shah Jahan in memory of his favourite wife, Mumtaz Mahal.

The Taj Mahal (also "the Taj") is considered the finest example of Mughal architecture, a style that combines elements from Persian, Indian, and Islamic architectural styles. In 1983, the Taj Mahal became a UNESCO World Heritage Site and was cited as "the jewel of Muslim art in India and one of the universally admired masterpieces of the world's heritage."

While the white domed marble mausoleum is its most familiar component, the Taj Mahal is actually an integrated complex of structures. Building began around 1632 and was completed around 1653, and employed thousands of artisans and craftsmen. The construction of the Taj Mahal was entrusted to a board of architects under imperial supervision including Abd ul-Karim Ma'mur Khan, Makramat Khan, and Ustad Ahmad Lahauri. Lahauri is generally considered to be the principal designer.

Origin and Inspiration

The Taj Mahal represents the finest and most sophisticated example of Mughal architecture. Its origins lie in the moving circumstances of its commission and the culture and history of an Islamic Mughal empire's rule of large parts of India.

The distraught Mughal Emperor Shah Jahan commissioned the mausoleum upon the death of his favourite wife, Mumtaz Mahal. Today it is one of the most famous and recognisable buildings in the world and while the white domed marble mausoleum is the most familiar part of the monument, the Taj Mahal is an extensive complex of buildings and gardens that extends over 22.44 Hectares and includes subsidiary tombs, waterworks infrastructure, the small town of 'Taj Ganji' and a 'moonlight garden' to the north of the river. Construction began in 1632 AD, (1041 AH), on the south bank of the River Yamuna in Agra, and was substantially complete by 1648 AD (1058 AH). The design was conceived as both an earthly replica of the house of Mumtaz in paradise and an instrument of propaganda for the emperor.

Who designed the Taj Mahal is unclear; although it is known that a large team of designers and craftsmen were responsible with Jahan himself taking an active role. Ustad Ahmad Lahauri is considered the most likely candidate as the principal designer.

Mumtaz and Jahan

In 1607 AD (1025 AH) the Mughal Prince Khurrum (later to become Shah Jahan) was betrothed to Arjumand Banu Begum, the grand daughter of a Persian noble. She would become the unquestioned love of his life. They were married five years later in 1612 AD (1021 AH). After their wedding celebrations, Khurram "finding her in appearance and character elect among all the women of the time," gave her the title Mumtaz Mahal (Jewel of the Palace).

The intervening years had seen Khurrum take two other wives known as Akbarabadi Mahal and Kandahari Mahal, but according to the official court chronicler Qazwini, the relationship with his other wives "had nothing more than the status of marriage. The intimacy, deep affection, attention and favour which His Majesty had for the Cradle of Excellence [Mumtaz] exceeded by a thousand times what he felt for any other."

Mumtaz died in Burhanpur in 1631 AD (1040 AH), after the childbirth of their fourteenth child, a daughter named Gauhara Begum. Typcially she had been accompanying her husband whilst he was fighting a campaign in the Deccan Plateau. Her body was temporarily buried in a garden called Zainabad on the banks of the Tapti River in Burhanpur. The contemporary court chroniclers paid an unusual amount of attention to this event and Shah Jahan's grief at her demise. Immediately after hearing the news the emperor was reportedly inconsolable. He was not seen for a week at court and considered abdicating and living his life as a religious recluse.

The court historian Muhammad Amin Qazwini, wrote that before his wife's death the emperor's beard had "not more than ten or twelve grey hairs, which he used to pluck out' turned grey and eventually white" and that he soon needed spectacles because his eyes deteriorated from constant weeping. Since Mumtaz had died on Wednesday, all entertainments were banned on that day. Jahan gave up listening to music, wearing jewelry or rich and colourful clothes and using perfumes for two years.

So concerned were the imperial family that an honoury uncle wrote to say that "if he continued to abandon himself to his mourning, Mumtaz might think of giving up the joys of Paradise to come back to earth, this place of misery — and he should also consider the children she had left to his care." The Austrian scholar Ebba Koch compares Shah Jahan to "Majnum, the ultimate lover of Muslim lore, who flees into the desert to pine for his unattainable Layla."

Jahan's eldest daughter, the devoted Jahanara Begum Sahib, gradually brought him out of grief and fulfilled the functions of Mumtaz at court. Immediately after the burial in Burhanpur, Jahan and the imperial court devoted themselves to the planning and design of the mausoleum and funery garden in Agra.

16th–17th Century Agra

The first Mughal garden was created in 1526 in Agra by Babur, the founder of the dynasty. Thereafter, gardens became important Mughal symbols of power, changing the emphasis from pre-Mughal symbols such as forts. The shift has been explained in terms of the introduction of a new ordered aesthetic — an artistic expression with religious and funerary aspects and as a metaphor for Babur's ability to control the arid Indian planes and hence the country at large.

Babur rejected much of the indigenous and Lodhi architecture on the opposite bank and attempted to create new ones inspired by Persian gardens and royal encampments. Ram Bagh was followed by an extensive, regular and integrated complex of gardens and palaces stretching for more than a kilometre along the river. A high continuous stone plinth bounded the transition between gardens and river and established the framework for future development in the city.

In the following century, a thriving riverfront garden city developed on both sides of the Yamuna. Subsequent Mughal emperors developed both sides of the river. This included the rebuilding of Agra Fort by Akbar, which was completed in 1573. By the time Jahan ascended to the throne, Agra's population had grown to approximately 700,000 and was, as Abdul Aziz writes, "a wonder of the age — as much a centre of the arteries of trade both by land and water as a meeting-place of saints, sages and scholars from all Asia.....a veritable lodestar for artistic workmanship, literary talent and spiritual worth".

Agra became a city centred on its waterfront and developed partly eastwards but mostly westwards from the rich estates that lined the banks. The prime sites remained those that had access to the river and the Taj Mahal was built in this context, but uniquely, on both sides of the river.

Mughal Tombs

The erection of Mughal tombs to honour the dead was the subject of a theological debate conducted in part, through built architecture over several centuries. For the majority of Muslims, the spiritual power (barakat) of visiting the resting places (ziyarat) of those venerated in Islam, was a force by which greater personal sanctity could be achieved. However, orthodox Islam found tombs problematic because a number of Hadith forbade the their construction.

As a culture also attempting to accommodate and assimilate the majority Hindu populace, opposition also came from these local traditions which believed dead bodies and the structures over them were impure. For many Muslims at the time of the Taj's construction, tombs could be considered legitimate providing they did not strive for pomp and were seen as a means to provide a reflection of paradise (Jannah) here on earth.

The ebb and flow of this debate can be seen in the Mughul's dynastic mausoleums stretching back to that of their ancestor Timur. Built in 1403 AD (810 AH) Timur is buried in the Gur-e Amir in Samarkand, under a fluted dome. The tomb employs a traditional Persian Iwan as an entrance. The 1528 AD (935 AH) Tomb of Babur in Kabul is much more modest in comparison, with a simple cenotaph exposed to the sky, laid out in the centre of a walled garden.

Humayun's tomb commissioned in 1562 AD, was one of the most direct influences on the Taj Mahal's design and was a response to the Gur-e Amir, borrowing a central dome, geometric symmetrical planning and iwan entrances, but incorporating the more specifically Indian Mughal devices of chhatris, red sandstone face work, and a 'Paradise garden' (Charbagh). Akbar's tomb c.1600 at Sikandra, Agra, retains many of the elements of Humayan's tomb but possesses no dome and reverts to a cenotaph open to the sky.

A theme which was carried forward in the Itmad-Ud-Daulah's Tomb also at Agra, built between 1622 and 1628, commissioned by his daughter Nur Jahan. The Tomb of Jahangir at Shahdara (Lahore), begun in 1628 AD (1037 AH), only 4 years before the construction of the Taj and again without a dome, takes the form of a simple plinth with a minaret at each corner.

Paradise Gardens

The concept of the paradise garden (Charbagh) was brought from Persia by the Mughals as a form of Timurid garden. They were the first architectural expression the new empire made in the Indian sub-continent, and fulfilled diverse functions with strong symbolic meanings. The symbolism of these gardens is derived from mystic Islamic texts describing paradise as a garden filled with abundant trees, flowers and plants, with water playing a key role: In Paradise four rivers source at a central spring or mountain. In their ideal form they were laid out as a square subdivided into four equal parts. These are often represented in the Charbagh as shallow canals which separate the garden by flowing towards the cardinal points. The canals represent the promised rivers of water, milk, wine and honey.

The centre of the garden, at the intersection of the divisions is highly symbolically charged and is where, in the ideal form, a pavilion, pool or tomb would be situated. The tombs of Humayun, Akbar and Jahangir, the previous Mughal emperors, follow this pattern. The cross axial garden also finds independent precedents within South Asia dating from the 5th century where the royal gardens of Sigiriya in Sri Lanka were laid out in a similar way. For the tomb of Jahan's late wife though, where the mausoleum is sited at the edge of the garden, there is a debate amongst scholars regarding why the traditional charbagh form has not been used. Ebba Koch suggests a variant of the charbagh was employed; that of the more secular waterfront garden found in Agra, adapted for a religious purpose. Such gardens were developed by the Mughuls for the specific conditions of the Indian plains where slow flowing rivers provide the water source, the water is raised from the river by animal driven devices known as purs and stored in cisterns.

A linear terrace is set close to the riverbank with low-level rooms set below the main building opening on to the river. Both ends of the terrace were emphasised with towers. This form was brought to Agra by Babur and by the time of Shah Jahan, gardens of this type, as well as the more traditional charbagh, lined both sides of the Jumna river. The riverside terrace was designed to enhance the views of Agra for the imperial elite who would travel in and around the city by river. Other scholars suggest another explanation for the eccentric siting of the mausoleum. If the Midnight Garden to the north of the river Jumna is considered an integral part of the complex, then the mausoleum can be interpreted as being in the centre of a garden divided by a real river and thus can be considered more in the tradition of the pure charbagh.

Mausolea

The favoured form of both Mughal garden pavilions and mausolea (seen as a funerary form of pavilion) was the hasht bihisht which translates from Persian as 'eight paradises'. These were a square or rectangular planned buildings with a central domed chamber surrounded by eight elements. Later developments of the hasht bihisht divided the square at 45 degree angles to create a more radial plan which often also includes chamfered corners; examples of which can be found in Todar Mal's Baradari at Fatehpur Sikri and Humayun's Tomb.

Each element of the plan is reflected in the elevations with iwans and with the corner rooms expressed through smaller arched niches. Often such structures are topped with chhatris (small pillared pavilions) at each corner. The eight divisions and frequent octagonal forms of such structures represent the eight levels of paradise for Muslims. The paradigm however was not confined solely to Islamic antecedents. The Chinese magic square was employed for numerous purposes including crop rotation and also finds a Muslim expression in the wafq of their mathematicians. Ninefold schemes find particular resonance in the Indian mandalas, the cosmic maps of Hinduism and Buddhism.

In addition to Humayun's tomb, the more closely contemporary Tomb of Itmad-Ud-Daulah marked a new era of Mughal architecture. It was built by the empress Nur Jehan for her father from 1622–1625 AD (1031–1034 AH) and is small in comparison to many other Mughal-era tombs. So exquisite is the execution of its surface treatments, it is often described as a jewel box. The garden layout, hierarchical use of white marble and sandstone, Parchin kari inlay designs and latticework presage many elements of the Taj Mahal. The cenotaph of Nur Jehan's father is laid, off centre, to the west of her mother. This break in symmetry was repeated in the Taj where Mumtaz was interred in the geometric centre of the complex and Jahan is laid to her side. These close similarities with the tomb of Mumtaz have earned it the sobriquet- *The Baby Taj*.

Minarets

Minarets did not become a common feature of Mughal architecture until the 17th century, particularly under the patronage of Shah Jahan. A few precedents exist in the 20 years before the construction of the Taj in the Tomb of Akbar and the Tomb of Jahangir. Their increasing use was influenced by developments elsewhere in the Islamic world, particularly in Ottoman and Timurid architecture and is seen as suggestive of an increasing religious orthodoxy of the Mughal dynasty.

Concepts, Symbolism and Interpretations

Under the reign of Shah Jahan, the symbolic content of Mughal architecture reached a peak. The Taj Mahal complex was conceived as a replica on earth of the house of the departed in paradise (inspired by a verse by the imperial goldsmith and poet Bibadal Khan. This theme, common in most Mughal funerary architecture, permeates the entire complex and informs the detailed design of all the elements. A number of secondary principles also inform the design, of which hierarchy is the most dominant. A deliberate interplay is established between the building's elements, its surface decoration, materials, geometric planning and its acoustics. This interplay extends from what can be experienced directly with the senses, into religious, intellectual, mathematical and poetic ideas. The constantly changing sunlight that illuminates the building reflected from its translucent marble is not a happy accident, it had a metaphoric role associated with the presence of god.

Symmetry and Hierachy

Symmetry and geometric planning played an important role in ordering the complex and reflected a trend towards formal systematisation that was apparent in all of the arts emanating from Jahan's imperial patronage. Bilateral symmetry expressed simultaneous ideas of pairing, counterparts and integration, reflecting intellectual and spiritual notions of universal harmony. A complex set of implied grids based on the Mughul Gaz unit of measurement provided a flexible means of bringing proportional order to all the elements of the Taj Mahal.

Hierarchical ordering of architecture is commonly used to emphasise particular elements of a design and to create drama. In the Taj Mahal, the hierarchical use of red sandstone and white marble contributes manifold *symbollic* significance. The Mughals were elaborating on a concept which traced its roots to earlier Hindu practices, set out in the Vishnudharmottara Purana, which recommended white stone for buildings for the Brahmins (priestly caste) and red stone for members of the Kshatriyas (warrior caste).

By building structures that employed such colour coding, the Mughals identified themselves with the two leading classes of Indian social structure and thus defined themselves as rulers in Indian terms. Red sandstone also had significance in the Persian origins of the Mughal empire where red was the exclusive colour of imperial tents. In the Taj Mahal the relative importance of each building in the complex is denoted by the amount of white marble (or sometimes white polished plaster) that is used.

The use of naturalist ornament demonstrates a similar hierarchy. Wholly absent from the more lowly jilaukhana and caravanserai areas, it can be found with increasing frequency as the processional route approaches the climactic Mausoleum.

Its symbolism is multifaceted, on the one hand evoking a more perfect, stylised and permanent garden of paradise than could be found growing in the earthly garden; on the other, an instrument of propaganda for Jahan's chroniclers who portrayed him as an 'erect cypress of the garden of the caliphate' and frequently used plant metaphors to praise his good governance, person, family and court. Plant metaphors also find common cause with Hindu traditions where such symbols as the 'vase of plenty' (Kalasha) can be found.

Sound was also used to express ideas of paradise. The interior of the mausoleum has a reverberation time (the time taken from when a noise is made until all of its echoes have died away) of 28 seconds providing an atmosphere where the words of those employed to continually recite the Qu'ran Hafiz, as prayer for the soul of Mumtaz, would linger in the air.

A Symbol of Love

The popular view of the Taj as one of the world's monuments to a great "love story" is born out by the contemporary accounts and most scholars accept this has a strong basis in fact. The building was also used to assert Jahani propaganda concerning the 'perfection' of the Mughal leadership. The extent to which the Taj uses propaganda is the subject of some debate amongst contemporary scholars. Wayne Begley put forward an interpretation in 1979 that exploits the Islamic idea that the 'Garden of paradise' is also the location of the 'throne of god' on the day of judgement. In his reading the Taj Mahal is seen as a monument where Shah Jahan has appropriated the authority of the 'throne of god' symbolism for the glorification of his own reign. Koch disagrees, finding this an overly elaborate explanation and pointing out that the 'Throne' sura from the Qu'ran is missing from the calligraphic inscriptions.

This period of Mughal architecture best exemplifies the maturity of a style that had synthesised Islamic architecture with its indigenous counterparts. By the time the Mughals built the Taj, though proud of their Persian and Timurid roots, they had come to see themselves as Indian. Copplestone writes "Although it is certainly a native Indian production, its architectural success rests on its fundamentally Persian sense of intelligible and undisturbed proportions, applied to clean, uncomplicated surfaces."

Architects and Craftsmen

We do not know precisely who designed the Taj Mahal today.

In the Islamic world at the time, the credit for a building's design was usually given to its patron rather than its architects. From the evidence of contemporary sources, it is clear that a team of architects were responsible for the design and supervision of the works, but they are mentioned infrequently. Shah Jahan's court histories emphasise his personal involvement in the construction and it is true that, more than any other Mughal emperor, he showed the greatest interest in building, holding daily meetings with his architects and supervisors.

The court chronicler Lahouri, writes that Jahan would make "appropriate alterations to whatever the skilful architects designed after many thoughts, and asked competent questions." Two architects *are* mentioned by name, Ustad Ahmad Lahauri and Mir Abdul Karim in writings by Lahauri's son Lutfullah Muhandis. Ustad Ahmad Lahauri had laid the foundations of the Red Fort at Delhi. Mir Abdul Karim had been the favourite architect of the previous emperor Jahangir and is mentioned as a supervisor, together with Makramat Khan, of the construction of the Taj Mahal.

- Expand and add craftsmen
- Bebadal Khan, the poet and goldsmith
- Hindu craftsmen.

Calligraphy and Decoration

The exquisite and highly skilled parchin kari work was developed by Mughal lapidarists from techniques taught to them by Italian craftsmen employed at court. The look of European herbals, books illustrating botanical species, was adapted and refined in Mughal parchin kari work.

Throughout the complex, passages from the Qur'an are used as decorative elements. Recent scholarship suggests that the passages were chosen by a persian calligrapher Abd ul-Haq, who came to India from Shiraz, Iran, in 1609. As a reward for his "dazzling virtuosity", Shah Jahan gave him the title of "Amanat Khan". This is supported by an inscription near the lines from the Qur'an at the base of the interior dome that reads "Written by the insignificant being, Amanat Khan Shirazi." The texts refer to themes of judgment and include:

- Surah 91 – The Sun
- Surah 112 – The Purity of Faith

- Surah 89 – Daybreak
- Surah 93 – Morning Light
- Surah 95 – The Fig
- Surah 94 – The Solace
- Surah 36 – Ya Sin
- Surah 81 – The Folding Up
- Surah 82 – The Cleaving Asunder
- Surah 84 – The Rending Asunder
- Surah 98 – The Evidence
- Surah 67 – Dominion
- Surah 48 – Victory
- Surah 77 – Those Sent Forth
- Surah 39 – The Crowds.

The calligraphy on the Great Gate reads *"O Soul, thou art at rest. Return to the Lord at peace with Him, and He at peace with you."*

Much of the calligraphy is composed of florid thuluth script, made of jasper or black marble, inlaid in white marble panels. Higher panels are written in slightly larger script to reduce the skewing effect when viewed from below. The calligraphy found on the marble cenotaphs in the tomb is particularly detailed and delicate.

Abstract forms are used throughout, especially in the plinth, minarets, gateway, mosque, jawab and, to a lesser extent, on the surfaces of the tomb. The domes and vaults of the sandstone buildings are worked with tracery of incised painting to create elaborate geometric forms. Herringbone inlays define the space between many of the adjoining elements. White inlays are used in sandstone buildings, and dark or black inlays on the white marbles. Mortared areas of the marble buildings have been stained or painted in a contrasting colour, creating geometric patterns of considerable complexity. Floors and walkways use contrasting tiles or blocks in tessellation patterns.

On the lower walls of the tomb there are white marble dados that have been sculpted with realistic bas relief depictions of flowers and vines. The marble has been polished to emphasise the exquisite detailing of the carvings and the dado frames and archway spandrels have been decorated with pietra dura inlays of highly stylised, almost geometric vines, flowers and fruits. The inlay stones are of yellow marble, jasper and jade, polished and levelled to the surface of the walls.

Construction & Interment

A site was chosen on the banks of the Yamuna River on the southern edge of Agra and purchased from Raja Jai Singh in exchange for four mansions in the city. The site, *"from the point of view of loftiness and pleasantness appeared to be worthy of the burial of that one who dwells in paradise"*. In January 1632 AD (1041 AH), Mumtaz's body was moved with great ceremony from Burhanpur to Agra while food, drink and coins were distributed amongst the poor and deserving along the way. Work had already begun on the foundations of the river terrace when the body arrived. A small domed building was erected over her body, thought to have been sited, and now marked, by an enclosure in the western garden near the riverfront terrace.

Foundations

The foundations represented the biggest technical challenge to be overcome by the Mughal builders. In order to support the considerable load resulting from the mausoleum, the sands of the riverbank needed to be stabilised. To this end, wells were sunk and then cased in timber and finally filled with rubble, iron and mortar — essentially acting as augured piles. After construction of the terrace was completed, work began simultaneously on the rest of the complex. Trees were planted almost immediately to allow them to mature as work progressed.

Dating

The initial stages of the build were noted by Shah Jahan's chroniclers in their description of the first two anniversary celebrations in honour of Mumtaz — known as the 'Urs. The first, held on the June 22, 1632 AD (1041 AH), was a tented affair open to all ranks of society and held in the location of what is now the entrance courtyard (jilaukhana). Alms were distributed and prayers recited. By the second Urs, held on May 26, 1633 AD (1042 AH), Mumtaz Mahal had been interred in her final resting place, the riverside terrace was finished; as was the plinth of the mausoleum and the tahkhana, a galleried suite of rooms opening to the river and under the terrace.

It was used by the imperial retinue for the celebrations. Peter Mundy, an employee of the British East India company and a western eye witness, noted the ongoing construction of the caravanserais and bazaars and that "There is alreadye[sic] about Her Tombe a raile[sic] of gold". To deter theft it was replaced in 1643 AD (1053 AH) with an inlaid marble jali.

After the second Urs further dating of the progress can be made from several signatures left by the calligrapher Amanat Khan. The signed frame of the south arch of the domed hall of the mausoleum indicates it was reaching completion in 1638/39 AD (1048/1049 AH). In 1643 AD (1053 AH) the official sources documenting the twelfth Urs give a detailed description of a substantially completed complex. Decorative work apparently continued until 1648 AD (1058 AH) when Amanat Khan dated the north arch of the great gate with the inscription "Finished with His help, the Most High".

Materials

The Taj Mahal was constructed using materials from all over India and Asia. The buildings are constructed with walls of brick and rubble inner cores faced with either marble or sandstone locked together with iron dowels and clamps. Some of the walls of the mausoleum are several metres thick. Over 1,000 elephants were used to transport building materials during the construction. The bricks were fired locally and the sandstone was quarried 28 miles away near Fatehpur Sikri. The white marble was brought 250 miles from quarries belonging to Raja Jai Singh in Makrana, Rajasthan. The jasper was sourced from the Punjab and the jade and crystal from China.

The turquoise was from Tibet and the Lapis lazuli from Afghanistan, while the sapphire came from Sri Lanka and the carnelian from Arabia. In all, 28 types of precious and semi-precious stones were inlaid into the white marble. Jean-Baptiste Tavernier records that the scaffolding and centering for the arches was constructed entirely in brick. Legend says that the emperor offered these scaffolding bricks to anyone who would remove them and that at the end of the construction and they removed within a week. Modern scholars dispute this and consider it much more likely that the scaffolding was made of bamboo and materials were elevated by means of timber ramps.

Cost

Initial estimates for the cost of the works of 4,000,000 rupees had risen to 5,000,000 by completion. A waqf (trust) was established for the perpetual upkeep of the mausoleum with an income of 300,000 rupees. One third of this income came from 30 villages in the district of Agra while the remainder came from taxes generated as a result of trade from the bazaars and caravanserais which had been built at an early stage to the south of the complex. Any surplus would be distributed by the emperor as he saw fit. As well as paying for routine maintenance, the waqf financed the expenses for the tomb attendants and the Hafiz, the Koran reciters who would sit day and night in the mausoleum and perform funery services praying for the eternal soul of Mumtaz Mahal.

Dimensional Organisation

The Taj complex is ordered by grids. The complex was originally surveyed by J.A. Hodgson in 1825, however the first detailed scholastic examination of how the various elements of the Taj might fit into a coordinating grid was not carried out until 1989 by Begley and Desai. Numerous 17th century accounts detail the precise measurements of the complex in terms of the gaz or *zira*, the Mughal linear yard, equivalent to approximately 80–92 cm. Begley and Desai concluded a 400-gaz grid was used and then subdivided and that the various discrepancies they discovered were due to errors in the contemporary descriptions.

Research and measurement by Koch and Richard Andre Barraud in 2006 suggested a more complex method of ordering that relates better to the 17th century records. Whereas Begley and Desai had used a simple fixed grid on which the buildings are superimposed, Koch and Barraud found the layout's proportions were better explained by the use of a *generated* grid system in which specific lengths may be divided in a number of ways such as halving, dividing by three or using decimal systems. They suggest the 374-gaz width of the complex given by the contemporary historians was correct and the Taj is planned as a tripartite rectangle of three 374-gaz squares.

Different modular divisions are then used to proportion the rest of the complex. A 17-gaz module is used in the jilaukhana, bazaar and caravanserais areas whereas a more detailed 23-gaz module is used in the garden and terrace areas (since their width is 368 gaz, a multiple of 23). The buildings were in turn proportioned using yet smaller grids superimposed on the larger organisational ones. The smaller grids were also used to establish elevational proportion throughout the complex.

Koch and Barraud explain such apparently peculiar numbers as making more sense when seen as part of Mughal geometric understanding. Octagons and triangles, which feature extensively in the Taj, have particular properties in terms of the relationships of their sides. A right-handed triangle with two sides of 12 will have a hypotenuse of 17; similarly if it has two sides of 17 its hypotenuse will be 24. An octagon with a width of 17 will have sides of exactly 7, which is the basic grid upon which the mausoleum, mosque and Mihman Khana are planned.

Discrepancies remain in Koch and Barraud's work which they attribute to numbers being rounded fractions, inaccuracies of reporting from third persons and errors in workmanship (most notable in the caravanserais areas further from the tomb itself).

A 2009 paper by Prof R. Balasubramaniam of the Indian Institute of Technology found Barraud's explanation of the dimensional errors and the transition between the 23 and 17 gaz grid at the great gate unconvincing. Balasubramaniam conducted dimensional analysis of the complex based on Barraud's surveys. He concluded that the Taj was constructed using the ancient Aegula as the basic unit rather than the Mughal 'gaz', noted in the contemporary accounts. The AEgula, which equates to 1.763 cm and the Vistasti (12 Angulams) were first mentioned in the Arthasastra in c. 300 BC and may have been derived from the earlier Indus Valley Civilisation. In this analysis the forecourt and caravanserai areas were set out with a 60 Vistasti grid, and the riverfront and garden sections with a 90-vistari grid. The transition between the grids is more easily accommodated, 90 being easily divisible by 60. The research suggests that older, pre-Mughal methods of proportion were employed as ordering principles in the Taj.

Components of the Complex

Mausoleum (Rauza-i Munauwara)

Base, dome, and minaret: The focus and climax of the Taj Mahal complex is the symmetrical white marble tomb; a cubic building with chamfered corners, with arched recesses known as pishtaqs. It is topped by a large dome and several pillared, roofed chhatris. In plan, it has a near perfect symmetry about 4 axes. It comprises 4 floors; the lower basement storey containing the tombs of Jahan and Mumtaz, the entrance storey containing identical cenotaphs of the tombs below in a much more elaborate chamber, an ambulatory storey and a roof terrace.

Minarets: At the corners of the plinth stand minarets: four large towers each more than 40 metres tall. The towers are designed as working minarets, a traditional element of mosques, a place for a muezzin to call the Islamic faithful to prayer. Each minaret is effectively divided into three equal parts by two balconies that ring the tower. At the top of the tower is a final balcony surmounted by a chhatri that echoes the design of those on the tomb. The minaret chhatris share the same finishing touches: a lotus design topped by a gilded finial. Each of the minarets was constructed slightly out of plumb to the outside of the plinth, so that in the event of collapse (a typical occurrence with many such tall constructions of the period) the structure would fall away from the tomb.

Elevations: The mausoleum is cubic with chamfered edges, xyz metres on each side. On the long sides, a massive *pishtaq*, or vaulted archway frames an arch-shaped doorway, with a similar arch-shaped balcony above. These main arches extend above the roof the building by use of an integrated facade. To either side of the main arch, additional pishtaqs are stacked above and below. This motif of stacked pishtaqs is replicated on the chamfered corner areas. The design is completely uniform and consistent on all sides of the building.

Dome: The marble dome that surmounts the tomb is its most spectacular feature. Its height is about the same size as the base building, about 35 m. Its height is accentuated because it sits on a cylindrical "drum" about 7 metres high. Because of its shape, the dome is often called an onion dome (also called an *amrud* or apple dome). The dome is topped by a gilded finial, which mixes traditional Islamic and Hindu decorative elements. The dome shape is emphasised by four smaller domed chhatris placed at its corners. The chhatri domes replicate the onion shape of main dome. Their columned bases open through the roof of the tomb, and provide light to the interior. The chhatris also are topped by gilded finials. Tall decorative spires (*guldastas*) extend from the edges of the base walls, and provide visual emphasis of the dome height.

Lower chamber: Muslim tradition forbids elaborate decoration of graves, so the bodies of Mumtaz and Shah Jahan are laid in a relatively plain chamber beneath the main chamber of the Taj. They are buried on a north-south access, with faces turned right (west) toward Mecca. The Taj has been raised over their cenotaphs (from Greek *keno taphas,* empty tomb). The cenotaphs mirror precisely the placement of the two graves, and are exact duplicates of the grave stones in the basement below. Mumtaz's cenotaph is placed at the precise centre of the inner chamber. On a rectangular marble base about 1.5 by 2.5 metres is a smaller marble casket. Both base and casket are elaborately inlaid with precious and semiprecious gems. Calligraphic inscriptions on the casket identify and praise Mumtaz. On the lid of the casket is a raised rectangular lozenge meant to suggest a writing tablet.

Main chamber: The inner chamber of the Taj Mahal contains the cenotaphs of Mumtaz and Shah Jahan. It is a masterpiece of artistic craftsmanship, virtually without precedent or equal. The inner chamber is an octagon. While the design allows for entry from each face, only the south (garden facing) door is used. The interior walls are about 25 metres high, topped by a "false" interior dome decorated with a sun motif.

Eight pishtaq arches define the space at ground level. As is typical with the exterior, each lower pishtaq is crowned by a second pishtaq about midway up the wall. The four central upper arches form balconies or viewing areas; each balcony's exterior window has an intricate screen or *jali* cut from marble. In addition to the light from the balcony screens, light enters through roof openings covered by the chhatris at the corners of the exterior dome. Each of the chamber walls has been highly decorated with dado bas relief, intricate lapidary inlay, and refined calligraphy panels.

The hierarchical ordering of the entire complex reaches its crescendo in the chamber. Mumtaz's cenotaph sits at the geometric centre of the building; Jahan was buried at a later date by her side to the west — an arrangement seen in other Mughal tombs of the period such as Itmad-Ud-Daulah. Marble is used exclusively as the base material for increasingly dense, expensive and complex parchin kari floral decoration as one approaches the screen and cenotpahs which are inlaid with semi-precious stones.

The use of such inlay work is often reserved in Shah Jahani architecture for spaces associated with the emperor or his immediate family. The ordering of this decoration simultaneously emphasises the cardinal points and the centre of the chamber with dissipating concentric octagons. Such hierarchies appear in both Muslim and Indian culture as important spiritual and atrological themes. The chamber is an abundant evocation of the garden of paradise with representations of flowers, plants and arabesques and the calligraphic inscriptions in both the thuluth and the less formal naskh script,

Shah Jahan's cenotaph is beside Mumtaz's to the western side. It is the only asymmetric element in the entire complex. His cenotaph is bigger than his wife's, but reflects the same elements: A larger casket on slightly taller base, again decorated with astonishing precision with lapidary and calligraphy which identifies Shah Jahan. On the lid of this casket is a sculpture of a small pen box. (The pen box and writing tablet were traditional Mughal funerary icons decorating men's and women's caskets respectively.)

An octagonal marble screen or *jali* borders the cenotaphs and is made from eight marble panels. Each panel has been carved through with intricate piercework. The remaining surfaces have been inlaid with semiprecious stones in extremely delicate detail, forming twining vines, fruits and flowers.

Riverfront Terrace (Chameli Farsh)

Plinth and terrace:

- Tahkhana
- Towers.

Minarets: At the corners of the plinth stand minarets — four large towers each more than 40 metres tall. The towers are designed as working minarets, a traditional element of mosques, a place for a muezzin to call the Islamic faithful to prayer. Each minaret is effectively divided into three equal parts by two working balconies that ring the tower. At the top of the tower is a final balcony surmounted by a chhatri that mirrors the design of those on the tomb. Each of the minarets was constructed slightly out of plumb to the outside of the plinth, so that in the event of collapse (a typical occurrence with many such tall constructions of the period) the material would tend to fall away from the tomb.

Garden (Charbagh)

The large *charbagh* (a formal Mughal garden divided into four parts) provides the foreground for the classic view of the Taj Mahal. The garden's strict and formal planning employs raised pathways which divide each quarter of the garden into 16 sunken parterres or flowerbeds. A raised marble water tank at the centre of the garden, halfway between the tomb and the gateway, and a linear reflecting pool on the North-South axis reflect the Taj Mahal. Elsewhere the garden is laid out with avenues of trees and fountains. The *charbagh* garden is meant to symbolise the four flowing Rivers of Paradise. The raised marble water tank (hauz) is called *al Hawd al-Kawthar*, literally meaning and named after the "Tank of Abundance" promised to Muhammad in paradise where the faithful may quench their thirst upon arrival.

Two pavilions occupy the east and west ends of the cross axis, one the mirror of the other. In the classic charbargh design, gates would have been located in this location. In the Taj they provide punctuation and access to the long enclosing wall with its decorative crenellations. Built of sandstone, they are given a tripartite form and over two storeys and are capped with a white marble chhatris supported from 8 columns.

The original planting of the garden is one of the Taj Mahal's remaining mysteries. The contemporary accounts mostly deal just with the architecture and only mention 'various kinds of fruit-bearing trees and rare aromatic herbs' in relation to the garden. Cypress trees are almost certainly to have been planted being popular similes in Persian poetry for the slender elegant stature of the beloved. By the end of the 18th century, Thomas Twining noted orange trees and a large plan of the complex suggests beds of various other fruits such as pineapples, pomegranates, bananas, limes and apples. The British, at the end of the 19th century thinned out a lot of the increasingly forested trees, replanted the cypresses and laid the gardens to lawns in their own taste.

The layout of the garden, and its architectural features such as its fountains, brick and marble walkways, and geometric brick-lined flowerbeds are similar to Shalimar's, and suggest that the garden may have been designed by the same engineer, Ali Mardan. Early accounts of the garden describe its profusion of vegetation, including roses, daffodils, and fruit trees in abundance. As the Mughal Empire declined, the tending of the garden declined as well. When the British took over management of the Taj Mahal, they changed the landscaping to resemble the formal lawns of London.

Great Gate (Darwaza-i Rauza)

The great gate stands to the north of the entrance forecourt (jilaukhana) and provides a symbollic transition between the worldly realm of bazaars and caravanserai and the spiritual realm of the paradise garden, mosque and the mausoleum. Its rectangular plan is a variation of the 9-part hasht bihisht plan found in the mausoleum. The corners are articulated with octagonal towers giving the structure a defensive appearance. External domes were reserved for tombs and mosques and so the large central space does not receive any outward expression of its internal dome. From within the great gate, the Mausoleum is framed by the pointed arch of the portal. Inscriptions from the Qu'ran are inlaid around the two northern and southern pishtaqs, the southern one 'Daybreak' invites believers to enter the garden of paradise.

Forecourt (Jilaukhana)

The jilaukhana (literally meaning 'in front of house') was a courtyard feature introduced to mughal architecture by Shah Jahan. It provided an area where visitors would dismount from their horses or elephants and assemble in style before entering the main tomb complex. The rectangular area divides north-south and east-west with an entry to the tomb complex through the main gate to the north and entrance gates leading to the outside provided in the eastern, western and southern walls. The southern gate leads to the Taj Ganji quarter.

Bazaar streets: Two identical streets lead from the east and west gates to the centre of the courtyard. They are lined by verandahed colonnades articulated with cusped arches behind which cellular rooms were used to sell goods from when the Taj was built until 1996. The tax revenue from this trade was used for the upkeep of the Taj complex. The eastern bazaar streets were essentially ruined by the end of the 19th century and were restored by Lord Curzon restored 1900 and 1908.

Inner Subsidiary Tombs (Saheli Burj)

Two mirror image tombs are located at the southern corners of the jilaukhana. They are conceived as miniature replicas of the main complex and stand on raised platforms accessed by steps. Each octagonal tomb is constructed on a rectangular platform flanked by smaller rectangular buildings in front of which is laid a charbargh garden. Some uncertainty exists as to whom the tombs might memorialise. Their descriptions are absent from the contemporary accounts either because they were unbuilt or because they were ignored, being the tombs of women. On the first written document to mention them, the plan drawn up by Thomas and William Daniel in 1789, the eastern tomb is marked as that belonging to Akbarabadi Mahal and the western as Fatehpuri Mahal (two of Jahan's other wives).

Northern Courtyards (Khawasspuras)

A pair of courtyards is found in the northern corners of the jilaukhana which provided quarters (Khawasspuras) for the tombs attendants and the Hafiz. This residential element provided a transition between the outside world and the other-worldy delights of the tomb complex. The Khawasspurs had fallen into a state of disrepair by the late 18th century but the institution of the Khadim continued into the 20th century. The Khawasspuras were restored by Lord Curzon as part of his repairs between 1900 and 1908, after which the western courtyard was used as a nursery for the garden and the western courtyard was used as a cattle stable until 2003.

Bazaar and Caravanserai (Taj Ganji)

The Bazaar and caravanserai were constructed as an integral part of the complex, initially to provide the construction workers with accommodation and facilities for their wellbeing, and later as a place for trade, the revenue of which supplemented the expenses of the complex. The area became a small town in its own right during and after the building of the Taj. Originally known as 'Mumtazabad', today it is called Taj Ganji or 'Taj Market'. Its plan took the characteristic form of a square divided by two cross axial streets with gates to the four cardinal points. Bazaars lined each street and the resultant squares to each corner housed the caravanserais in open courtyards accessed from internal gates from where the streets intersected (Chauk). Contemporary sources pay more attention to the north eastern and western parts of the Taj Ganji (Taj Market) and it is likely that only this half received imperial funding. Thus, the quality of the architecture was finer than the southern half.

The distinction between how the sacred part of the complex and the secular was regarded is most acute in this part of the complex. Whilst the rest of the complex only received maintenance after its construction, the Taj Ganji became a bustling town and the centre of Agra's economic activity where "different kinds of merchandise from every land, varieties of goods from every country, all sorts of luxuries aof the time, and various kinds of necessitities of civilisation and comfortable living brought from all parts of the world" were sold. An idea of what sort of goods might have been traded is found in the names for the caravanserais; the north western one was known as Katra Omar Khan (Market of Omar Khan), the north eastern as Katra Fulel (Perfume Market), the south western as Katra Resham (Silk Market) and the south-eastern as Katra Jogidas.

It has been constantly redeveloped ever since its construction, to the extent that by the 19th century it had become unrecognisable as part of the Taj Mahal and no longer featured on contemporary plans and its architecture was largely obliterated. Today, the contrast is stark between the Taj Mahal's elegant, formal geometric layout and the narrow streets with organic, random and un-unified constructions found in the Taj Ganji. Only fragments of the original constructions remain, most notably the gates.

Perimeter Walls and Ancillary Buildings

The Taj Mahal complex is bounded on three sides by crenellated red sandstone walls, with the river-facing side left open. The garden-facing inner sides of the wall are fronted by columned arcades, a feature typical of Hindu temples which was later incorporated into Mughal mosques. The wall is interspersed with domed chhatris, and small buildings that may have been viewing areas or watch towers.

Outside the walls are several additional mausolea. These structures, composed primarily of red sandstone, are typical of the smaller Mughal tombs of the era. The outer eastern tomb has an associated mosque called the Black Mosque (Kali Masjid) or the Sandalwood Mosque (Sandli Masjid). The design is closely related to the inner subsidiary tombs found in the Jilhaukhana – small, landlocked versions of the riverfront terrace with a garden separating the mosque from the tomb. The person interred here is unknown, but was likely a female member of Jahan's household.

Waterworks

Water for the Taj complex was provided through a complex infrastructure. It was first drawn from the river by a series of *purs*- an animal-powered rope and bucket mechanism. The water then flowed along an arched aqueduct into a large storage tank, where, by thirteen additional purs, it was raised to large distribution cistern above the Taj ground level located to the west of the complex's wall. From here water passed into three subsidiary tanks and was then piped to the complex. The head of pressure generated by the height of the tanks (9.5m) was sufficient to supply the fountains and irrigate the gardens.

A 0.25 metre diameter earthenware pipe lies 1.8 metres below the surface, in line with the main walkway which fills the main pools of the complex. Some of the earthenware pipes were replaced in 1903 with cast iron. The fountain pipes were not connected directly to the fountain heads, instead a copper pot was provided under each fountain head: water filled the pots ensuring an equal pressure to each fountain. The purs no longer remain, but the other parts of the infrastructure have survived with the arches of the aqueduct now used to accommodate offices for the Archaeological Survey of India's Horticultural Department.

Moonlight garden (Mahtab Bagh)

To the north of the Taj Mahal complex, across the river is another Charbagh garden. It was designed as an integral part of the complex in the riverfront terrace pattern seen elsewhere in Agra. Its width is identical to that of the rest of the Taj. The garden historian Elizabeth Moynihan suggests the large octagonal pool in the centre of the terrace would reflect the image of the Mausoleum and thus the garden would provide a setting to view the Taj Mahal. The garden has been beset by flooding from the river since Mughal times.

As a result, the condition of the remaining structures is quite ruinous. Four sandstone towers marked the corners of the garden, only the south-eastward one remains. The foundations of two structures remain immediately north and south of the large pool which were probably garden pavilions. From the northern structure a stepped waterfall would have fed the pool. The garden to the north has the typical square, cross-axial plan with a square pool in its centre. To the west an aqueduct fed the garden.

History

Soon after the Taj Mahal's completion, Shah Jahan was deposed by his son Aurangzeb and put under house arrest at nearby Agra Fort. Upon Shah Jahan's death, Aurangzeb buried him in the mausoluem next to his wife.

By the late 19th century, parts of the buildings had fallen badly into disrepair. During the time of the Indian rebellion of 1857, the Taj Mahal was defaced by British soldiers and government officials, who chiseled out precious stones and lapis lazuli from its walls. At the end of the 19th century, British viceroy Lord Curzon ordered a massive restoration project, which was completed in 1908. He also commissioned the large lamp in the interior chamber, modeled after one in a Cairo mosque. During this time the garden was remodeled with British-style lawns that are still in place today.

Myths: Ever since its construction, the building has been the source of an admiration transcending culture and geography, and so personal and emotional responses have consistently eclipsed scholastic appraisals of the monument.

A longstanding myth holds that Shah Jahan planned a mausoleum to be built in black marble across the Yamuna river. The idea originates from fanciful writings of Jean-Baptiste Tavernier, a European traveller who visited Agra in 1665. It was suggested that Shah Jahan was overthrown by his son Aurangzeb before it could be built. Ruins of blackened marble across the river in *Moonlight Garden,* Mahtab Bagh, seemed to support this legend. However, excavations carried out in the 1990s found that they were discolored white stones that had turned black. A more credible theory for the origins of the black mausoleum was demonstrated in 2006 by archeologists who reconstructed part of the pool in the Moonlight Garden. A dark reflection of the white mausoleum could clearly be seen, befitting Shah Jahan's obsession with symmetry and the positioning of the pool itself.

No evidence exists for claims that describe, often in horrific detail, the deaths, dismemberments and mutilations which Shah

Jahan supposedly inflicted on various architects and craftsmen associated with the tomb. Some stories claim that those involved in construction signed contracts committing themselves to have no part in any similar design. Similar claims are made for many famous buildings. No evidence exists for claims that Lord William Bentinck, governor-general of India in the 1830s, supposedly planned to demolish the Taj Mahal and auction off the marble. Bentinck's biographer John Rosselli says that the story arose from Bentinck's fund-raising sale of discarded marble from Agra Fort.

In 2000, India's Supreme Court dismissed P.N. Oak's petition to declare that a Hindu king built the Taj Mahal. Oak claimed that origins of the Taj, together with other historic structures in the country currently ascribed to Muslim sultans predate Muslim occupation of India and thus, have a Hindu origin. A more poetic story relates that once a year, during the rainy season, a single drop of water falls on the cenotaph, as inspired by Rabindranath Tagore's description of the tomb as *"one tear-drop...upon the cheek of time"*. Another myth suggests that beating the silhouette of the finial will cause water to come forth. To this day, officials find broken bangles surrounding the silhouette.

Ustad Ahmad Lahauri

Ustad Ahmad Lahouri was a Persian architect and the most likely candidate as the chief architect of the Taj Mahal. The assertion is based on a claim made in writings by Lahauri's son Lutfullah Muhandis.

Shah Jahan's court histories emphasise his personal involvement in the construction and it is true that, more than any other Mughal emperor, he showed the greatest interest in building, holding daily meetings with his architects and supervisors. The court chronicler Lahouri, writes that Jahan would make "appropriate alterations to whatever the skilful architects designed after many thoughts, and asked competent questions."

In writings by Lahauri's son Lutfullah Muhandis, two architects are mentioned by name; Ustad Ahmad Lahauri and Mir Abdul Karim. Ustad Ahmad Lahauri had laid the foundations of the Red Fort at Delhi. Mir Abdul Karim had been the favourite architect of the previous emperor Jahangir and is mentioned as a supervisor, together with Makramat Khan, of the construction of the Taj Mahal.

Replicas

Among the buildings modeled on the Taj Mahal are the Taj Mahal Bangladesh, the Bibi Ka Maqbara in Aurangabad, Maharashtra, and the Tripoli Shrine Temple in Milwaukee, Wisconsin.

Old Delhi

Old Delhi, walled city of Delhi, was founded as Shahjahanabad by Indian Emperor Shahjahan in 1639. It remained the capital of the Mughals until the end of the Mughal dynasty.

It was once filled with mansions of nobles and members of the royal court, along with elegant mosques and gardens. Today, despite having become extremely crowded and dilapidated, it still serves as the symbolic heart of metropolitan Delhi.

The site of Shahjahanabad is north of earlier settlements of Delhi, its southern part overlaps some of the area settled during the Tughlaqs. The British city ("Lutyens' Delhi") was developed just south-west of Shahjahanabad.

Walls and Gates

It is approximately shaped like a quarter circle, with the Red Fort as the focal point. The old city was surrounded by a wall enclosing about 1500 acres, with several gates:

1. Nigambodh Gate:North/East, leading to historic Nigambodh ghat on Jamuna
2. Kashmiri Gate: North
3. Mori Gate: North
4. Kabuli gate: West
5. Lahori gate: West
6. Ajmeri Gate: South East, leading to Ghaziuddin Khan's Madrassa and Connaught Place, a focal point in New Delhi.
7. Turkman Gate: South East, close to some pre-Shahjahan remains which got enclosed within the walls, including the tomb of Hazrat Shah Turkman Bayabani.
8. Delhi Gate: South leading to Feroz Shah Kotla and what was then older habitation of Delhi then.

The surrounding walls, 12 feet wide and 26 feet tall, originally of mud, were replaced by red stone in 1657. In the Mughal period, the gates were kept locked at night. The walls have now largely disappeared, but most of the gates are still present. The township of old Delhi is still identifiable in a satellite image because of density of houses.

The famous Khooni Darwaza south of Delhi Gate, was just outside the walled city, it was originally constructed by Sher Shah Suri.

Red Fort

The Red Fort is a 17th century fort complex constructed by the Mughal emperor Shahjahan in the walled city of Old Delhi (in present day Delhi, India). It served as the capital of the Mughals until 1857, when Mughal emperor Bahadur Shah Zafar was exiled by the British Indian government. The British used it as a military camp until India was made independent in 1947. It is now a popular tourist site, as well as a powerful symbol of India's sovereignty: the Prime Minister of India raises the flag of India on the rampants of the Lahori Gate of the fort complex every year on Independence Day. It was designated a UNESCO World Heritage Site in 2007.

History

Mughal Emperor Shahjahan started construction of the massive fort in 1638 and work was completed in 1648. The Red Fort was originally referred to as "Qila-i-Mubarak" (the blessed fort), because it was the residence of the royal family. The layout of the Red Fort was organised to retain and integrate this site with the Salimgarh Fort. The fortress palace is an important focal point of the medieval city of Shahjahanabad. The planning and aesthetics of the Red Fort represent the zenith of Mughal creativity which prevailed during the reign of Emperor Shah Jahan.

This Fort has had many developments added on after its construction by Emperor Shahjahan. The significant phases of development were under Aurangzeb and later Mughal rulers. Important physical changes were carried out in the overall settings of the site after the First War of Independence during British Rule in 1857. After Independence, the site experienced a few changes in terms of addition/alteration to the structures. During the British period the Fort was mainly used as a cantonment and even after

Independence, a significant part of the Fort remained under the control of the Indian Army until the year 2003.

The Red Fort was the palace for Mughal Emperor Shah Jahan's new capital, Shahjahanabad, the seventh greatcity in the Delhi site. He moved his capital from Agra in a move designed to bring prestige to his reign, and to provide ample opportunity to apply his ambitious building schemes and interests.

The fort lies along the Yamuna River, which fed the moats that surround most of the wall. The wall at its north-eastern corner is adjacent to an older fort, the Salimgarh Fort, a defense built by Islam Shah Suri in 1546.The construction of the Red Fort began in 1638 and was completed by 1648.

On 11 March 1783, Sikhs briefly entered Red Fort in Delhi and occupied the Diwan-i-Am. The city was essentially surrendered by the Mughal wazir in cahoots with his Sikh Allies. This task was carried out under the command of the Sardar Baghel Singh Dhaliwal of the Karor Singhia misl.

The last Mughal emperor to occupy the fort was Bahadur Shah II "Zafar". Despite being the seat of Mughal power and its defensive capabilities, the Red Fort was not defended during the 1857 uprising against the British. After the failure of the 1857 rebellion, Zafar left the fort on 17 September. He returned to Red Fort as a prisoner of the British. Zafar was tried on in a trial starting on 27 January 1858, and was exiled on 7 October.

On 15 August 1947, India became an independent nation. This was marked by Jawahar Lal Nehru, the Prime Minister of India, unveiling the flag of independent India on 15 August 1947. This practice of unfurling the national flag with a speech by the Prime Minister on Independence Day continues to this day. Just after World War II, the Red Fort had been the scene of the famous trial of the Indian National Army.

Architectural Design

Red Fort showcases the very high level of art form and ornamental work. The art work in the Fort is a synthesis of Persian, European and Indian art which resulted in the development of unique Shahjahani style which is very rich in form, expression and colour. Red Fort, Delhi is one of the important building complexes of India which encapsulates a long period of Indian history and its arts. Its significance has transcended time and space. It is relevant as a symbol of architectural brilliance and power. Even before its notification as a monument of national importance in the year 1913, efforts were made to preserve and conserve the Red Fort, for posterity. The walls of the fort are smoothly dressed, articulated by heavy string-courses along the upper section. They open at two major gates, the Delhi and the Lahore gates. The Lahore Gate is the main entrance; it leads to a long covered bazaar street, the Chatta Chowk, whose walls are lined with stalls for shops. The Chatta Chowk leads to a large open space where it crosses the large north-south street that was originally the division between the fort's military functions, to its west, and the palaces, to its east. The southern end of this street is the Delhi Gate.

Important Buildings Inside Fort

Diwan-i-Aam

Beyond this gate is another, larger open space, which originally served as the courtyard of the Diwan-i-Aam, the large pavilion for public imperial audiences with an ornate throne-balcony (*jharokha*) for the emperor. The columns were painted in gold and there was a gold and silver railing separating the throne from the public.

Diwan-i-Khas

The Diwan-i-Khas is a pavilion clad completely in marble, the pillars decorated with floral carvings and inlay work with semi-precious stones.

Nahr-i-Behisht

The imperial private apartments lie behind the throne. The apartments consist of a row of pavilions that sits on a raised platform along the eastern edge of the fort, looking out onto the river Yamuna. The pavilions are connected by a continuous water channel, known as the Nahr-i-Behisht, or the "Stream of Paradise", that runs through the centre of each pavilion. The water is drawn from the river Yamuna, from a tower, the *Shah Burj*, at the north-eastern corner of the fort. The palace is designed as an imitation of paradise as it is described in the Koran; a couplet repeatedly inscribed in the palace reads, "If there be a paradise on earth, it is here, it is here". The planning of the palace is based on Islamic prototypes, but each pavilion reveals in its architectural elements the Hindu influences typical of Mughal building. The palace complex of the Red Fort is counted among the best examples of the Mughal style.

Zenana

The two southernmost pavilions of the palace are *zenanas*, or women's quarters: the Mumtaz Mahal (now a museum), and the larger, lavish Rang Mahal, which has been famous for its gilded, decorated ceiling and marble pool, fed by the *Nahr-i-Behisht*.

Moti Masjid

To the west of the hammam is the Moti Masjid, the Pearl Mosque. This was a later addition, built in 1659 as a private mosque for Aurangzeb, Shah Jahan's successor. It is a small, three-domed mosque in carved white marble, with a three-arched screen which steps down to the courtyard.

Hayat Bakhsh Bagh

To its north lies a large formal garden, the Hayat Bakhsh Bagh, or "Life-Bestowing Garden", which is cut through by two bisecting channels of water. A pavilion stands at either end of the north-south channel, and a third, built in 1842 by the last emperor, Bahadur Shah Zafar, stands at the centre of the pool where the two channels meet.

The Fort Today

The Red Fort is one of the most popular tourist destinations in Old Delhi, attracting thousands of visitors every year. The fort is also the site from which the Prime Minister of India addresses the nation on 15 August, the day India achieved independence from the British. It also happens to be the largest monument in Old Delhi. At one point in time, more than 3,000 people lived within the premises of the Delhi Fort complex. But after the Sepoy Mutiny of 1857, the fort was captured by Britain and the residential palaces destroyed. It was made the headquarters of the British Indian Army. Immediately after the mutiny, Bahadur Shah Zafar was tried at the Red Fort.

Jama Masjid, Delhi

The Masjid-i Jahan-Numa commonly known as the Jama Masjid of Delhi, is the principal mosque of Old Delhi in India.

Commissioned by the Mughal Emperor Shah Jahan, builder of the Taj Mahal, and completed in the year 1656 AD, it is the largest and best-known mosque in India. The name Jahan-Numa comes from Persian meaning "World-reflecting". It lies at the origin of a very busy central street of Old Delhi, Chandni Chowk.

The later name, Jami Masjid, is a reference to the weekly Friday noon congregation prayers of Muslims, Jummah, which are usually done at a mosque, the "congregational mosque" or "jami' masjid". The courtyard of the mosque can hold up to twenty-five thousand worshippers. The mosque also houses several relics in a closet in the north gate, including an antique copy of the Qur'an written on deer skin.

Construction

The foundation of the historic Jama Masjid (Friday Mosque) was laid on a hillock in Shahjahanabad by fifth Mughal Emperor of India, Shahjahan, on Friday the October 6, 1650 AD, (10th Shawwal 1060 AH). The mosque was the result of the efforts of over 5,000 workers, over a period of six years.. The cost incurred on the construction in those times was 10 lakh (1 million) Rupees, and it was same Emperor who also built the Taj Mahal, at Agra and the Red Fort, which stands across the Jama Masjid, which was finally ready in 1656 AD (1066 AH), complete with three great gates, four towers and two 40 m-high minarets constructed of strips of red sandstone and white marble.

Shah Jahan built several important mosques in Delhi, Agra, Ajmer and Lahore. The Jama Masjid's floorplan is very similar to the Jama Masjid, Fatehpur Sikri near Agra, but the Jamia Masjid is the bigger and more imposing of the two. Its majesty is further enhanced because of the high ground that he selected for building this mosque. The architecture and design of the slightly larger Badshahi Mosque of Lahore built by Shah Jahan's son Aurangzeb in 1673 is closely related to the Jamia Masjid in Delhi.

Architecture

The courtyard of the mosque can be reached from the east, north and south by three flights of steps, all built of red sandstone. The northern gate of the mosque has 39 steps. The southern side of the mosque has 33 steps. The eastern gate of the mosque was the royal entrance and it has 35 steps. These steps used to house food stalls, shops and street entertainers. In the evening, the eastern side of the mosque used to be converted into a bazaar for poultry and birds in general. Prior to the 1857 War of Indian Independence, there was a madrassah near the southern side of the mosque, which was pulled down after the mutiny.

The mosque faces west. Its three sides are covered with open arched colonnades, each having a lofty tower-like gateway in the centre. The mosque is about 261 feet (80 m) long and 90 feet (27 m) wide, and its roof is covered with three domes with alternate stripes of black and white marble, with its topmost parts covered with gold. Two lofty minarets, 130 feet (41 m) high, and containing 130 steps, longitudinally striped with white marble and red sandstone, flank the domes on either side. The minarets are divided by three projecting galleries and are surmounted by open twelve-sided domed pavilions. On the back of the mosque, there are four small minarets crowned like those in the front.

Under the domes of the mosque, is a hall with seven arched entrances facing the west and the walls of the mosque, up to the height of the waist, are covered with marble. Beyond this is a prayer hall, which is about 61 meters X 27.5 meters, with eleven arched entrances, of which the centre arch is wide and lofty, and in the form of a massive gateway, with slim minarets in each corner, with the usual octagonal pavilion surmounting it. Over these arched entrances there are tablets of white marble, four feet (1.2 m) long and 2.5 feet (760 mm) wide, inlaid with inscriptions in black marble. These inscriptions give the history of the building of the mosque, and glorify the reign and virtues of Shah Jahan. The slab over the centre arch contains simply the words "The Guide!"

The mosque stands on a platform of about five feet (1.5 m) from the pavement of the terrace, and three flight of steps lead to the interior of the mosque from the east, north, and the south. The floor of the mosque is covered with white and black marble ornamented to imitate the Muslim prayer mat; a thin black marble border is marked for the worshippers, which is three feet long and 1 ½ feet wide. In total there are 899 such spaces marked in the floor of the mosque. The back of the mosque is cased over to the height of the rock on which the mosque stands with large hewn stones.

Aurangzeb and Later Mughal Architecture

In Aurangzeb's reign (1658–1707) squared stone and marble gave way to brick or rubble with stucco ornament. Srirangapatna and Lucknow have examples of later Indo-Muslim architecture. He also added his mark to the Lahore Fort. He also built one of the thirteen gates, and it was later named after him, Alamgir. The most impressive building of Aurangzeb's reign, is the Badshahi Mosque which was constructed in 1674 under the supervision of Fida'i Koka. This mosque is adjacent to the Lahore Fort.

Badshahi Mosque is the last in the series of great congregational mosques in red sandstone and is closely modeled on the one Shah Jahan built at Shahjahanabad. The red sandstone of the walls contrasts with the white marble of the domes and the subtle intarsia decoration. The materials depart from the local tradition of tile revetment that is seen in the Wazir Khan Mosque. According to Blair and Bloom, the cusped arches and arabesque floral patterns inlaid in white marble give the building, despite its vast proportions, a lighter appearance than its prototype.

Additional monuments from this period are associated with women from Aurangzeb's imperial family. The construction of the elegant Zinat al-Masjid in Daryaganij was overseen by Aurangzeb's second daughter Zinat al-Nisa. The delicate brick and plaster mausoleum in the Roshan-Ara-Bagh in Sabzimandi was for Aurangzeb's sister Roshan-Ara who died in 1671. Unfortunately, the tomb of Roshanara Begum and the beautiful garden surrounding it were neglected for a long time and are now in an advanced state of decay. Bibi Ka Maqbara a mausoleum was built by Prince Azam Shah, son of Emperor Aurangzeb, in the late 17th century as a loving tribute to his mother, Dilras Bano Begam in Aurangabad, Maharashtra. The Alamgiri Gate, built in 1673 A.D., is the main entrance to the Lahore Fort in present day Lahore, Pakistan. It was constructed to face west towards the Badshahi Mosque in the days of the Mughal Emperor Aurangzeb. The monumental gateway is an imposing vestibule flanked by two semi-circular bastions that have boldly fluted shafts and lotus petalled bases and are crowned with domed pavilions.

Badshahi Mosque

The Badshahi Mosque or the 'Emperor's Mosque', in Lahore is the second largest mosque in Pakistan and South Asia and the fifth largest mosque in the world. It is Lahore's most famous landmark and a major tourist attraction epitomising the beauty, passion and grandeur of the Mughal era.

Capable of accommodating 10,000 worshippers in its main prayer hall and 100,000 in its courtyard and porticoes, it remained the largest mosque in the world from 1673 to 1986 (a period of 313 years), when overtaken in size by the completion of the Faisal Mosque in Islamabad. Today, it remains the second largest mosque in Pakistan and South Asia and the fifth largest mosque in the world after the Masjid al-Haram (Grand Mosque) of Mecca, the Al-Masjid al-Nabawi (Prophet's Mosque) in Medina, the Hassan II Mosque in Casablanca and the Faisal Mosque in Islamabad.

To appreciate its large size, the four minarets of the Badshahi Mosque are 13.9 ft (4.2 m) taller than those of the Taj Mahal and the main platform of the Taj Mahal can fit inside the 278,784 sq ft (25,899.9 m) courtyard of the Badshahi Mosque, which is the largest mosque courtyard in the world.

History

Construction of the Badshahi Mosque was ordered in May 1671 by the sixth Mughal Emperor, Aurangzeb, who assumed the title 'Alamgir'. Construction took about two years and was completed in April 1673. The construction work was carried out under the supervision of Aurangzeb's foster brother Muzaffar Hussain (also known as Fidaie Khan Koka) who was appointed Governor of Lahore in May 1671 and held this post until 1675. He was also Master of Ordnance to the Emperor. The mosque was built opposite the Lahore Fort, illustrating its stature in the Mughal Empire. In conjunction with the building of the mosque, a new gate was built at the Fort, named Alamgiri Gate after the Emperor.

Badshahi Mosque was somewhat damaged and misused during the glorious reign of Maharaja Ranjit Singh, some claim it was converted into a stable for his horses, other sources say it was used as a gun powder magazine for military stores.

When the British took control of India, they would use the mosque for their military purposes by using the mosque for gun practices, cannons, etc. Even though they sensed Muslim hate for the British, they demolished a large portion of the wall of the mosque so the Muslims could not use it as a kind of "fort" for anti-British reasons. After a while, they finally returned it to the

Muslims as a good will gesture, even though it was in terrible condition. It was then given to Badshahi Mosque Authority to restore it to its original glory.

From 1852 onwards, piecemeal repairs were carried out under the supervision of the Badshahi Mosque Authority. Extensive repairs were carried out from 1939 to 1960 at a cost of about 4.8 million rupees, which brought the mosque to its original shape and condition. The blueprint for the repairs was prepared by the late architect Nawab Zen Yar Jang Bahadur.

On the occasion of the second Islamic Summit held at Lahore on February 22, 1974, thirty-nine heads of Muslim states offered their Friday prayers in the Badshahi Masjid, led by Mawlana Abdul Qadir Azad, the *Khatib* of the mosque.

A small museum is also attached to the mosque complex. It contains relics of the Prophet Muhammad, his cousin Ali, and his daughter, Fatimah.

In 2000, the marble inlay in the main vault was repaired under the supervision of Saleem Anjum Qureshi. In 2008, replacement work began to be carried out on the red sandstone tiles on the mosque's large courtyard, using red sandstone especially imported from the original source in Rajasthan, India.

Design

The architecture and design of the Badshahi Mosque closely resembles that of the slightly smaller Jama Mosque in Delhi, India, which was built in 1648 by Aurangzeb's father and predecessor, Emperor Shah Jahan.

Like the character of its founder, the mosque is bold, vast and majestic in its expression. Its design was inspired by Islamic, Persian, Central Asian and Indian influences.

The interior of the mosque has rich embellishment in stucco tracery (Manbatkari) and a fresco touch on the ceiling panels, all in bold relief, as well as marble inlay.

The exterior is decorated with stone carving as well as marble inlay on red sandstone, specially of lotiform motifs in bold relief. The embellishment has Indo-Greek, Central Asian and Indian architectural influence both in technique and motifs.

The skyline is furnished by beautiful ornamental merlons inlaid with marble lining adding grace to the perimeter of the mosque. In its various architectural features like the vast square courtyard, the side aisles (dalans), the four corner minars, the projecting central transept of the prayer chamber and the grand entrance gate, is summed up the history of development of mosque architecture of the Muslim world over the thousand years prior to its construction in 1673.

The north enclosure wall of the mosque was laid close to the Ravi River bank, so a majestic gateway could not be provided on that side and, to keep the symmetry the gate had to be omitted on the south wall as well. Thus, a four Aiwan plan like the earlier Delhi, Jamia Masjid could not be adopted here.

The walls were built with small kiln-burnt bricks laid in kankar, lime mortar (a kind of hydraulic lime) but have a veneer of red sandstone. The steps leading to the prayer chamber and its plinth are in variegated marble.

The prayer chamber is very deep and is divided into seven compartments by rich engraved arches carried on very heavy piers. Out of the 7 compartments, three double domes finished in marble have superb curvature, whilst the rest have curvilinear domes with a central rib in their interior and flat roof above. In the eastern front aisle, the ceiling of the compartment is flat (Qalamdani) with a curved border (ghalatan) at the cornice level.

The original floor of the courtyard was laid with small kiln-burnt bricks laid in the Mussalah pattern. The present red sandstone flooring was laid during the last thorough repairs (1939-60). Similarly, the original floor of the prayer chamber was in cut and dressed bricks with marble and Sang-i-Abri lining forming Mussalah and was also replaced by marble Mussalah during the last repairs.

There are only two inscriptions in the mosque:

- one on the gateway
- the other of Kalimah in the prayer chamber under the main high vault.

Dimensions

- Courtyard: 528 ft 8 in (161.14 m) x 528 ft 4 in (161.04 m) (area: 278,784 sq ft (25,899.9 m^2)) (the world's largest mosque courtyard) (compared to 186 ft × 186 ft (57 m × 57 m) for the main platform of the Taj Mahal), divided into two levels: the upper and the lower. In the latter, funeral prayers can also be offered.

- Prayer Chamber: 275 ft 8 in (84.02 m) x 83 ft 7 in (25.48 m) x 50 ft 6 in (15.39 m) high, with its main vault 37 ft 3 in (11.35 m) x 59 ft 4 in (18.08 m) high but with the merlons 74 ft (22.555200 m). (area: 22,825 sq ft (2,120.5 m^2))
- 4 Corner Minarets: 176 ft 4 in (53.75 m) high and 67 ft (20 m) in circumference, are in four stages and have a contained staircase with 204 steps (compared with 162.5 ft (49.5 m) for the minarats of the Taj Mahal).
- Central Dome: Diameter 65 ft (20 m) at bottom (at bulging 70 ft 6 in (21.49 m)); height 49 ft (15 m); pinnacle 24 ft (7.3 m) and neck 15 ft (4.6 m) high.
- 2 Side Domes: Diameter 51 ft 6 in (15.70 m) (at bulging 54 ft (16.46 m)); height 32 ft (9.8 m); pinnacle 19 ft (5.8 m); neck 9 ft 6 in (2.90 m) high.
- Gateway: 66 ft 7 in (20.29 m) x 62 ft 10 in (19.15 m) x 65 ft (20 m) high including domelets; vault 21 ft 6 in (6.55 m) x 32 ft 6 in (9.91 m) high. Its three sided approach steps are 22 in number.
- Side Aisles (Dalans). 80 in number. Height above floor 23 ft 9 in (7.24 m); plinth 2 ft 7 in (0.79 m).
- Central Tank: 50 ft (15 m) x 50 ft (15 m) x 3 ft (0.91 m) deep (area: 2,500 sq ft (230 m^2))

Mughal gardens

Mughal gardens are a group of gardens built by the Mughals in the Islamic style of architecture. This style was influenced by Persian gardens and Timurid gardens. Significant use of rectilinear layouts are made within the walled enclosures. Some of the typical features include pools, fountains and canals inside the gardens.

History

The founder of the Mughal empire, Babur, described his favourite type of garden as a charbagh. This word developed a new meaning in India, because as Babur explains, India lacked the fast-flowing streams required for the Central Asian charbagh. The Agra garden, now known as the Ram Bagh, is thought to have been the first charbagh. India, Bangladesh and Pakistan have a number of Mughal gardens which differ from their Central Asian predecessors with respect to "the highly disciplined geometry". An early textual references about Mughal gardens are found in the memoirs and biographies of the Mughal emperors, including those of Babur, Humayun and Akbar. Later references are found from "the accounts of India" written by various European travellers (Bernier for example). The first serious historical study of Mughal gardens was written by Constance Villiers-Stuart, with the title *Gardens of the Great Mughals* (1913). Her husband was a Colonel in Britain's Indian army.

This gave her a good network of contacts and an opportunity to travel. During their residence at Pinjore Gardens, Mrs. Villiers-Stuart also had an opportunity to direct the maintenance of an important Mughal garden. Her book makes reference to the forthcoming design of a garden in the Government House at New Delhi (now known as Rashtrapati Bhavan). She was consulted by Edwin Lutyens, and this may have influenced his choice of Mughal style for this project.

Recent scholarly work on "the history of Mughal gardens" has been carried out under the auspicious guidance of Dumbarton Oaks (including *Mughal Gardens: Sources, Places, Representations, and Prospects* edited by James L. Wescoat, Jr. and Joachim Wolschke-Bulmahn) and the Smithsonian Institution. Some examples of Mughal gardens are Shalimar Gardens (Lahore), Lalbagh Fort at Dhaka, and Shalimar Gardens (Jammu and Kashmir).

From the beginnings of the Mughal Empire, the construction of gardens was a beloved imperial pastime. Babur, the first Mughal conqueror-king, had gardens built in Lahore and Dholpur. Humayun, his son, does not seem to have had much time for building—he was busy reclaiming and increasing the realm—but he is known to have spent a great deal of time at his father's gardens. Akbar built several gardens first in Delhi, then in Agra, Akbar's new capital. These tended to be riverfront gardens rather than the fortress gardens that his predecessors built.

Building riverfront rather than fortress gardens influenced later Mughal garden architecture considerably. Akbar's heir, Jahangir, did not build as much, but he helped to lay out the famous Shalimar garden and was known for his great love for flowers. Indeed, his trips to Kashmir are believed to have begun a fashion for naturalistic and abundant floral design.

Jahangir's son, Shah Jahan, marks the apex of Mughal garden architecture and floral design. He is famous for the construction of the Taj Mahal, a sprawling funereal paradise in memory of his favourite wife, Mumtaz Mahal. He is also responsible for the Red Fort at Delhi which contains the Mahtab Bagh, a night garden that was filled with night-blooming jasmine and other pale flowers. The pavilions within are faced with white marble to glow in the moonlight. This and the marble of the Taj Mahal are inlaid with semiprecious stone depicting scrolling naturalistic floral motifs, the most important being the tulip, which Shah Jahan adopted as a personal symbol.

The Mughals were obsessed with symbol and incorporated it into their gardens in many ways. The standard Quranic references to paradise were in the architecture, layout, and in the choice of plant life; but more secular references, including numerological and zodiacal significances connected to family history or other cultural significance, were often juxtaposed. The numbers eight and nine were considered auspicious by the Mughals and can be found in the number of terraces or in garden architecture such as octagonal pools.

Mughal garden design derives primarily from the medieval Islamic garden, although there are nomadic influences that come from the Mughals' Turkish-Mongolian ancestry. Julie Scott Meisami describes the medieval Islamic garden as "a hortus conclusus, walled off and protected from the outside world; within, its design was rigidly formal, and its inner space was filled with those elements that man finds most pleasing in nature.

Its essential features included running water (perhaps the most important element) and a pool to reflect the beauties of sky and garden; trees of various sorts, some to provide shade merely, and others to produce fruits; flowers, colorful and sweet-smelling; grass, usually growing wild under the trees; birds to fill the garden with song; the whole cooled by a pleasant breeze.

The garden might include a raised hillock at the centre, reminiscent of the mountain at the centre of the universe in cosmological descriptions, and often surmounted by a pavilion or palace." The Turkish-Mongolian elements of the Mughal garden are primarily related to the inclusion of tents, carpets and canopies reflecting nomadic roots. Tents indicated status in these societies, so wealth and power were displayed through the richness of the fabrics as well as by size and number.

Sites of Mughal Gardens

Afghanistan

- Bagh-e Babur (Kabul).

India

- Humayun's Tomb, Delhi (Nizamuddin)
- Taj Mahal, Agra
- Ram Bagh, Agra
- Mehtab Bagh, Agra
- Safdarjung's Tomb
- Shalimar Bagh (Srinagar), Jammu and Kashmir
- Nishat Gardens, Jammu and Kashmir
- Yadvindra Gardens, Pinjore
- Khusro Bagh, Allahabad
- Roshanara Bagh.

Pakistan

- Chauburji (The Gate to the Mughal Gardens)
- Lahore Fort
- Shahdara Bagh
- Shalimar Gardens (Lahore)
- Hazuri Bagh
- Hiran Minar (Sheikhupura)
- Mughal Garden Wah
- Vernag.

Bagh-e Babur

Bagh-e Babur is an historic park in Kabul, Afghanistan, and also the last resting-place of the first Mughal emperor Babur. The garden is thought to have been developed around 1528 AD (935 AH) when Babur gave orders for the construction of an 'avenue garden' in Kabul, described in some detail in his memoirs, the Baburnama. It was the tradition of Moghul princes to develop sites for recreation and pleasure during their lifetime, and choose one of these as a last resting-place. The site continued to be of significance to Babur's successors, and Jehangir made a pilgrimage to the site in 1607 AD (1016 AH) when he ordered that all gardens in Kabul be surrounded by walls, that a prayer platform be laid in front of Babur's grave, and an inscribed headstone placed at its head. During the visit of the Emperor Shah Jahan in 1638 (1047 AH) a marble screen was erected around the group of tombs, and a mosque built on the terrace below. There are accounts from the time of the visit to the site of Shah Jahan in 1638 (1047AH) of a stone water-channel that ran between an avenue of trees from the terrace below the mosque, with pools at certain intervals.

History

Since Babur had such a high rank, he would have been buried in a site the befitted him. The garden where it is believed Babur requested to be buried in is known as Bagh-e Babur. Mughul rulers saw this site as significant and aided in further development of the site and other tombs in Kabul. In an article written by the Aga Khan Historic Cities Program, describes the marble screen built around tombs by Emperor In 1638 the Emperor Shahjahan in 1683 with the following inscription: "only this mosque of beauty, this temple of nobility, constructed for the prayer of saints and the epiphany of cherubs, was fit to stand in so venerable a sanctuary as this highway of archangels, this theatre of heaven, the light garden of the godforgiven angel king whose rest is in the garden of heaven, Zahiruddin Muhammad Babur the Conqueror."

Although the additions of the screens by Shajahan contained references to Babur, Salome Zajadacz-Hastenrath, in her article "A Note on Babur's Lost Funerary and Enclosure at Kabul" suggests that Shajahan work transformed Bagh-e Babur into a graveyard. She states that a "mosque was built on the thirteenth terrace, the terrace nearest to Mecca; the next, the fourteenth terrace, was to contain the funerary enclosure of Babur's tomb and the tombs of some of his male relatives." This transformation towards a proper graveyard, with an enclosure around Babur's tomb, points towards the importance of Babur. By enclosing Babur's tomb, Shajahan separates the tomb of the king from others.

The only hint of the design lies in a sketch and short description by Charles Masson, a British soldier, in 1832 and published in 1842, the year the tomb was destroyed by and earthquake. One description of the tomb praised it, "although obviously-in a poor state of preservation, reveals fine workmanship in stone carving: high walls with lavish jali-work and relief decoration." Mason described the tomb as being "accompanied by many monuments of similar nature, commemorative of his relatives, and they are surrounded by an enclosure of white marble, curiously and elegantly carved... No person superintends them, and great liberty has been taken with the stones employed in the enclosing walls." Mason's sketch and Mason's description gives us the only modern view of how extravagant the tomb was.

Bagh-e Babur has changed drastically from the Mughul impression of the space to the present. Throughout the years outside influences have shaped the use of the site. For example, the Aga Khan Historic Cities Programme describes how by 1880, Amir Abdurahman Khan constructed a pavilion and a residence for his wife, Bibi Halima. In 1933, the space was converted into a public recreation space with pools and fountains becoming the central focal point. A modern greenhouse and swimming pool were added in 1980. Although the enclosure of the Babur's tomb is no longer present, Bagh-e Babur still remains a major historically important site in Kabul.

Over the past few years, attempts at rebuilding and reconstructing the city of Kabul and Babur's tomb have been undertaken. Zahra Breshna, an architect with the Department for Preservation & Rehabilitation of Afghanistan's Urban Heritage, argues that, "emphasis should be on developing and strengthening the partially forgotten local and traditional aspects, whilst placing them in a contemporary global context. The goal is to preserve the tradition without hindering the development of a modern social, ecological and economical institution." Planners also discuss the importance of 'a revival of cultural identity' in the development of Kabul. These ideas seem to fall in line with the plan of Aga Khan.

The plan put forth by Aga Khan calls for the reconstruction of the Bagh-e Babur and includes several key components. The rebuilding of the perimeter walls, the rehabilitation of the Shahjahani mosque, and the restoration of Babur's grave enclosure are all important parts of the rehabilitation of the garden and aid in the 'revival of cultural identity.' The perimeter walls, common throughout many Islamic cities, would provide for closure of the area. This enclosure of orchids is traditional in the area. Also, the restoration of the Shahjahani mosque, a place for prayer and meditation for visitors to the gardens would be restored.

The biggest idea proposed is the restoration of Babur's tomb. The reconstruction of Babur's garden would bring about a unity fixed around the ruler responsible for the importance of Kabul and the restoration of the historic quarters would restore the pride of the citizens of the city.

Architect Abdul Wasay Najimi writes that, "Restoration of confidence, pride and hope would be the main outcome in reintegrating the historic quarters in the mainstream rehabilitation and development of Kabul. This would have a direct impact on the revival of identity."

Ram Bagh

The Ram Bagh is the oldest Mughal Garden in India, originally built by the Mughal Emperor Babur in 1528 A.D., located about five kilometers northeast of the Taj Mahal in Agra, India. Babur was temporarily buried there before being interred in Kabul.

The garden is a Paradise garden or Charbagh, where pathways and canals divide the garden to represent the Islamic ideal of paradise, an abundant garden through which rivers flow. The Ram Bagh provides an example of a variant of the charbagh in which water cascades down three terraces in a sequence of cascades. Two viewing pavilions face the Jumna river and incorporates a subterranean 'tahkhana' which was used during the hot summers to provide relief for visitors. The garden has numerous water courses and fountains.

The name is a corruption of the Persian *Aaram Bagh* meaning 'Garden of Rest'. It is also variously known as *Bagh-i Nur Afshan* 'Light-Scattering Garden', *Aalsi Bagh* or 'Lazy Garden': according to legend, Emperor Akbar proposed to his third wife, who was a gardner there, by lying idle for 6 days until she agreed to marry him.

Jahangir waited in the garden in early March 1621 for the most astrologically auspicious hour for him to enter Agra after he took the Fort of Kangra. The preserved, surviving architecture dates to his reign and demonstrates the skill of his wife Nur Jahan as a garden designer.

Mehtab Bagh

Mehtab Bagh, is a charbagh located to the north of the Taj Mahal complex, across the Yamuna River. It was designed as an integral part of the complex in the riverfront terrace pattern seen elsewhere in Agra, Uttar Pradesh, India. Its width is identical to that of the rest of the Taj. The garden historian Elizabeth Moynihan suggests the large octagonal pool in the centre of the terrace would reflect the image of the Mausoleum and thus the garden would provide a setting to view the Taj Mahal.

The garden has been beset by flooding from the river since Mughal times. As a result, the condition of the remaining structures is quite ruinous. Four sandstone towers marked the corners of the garden, only the south-eastward one remains. The foundations of two structures remain immediately north and south of the large pool which were probably garden pavilions. From the northern structure a stepped waterfall would have fed the pool. The garden to the north has the typical square, cross-axial plan with a square pool in its centre. To the west an aqueduct fed the garden.

Safdarjung's Tomb

Safdarjung's Tomb is a garden tomb in a marble mausoleum in Delhi, India. It was built in 1754 in the style of late Mughal architecture. The top story of the edifice houses the Archaeological Survey of India. The garden, in the style evolved by the Mughal Empire that is now known as the Mughal gardens style known as a *charbagh,* is entered through an ornate gate. Its facade is decorated with elaborate plaster carvings.

Description

The tomb was built for Safdarjung, the powerful prime minister of Muhammad Shah who was the weak Mughal emperor from 1719 to 1748. The central tomb has a huge dome. There are four water canals leading to four buildings. One has an ornately decorated gateway while the other three are pavilions, with living quarters built into the walls. Octagonal towers are in the corners. The canals are four oblong tanks, one on each side of the tomb

Shalimar Bagh (Srinagar)

Shalimar Bagh, is a Mughal garden linked through a channel to the northeast of Dal Lake. Its other names are Shalamar Garden,

Shalamar Bagh, Farah Baksh and Faiz Baksh, and the other famous shore line garden in the vicinity is the Nishat Bagh. The Bagh was built by Mughal Emperor Jahangir for his wife Nur Jahan, in 1619. The Bagh is considered the high point of Mughal horticulture. It is now public park.

History

While the recent history and development of the Mughal types of gardens is credited to Emperor Jahangir of the Mughal Dynasty, the ancient history of the garden that existed here is traced to the 2nd century when it was built during the reign of Pravarsena II. Praversena II founded the city of Srinagar and ruled in Kashmir from 79 AD to 139 AD. He had built a cottage for his stay at the northeastern corner of the Dal Lake and had named it as Shalimar ('Shalimar' in Sanskrit means "Abode or Hall of Love").

The King, on his visits to a local saint by the name Sukarma Swami at Harwan, used to halt at this cottage. Over the years, the cottage fell into ruins and later could not be located also. However, the village name remained as 'Shalimar'. It is at this location that Emperor Jahangir built his celebrated Shalimar Bagh, his dream project to please his queen. He enlarged the ancient garden in 1619 into a royal garden and called it as 'Farah Baksh' (meaning: 'the delightful'). He built this for his wife Nur Jahan (meaning: 'light of the world').

In 1630, under Emperor Shah Jahan's orders, Zafar Khan the Governor of Kashmir got it extended He named it 'Faiz Baksh' ('the bountiful'). It then became a pleasure place for the Pathan and Sikh governors who followed Zafar Khan. During the rule of Maharaja Ranjit Singh the marble pavilion was the guest house for the European visitors. Electrification of the premises was done during Maharaja Hari Singh's rule. Thus, over the years, the garden was extended and improved by many rulers and called by different names, but the most popular name 'Shalimar Bagh' continues to this day.

During the Mughal period in particular, Emperor Jahangir and his wife Nur Jahan were so enamoured of Kashmir that during summer they moved to Srinagar with their full court entourage from Delhi, at least 13 times. Shalimar Bagh was their imperial summer residence, and also the Royal Court. They used to cross the arduous snowy passes of the Pir Panjal mountain range on elephants to reach Srinagar.

Layout

The layout of the garden is an adaptation of another Islamic garden layout known as the Chahar Bagh in Persia. This garden built on a flat land on a square plan with four radiating arms from a central location as the water source, could not be exactly replicated to the hilly conditions in the Kashmir valley. It needed to be modified to suit the hilly terrain and availability of a source of water, which could be diverted from a higher elevation by gravity to the planned gardens. Thus, modifications to suit the location were designed, which involved the main channel running through the garden axially from top to the lowest point. This central channel, known as the Shah Nahar, is the main axis of the garden. It runs through three terraces. This layout saved on radial arms and the shape became rectangular, instead of a square plan of the Chahar Bagh.

The garden, as finally laid, extends to an area of 12.4 hectares (31 acres) built with a size of 587 metres (1,930 ft) length on the main axis channel and with a total width of 251 metres (820 ft). The garden has three terraces fitted with fountains and with chinar (sycamore) tree-lined vistas. The Shahnahar is the main feeder channel to all the terraces. Each one of the three terraces has a specific role.

The garden was linked to the open Dal Lake water through a canal of about 1 mile (1.6 km) length and 12 yards (11 m) in width that ran through swampy quagmire. Willow groves and rice terraces fringed the lake edge. Broad green paths bordered the lake with rows of chinar trees. The garden was laid in trellised walkways lined by avenues of aspen trees planted at 2 feet (0.61 m) interval.

Architecture

The architectural details of the three terraces of the garden are elaborated.

The first terrace is a public garden or the outer garden ending in the Diwan-e-Aam (public audience hall). In this hall, a small black marble throne was installed over the waterfall. The second terrace garden along the axial canal, slightly broader, has two shallow terraces. The Diwan-i-Khas (the Hall of Private Audience), which was accessible only to the noblemen or guests of the court, now derelict, is in its centre. However, the carved stone bases and a fine platform surrounded by fountains are still seen. The royal bathrooms are located on the north-west boundary of this enclosure. The fountain pools of the Diwan-i Khas, the Diwan-i-Amm, and in turn, the Zenana terrace are supplied in succession.

In the third terrace, the axial water channel flows through the Zenana garden, which is flanked by the Diwan-i-Khas and chinar trees. At the entrance to this terrace, there are two small pavilions or guard rooms (built in Kashmir style on stone plinth) that is the restricted and controlled entry zone of the royal harem. Shahajahan built a baradari of black marble, called the Black Pavilion in the zenana garden. It is encircled by a fountain pool that receives its supply from a higher terrace.

A double cascade falls against a low wall carved with small niches (chini khanas), behind the pavilion. Two smaller, secondary water canals lead from the Black Pavilion to a small baradari. Above the third level, two octagonal pavilions define the end wall of the garden. The baradari has a lovely backdrop of the snow mountains, which is considered a befitting setting for the Bagh.

The Shalimar Bagh is well known for *chini khanas*, or arched niches, behind garden waterfalls. They are a unique feature in the Bagh. These niches were lighted at night with oil lamps, which gave a fairy tale appearance to the water falls. However, now the niches hold pots of flower pots that reflect their colours behind the cascading water.

Another unusual architectural feature mentioned is about the doors of the Baradari. In the garden complex, the Baradari had four exquisite doors made of stones supported by pillars. It is conjectured that these stone doors were ruins from old temples that were demolished by Shahajahan. The garden also provided large water troughs where a variety of fountains were fixed.

It has been aptly described by a chronicler glowingly:

A subtle air of leisure and repose, a romantic indefinable spell, pervades the royal Shalimar: this leafy garden of dim vistas, shallow terraces, smooth sheets of falling water, and wide canals, with calm reflections broken only by the stepping stones across the streams.

Even in later years, during Maharaja's rule, the gardens were well maintained and continue to be so even now as it is one of the prominent visitor attractions around the Dal Lake.

The garden is considered to be very beautiful during the autumn and spring seasons due to the colour change in leaves of the famed Chinar trees.

The gardens were the inspiration for other gardens of the same name, notably the Shalimar Bagh, Delhi in Delhi (built in 1653, which now also has an upscale colony) and Shalimar Gardens in Lahore, Pakistan built by Emperor Shah Jahan in 1641.

The black pavilion built during the early part of Jahangir's reign (1569-1627), in the top terrace of the Shalimar Bagh, has the famous inscription in Persian, which says:

Gar Firduas ruhe zamin ast, hamin asto hamin asto hamin asto.

This is a couplet by the Persian poet Jami, which is inscribed on many other buildings also in India and Pakistan.

Nishat Bagh

Nishat Bagh, is a Mughal garden built on the eastern side of the Dal Lake, close to the Srinagar city in the state of Jammu and Kashmir in India. It is the second largest Mughal garden in the Kashmir Valley. The largest in size is the Shalimar Bagh, which is also located on the bank of the Dal Lake. 'Nishat Bagh'is a Urdu word, which means "Garden of Joy," "Garden of Gladness" and "Garden of Delight."

History

An interesting anecdote of jealousy of the Emperor Shah Jahan on beholding such a delightful garden, which almost shutdown the garden for some time, is narrated. When Shah Jahan saw this garden, after its completion in 1633, he expressed great appreciation of its grandeur and beauty. He is believed to have articulated his appreciation three times to Asif Khan, his father-in-law, with the hope that he would gift it to him. As no such offer was made by Asif Khan, Shah Jahan was piqued and ordered closure of the water supply to the garden.

Then, for some time, the garden was deserted. Asif Khan was desolate and heartbroken; he was uninterested in the sequence of events. When he was resting under the shade of a tree, in one of the terraces, his servant was bold enough to turn on the water supply source from the Shalimar Bagh. When Asif Khan heard the sound of water and the fountains in action he was startled and immediately order closure of water supply as he feared the worst reaction from the emperor for this wanton act of disobedience.

Fortunately for the servant and Asif Khan, Shaha Jahan, who had heard about this incident at the garden, was not disturbed or annoyed by the disobedience of his orders. Instead, he appreciated the servant for loyal service to his master and then ordered full restoration rights for the supply of water to the garden to Asif Khan, his Prime Minister and father-in-law.

Layout

Even though the layout of Nishat Bagh was based on the basic conceptual model of the Chahar Bagh (four gardens) in Persia, it had to be remodelled to fit the topographic and water source conditions at the site chosen in the Kashmir valley. The plan, instead of being central with four radiating arms in a square pattern as in the case of Chahar (suited for a flat country side), was changed to an axial stream flow design to fit the hill condition with water source originating at the top of the hill end. This resulted in planning a rectangular layout rather than a square layout. This helped in dispensing with the long side arms. Thus, a rectangular layout with east-west length of 548 metres (1,800 ft) and width of 338 metres (1,110 ft) was adopted.

Architecture

Thus, Nishat Bagh as laid out now is a broad cascade of terraces lined with avenues of chinar and cypress trees, which starts from the lakeshore and reaches up to an artificial facade at the hill end. Rising from the edge of the Dal Lake, it has twelve 12 terraces representing twelve Zodiacal signs. However, it has only two sections, namely the public garden and the private garden for the Zanana or harem vis-a-vis the four sections of the Shalimar Bagh; this difference is attributed to the fact that the latter Bagh catered to the Mughal Emperor, while Nishad Bagh belonged to a man of his court, a noble.

There are, however, some similarities with the Shalimar Bagh, such as the polished stone channel and terraces. The source of water supply to the two gardens is the same. Built in an east-west direction, the top terrace has the Zenana garden while the lowest terrace is connected to the Dal Lake. In recent years, the lowest terrace has merged with the approach road. A spring called the Gopi Thirst provides clear water supply to the gardens. There are a few old Mughal period buildings in the vicinity of the Bagh.

The central canal, which runs through the garden from the top end, is 4 metres (13 ft) wide and has a water depth of 20 centimetres (7.9 in). Water flows down in a cascade from the top to the first terrace at the road level, which could be also approached from the Dal Lake through a shikara ride. The water flow from one terrace to the next is over stepped stone ramps that provide the sparkle to the flow. At all the terraces fountains with pools are provided, along the water channel. At channel crossings, benches are provided for people to sit and enjoy the beauty of the garden and the cascading flows and fountain jets.

Terraces

The details of the twelve terraces have been recorded, as originally built. The first terrace is a water collection chamber that is also linked to the side flow from the garden. The second terrace is accessed through a gate. This terrace has five fountains that is supplied water from the third terrace, from where it flowed to the lowest terrace. The third terrace has a different design. The water chute has five arched open niches in the front and similar niches on the sides. A pavilion (baradari), a two-storied structure, which existed here when it was originally built, has since been dismantled. Stairways, on either side of the channel lead to the third terrace, which has a square chamber with five fountains.

Moving up the flight of steps (four steps) on either side of the channel leads to the fourth terrace. This terrace has two levels namely, a water channel and a square pool. Stairways with 7 steps lead to the fifth terrace, where a stone bench is provided across the channel to enjoy the scenic beauty. This also has a square chamber with five fountains. Further up, the sixth terrace is at two levels with five fountains and the same pattern continues on the seventh terrace. The eighth terrace is only a water channel or chute. Moving further up to the ninth terrace, at the end of two stairways, there is an octagonal bench.

The pool in this terrace has nine fountains. The stairways to the tenth terrace are along the side retaining walls where only the water chute with fountains is provided. Engraved paths lead to an impressive eleventh terrace, which has twenty five fountains in a pool. Up this terrace is the last terrace, the Zenana chamber, the twelfth terrace, which is covered in the front by 5.5 metres (18 ft) high wall with a facade of blind arches. Only one arch in this blind facade provides an opening to the twelfth terrace. Two small octagonal towers on either side of the retaining walls provide views of the lower level terraces. A two-storey pavilion here is surrounded by a lovely garden with lots of plants.

Out of all the terraces, the second terrace is considered the most impressive in view of the twenty three niches provided in the arched recess just behind the cascade. Originally lighted lamps used to be placed at these niches. The second terrace also has abundance of Persian lilacs and pansies coupled with sparkling cascading water over the chute, which provided a lovely sight. Another interesting feature in the Nishat Bagh is of the many marble thrones like setas placed at the head of the waterfall, across the channel.

Pinjore Gardens

Pinjore Gardens (also known as Pinjor Gardens or Yadavindra Gardens) is an example of the Mughal Gardens style. The garden is in the village of Pinjore lie 22 km from Chandigarh on the Ambala-Shimla road. The Gardens were designed by the Nawab Fidal Khan. He was an architect and foster brother to Aurangzeb.

CM Villiers-Stuart was resident for the gardens for a time and included a description in her book on Gardens of the Great Mughals (1913). She wrote that "A quaint story still survives, how, when at length the work was finished, and Fadai came in state to spend his first summer there, bis enjoyment of the garden and its beauties was short-lived; for the Rajas quickly frightened him away In the districts round Pinjor, and in fact all along the foot of the Himalayas, occasional cases of goitre are to be seen; so from far and wide these poor people were collected by the wily Brahmins, and produced as the ordinary inhabitants of the place.

The gardeners all suffered from goitre; every coolie had this dreadful complaint; even the countrywomen carrying up the big flat baskets of fruits and flowers to the zenana terraces were equally disfigured. The ladies of the harem naturally were horrified;

it was bad enough to be brought into these wild outlandish jungles, without this new and added terror. For the poor coolie women, well instructed beforehand, had told how the air and water of Pinjor caused this disease, which no one who lived there long ever escaped.

A panic reigned in the zenana; its inmates implored to be removed at once from such a danger; and finally, Fadai Khan had to give way, and take his ladies to some other place less threatening to their beauty. Had it been the terrible Emperor himself instead of his foster-brother, the cunning Rajas would have met their match. But Fadai Khan, thoroughly deceived, rarely came back to visit his lovely gardens, and the Rajas and their fields were left in peace for a time."

Roshanara Bagh

Roshanara Garden is a Mughal-style garden was built by Roshanara Begum, the second daughter of the Mughal emperor Shah Jahan. It is situated at Chandni Chowk in Shahjahanabad.

The garden has a raised canal with flowering plants on both sides. Today the garden holds a white marble pavilion built in memory of the princess Roshanara, who died in 1671 and was buried there. The elite club, Roshanara club was started here in 1875 by the British.

Chauburji

In the historic city of Lahore, on the road that led southwards to Multan, the Chauburji gateway remains of an extensive garden known to have existed in Mughal times. The establishment of this garden is attributed to Mughal Princess Zeb-un-Nissa, 1646 A.D., which appears in one of the inscriptions on the gateway. The gateway consists of four towers (chau: four, burji: tower) and contains much of the brilliant tile work with which the entire entrance was once covered.

During a severe earthquake in 1843, the north-western minaret collapsed and cracks appeared in the central arch. This has however been restored as much as was reasonably possible and the gateway now looks quite as it might have been during the time of its Mughal patroness. The restoration was carried out by the Department of Archeology in the late in 1960's.

The architecture of Chauburji represents a strong blend of Mughal architecture with ancient Muslim style of building. Its distinguishing features are the minarets which expand from the top, not present anywhere in the sub-continent. Some, however, believe that there were cupolas upon these minarets which collapsed with the passage of time. Arches are of the so-called 'Tudor' style, adapted to Islamic architecture, particularly in Mughal mausoleums and mosques.

The red brickwork is typical of the Muslim buildings of the sub-continent; the doorways and windows running through the interior corridors are examples of the living style that characterized the Mughal buildings. However, the main purpose of building Chauburji appears to be strictly monumental. The decrepit building, which has not lost its elegance, stands alone surrounded by hoardings and bustling traffic on the busy Multan Road.

Dr. Ajaz Anwar wrote in an article published in The Pakistan Times in April, 1985: "But the real prototype of Chauburji is the Char Minar of Hyderabad Deccan constructed in 1591 by Muhammad Quli as a triumphal arch at the junction of four roads, leading to the four quarters of the old city. Octagonal minarets were later used along the corners of Jehangir's tomb itself. This became a motif and was incorporated in the Taj where the minarets flank the corners of the platform.

The Char Minar, though it comes closest to Chauburji, has a striking contrast and a sense of negation between the very simple lower portion and the heavily decorated upper portion. In the tomb of Akbar, the white marble and variegated stone give the feeling of having been added later... Chauburji, because of the colour of the brick adorned with glazed tiles having the look of flowering creepers, retains a distinctive unity."

Originally it was gateway to the Garden of Zeb-un-nisa or Zebinda Begum, the accomplished daughter of Aurangzeb. This garden is believed to have been extended from Nawankot in the south to the main city of Lahore towards north. However, no traces of such an expansive garden are now available. A fragmentary inscription on the eastern archway records that the garden was built in A.H. 1056 i.e. 1646 A.D. Although most of the inscriptions have been lost, on the upper-most part of the construction Ayat-ul-Kursi can be seen in Arabic script in blue and worked in porcelain. Others include two couplets written in Persian above the arch: "This garden, in the pattern of the garden of Paradise, has been founded (missing line)...

The garden has been bestowed on Mian Bai. By the bounty of Zebinda Begum, the Lady of the Age." It is thus understood that it was commissioned by Sahib-e-Zebinda (one endowed with elegance), Begum-e-Dauran (Lady of Ages) and was bestowed upon Mian Bai Fakhrunnisa (Pride of Women), the favourite female attendant of the princess.

Shalimar Gardens (Lahore)

The Shalimar Gardens, sometimes written Shalamar Gardens, is a Persian garden and it was built by the Mughal emperor Shah Jahan in Lahore, modern day Pakistan. Construction began in 1641 A.D. (1051 A.H.) and was completed the following year. The project management was carried out under the superintendence of Khalilullah Khan, a noble of Shah Jahan's court, in cooperation with Ali Mardan Khan and Mulla Alaul Maulk Tuni.

Architecture

The Shalimar Gardens are laid out in the form of an oblong parallelogram, surrounded by a high brick wall, which is famous for its intricate fretwork. The gardens measure 658 meters north to south and 258 meters east to west. In 1981, Shalimar Gardens was included as a UNESCO World Heritage Site along with the Lahore Fort, under the UNESCO Convention concerning the protection of the world's cultural and natural heritage sites in 1972.

The Three Level Terraces of the Gardens

The Gardens have been laid out from south to north in three descending terraces, which are elevated by 4-5 metres (13-15 feet) above one another. The three terraces have names in Urdu as follows:

- The upper terrace named *Farah Baksh* meaning *Bestower of Pleasure.*
- The middle terrace named *Faiz Baksh* meaning *Bestower of Goodness.*
- The lower terrace named *Hayat Baksh* meaning *Bestower of life.*

Shah Nahar : Irrigation of the Gardens

To irrigate the Gardens, a canal named *Shah Nahar* meaning *Royal canal,* later also known as *Hansti nahar,* meaning *Laughing canal* was brought from *Rajpot* (present day Madhpur in India), a distance of over 161 kilometers. The canal intersected the Gardens and discharged into a large marble basin in the middle terrace.

410 Fountains

From this basin, and from the canal, rise 410 fountains, which discharge into wide marble pools. The surrounding area is rendered cooler by the flowing of the fountains, which is a particular relief for visitors during Lahore's blistering summers, with temperature sometimes exceeding 120 degrees fahrenheit. It is a credit to the ingenuity of the Mughal engineers that even today scientists are unable to fathom how the fountains were operated originally. The distribution of the fountains is as follows:

- The upper level terrace has 105 fountains.
- The middle level terrace has 152 fountains.
- The lower level terrace has 153 fountains.
- All combined, the Gardens therefore have 410 fountains.

Water Cascades

The Gardens have 5 water cascades including *the great marble cascade* and *Sawan Bhadoon....*

Site History

The site of the Shalimar Gardens originally belonged to one of the noble *Zaildar* families in the region, well known as Mian Family Baghbanpura. The family was also given the Royal title of 'Mian' by the Mughal Emperor, for its services to the Empire. Mian Muhammad Yusuf, then the head of the Mian family, donated the site of Ishaq Pura to the Emperor Shah Jahan, after pressure was placed on the family by the royal engineers who wished to build on the site due to its good position and soil. In return, Shah Jahan granted the Mian family governance of the Shalimar Gardens. The Shalimar Gardens remained under the custodianship of this family for more than 350 years.

In 1962, the Shalimar Gardens were nationalised by General Ayub Khan because leading Mian family members had opposed his imposition of martial law in Pakistan.

The Mela Chiraghan festival used to take place in the Gardens, until President Ayub Khan ordered against it in 1958.

Hazuri Bagh

Hazuri is a garden in Lahore, Pakistan, bounded by the Lahore Fort (east side), Badshahi Mosque (west side), the Samadhi of Ranjit Singh (north side) and the Roshnai Gate (south side). In the centre stands the Hazuri Bagh Baradari, built by Ranjit Singh.

The Hazuri Bagh is a small enclosure between the Alamgiri Gate of the Lahore Fort and eastern gate of the Badshahi Mosque. This garden was built by Maharajah Ranjit Singh in 1813 to celebrate the capture of the famous Koh-i-Noor Diamond from Shah Shujah of Afghanistan. The Serai Alamgiri formerly stood here.

The garden was planned and built under the supervision of Faqir Azizuddin. After its completion, it is said, Maharajah Ranjit Singh, at the suggestion of Jamadar Khushhal Singh, ordered that marble be removed from various mausoleums of Lahore to construct a baradari (pavilion) here. This task was given to Khalifa Nooruddin. Elegant carved marble pillars support the baradari's delicate cusped arches. The central area, where Ranjit Singh held court, has a mirrored ceiling. Both the garden and the baradari, originally a 45-foot, three-storey square with a basement approached by fifteen steps, suffered extensive damage during the fratricidal Sikh wars and was only reclaimed and laid out according to the original plan during the British period. On 19 July 1932, the uppermost story collapsed and was never reconstructed.

Every Sunday afternoon, people gather in the gardens to hear reciters recite traditional Punjabi Qisse, such as Heer Ranjha and Sassi Punnun, and other Punjabi Sufi poetry.

Vernag

is a water garden built for the Mughal emperor Jahangir in what is today Pakistan. The garden was built around a natural spring of pre-Islamic religious significance. The water is collected in a pool surrounded by arched recesses, and then flows down a 300-yard canal to the Bihat river. Jahangir wished to be buried at Vernag gardens, but his wife, Nur Jahan, disobeyed his wishes. Today nothing remains of the pavilions which once decorated the area.

Hiran Minar

Hiran Minar is set in peaceful environs near Lahore in Sheikhupura, Pakistan. It was constructed by Emperor Jahangir as a monument to Mansraj, one of his pet deer. The structure consists of a large, almost-square water tank with an octagonal pavilion in its centre, built during the reign of Mughal emperor Shah Jahan; a causeway with its own gateway connects the pavilion with the mainland and a 100-foot (30 m)-high minar, or minaret.

At the centre of each side of the tank, a brick ramp slopes down to the water, providing access for royal animals and wild game. The minar itself was built by Emperor Jahangir in 1606 to honor the memory of a pet hunting antelope named Mansraj.

Unique features of this particular complex are the antelope's grave and the distinctive water collection system. At each corner of the tank (approximately 750 by 895 feet (273 m) in size), is a small, square building and a subsurface water collection system which supplied the tank; only one of these water systems is extensively exposed today. Another special feature of Hiran Minar is its location and environment: the top of the minar is perhaps the best place in the province of Punjab to get a feel for the broader landscape and its relationship to a Mughal site.

Looking north from the top of the minar, one can see a patch of forest which is similar to the scrub forest vegetation of Mughal times, while to the west are extensively-irrigated fields, a product of the late nineteenth and early twentieth centuries, but similar in size and appearance to the well-irrigated fields of the Mughal period.

Mughal Painting

Mughal painting is a particular style of South Asian painting, generally confined to miniatures either as book illustrations or as single works to be kept in albums, which emerged from Persian miniature painting, with Indian Hindu, Jain, and Buddhist influences, and developed during the period of the Mughal Empire (16th-19th centuries).

Genesis

When the second Mughal emperor, Humayun (reigned 1530–1540 and 1555-1556) was in Tabriz in the Safavid court of Shah Tahmasp I, he was exposed to Persian miniature painting. When

Humayun returned to India, he brought with him two accomplished Persian artists, *Sayyid Ali* and *Abdus Samad*. Their works, and the assimilation of local styles during succeeding decades, gave shape to a distinct style, which became known as Mughal painting.

The *Tutinama* (literal meaning "Tales of a Parrot"), now in the Cleveland Museum of Art, is among the earliest examples of Mughal painting. The manuscript was made in the reign of Humayun's son, Akbar (r. 1556-1605). Another manuscript the Hamzanama, also made early in Akbar's reign, is said to have contained about 1400 large paintings on cotton (only a fraction have survived) and took about 15 years to complete.

Themes

Mughal painting was rich in variety and included portraits, events and scenes from court life, wild life and hunting scenes, and illustrations of battles.

Development

Mughal painting developed and flourished during the reigns of Akbar, Jahangir and Shah Jahan.

During the reign of Akbar (1556-1605), the imperial court, apart from being the centre of administrative authority to

manage and rule the vast Mughal empire, also emerged as a centre of cultural excellence. Mughal painting thrived and hundreds of painters created innumerable paintings depicting scenes from various Hindu epics including the Ramayana and the Mahabharata; themes with animal fables; individual portraits; and paintings on scores of different themes. Mughal style during this period continued to refine itself with elements of realism and naturalism coming to the fore.

Jahangir (1605-27) had an artistic inclination and during his reign Mughal painting developed further. Brushwork became finer and the colors lighter. Jahangir was also deeply influenced by European painting. During his reign he came into direct contact with the English Crown and was sent gifts of oil paintings, which included portraits of the King and Queen. He encouraged his royal atelier to take up the single point perspective favoured by European artists, unlike the flattened multi-layered style used in traditional miniatures.

He particularly encouraged paintings depicting events of his own life, individual portraits, and studies of birds, flowers and animals. The Jahangirnama, written during his lifetime, which is a biographical account of Jahangir, has several paintings, including some unusual subjects such as the sexual union of a saint with a tigress, and fights between spiders.

During the reign of Shah Jahan (1628-58), Mughal paintings continued to develop, but they gradually became cold and rigid. Themes including musical parties; lovers, sometimes in intimate positions, on terraces and gardens; and ascetics gathered around a fire, abound in the Mughal paintings of this period.

Govardhan was a noted painter during the reigns of Akbar, Jahangir and Shah Jahan.

Decline

Aurangzeb (1658-1707) did not actively encourage Mughal paintings, but as this art form had gathered momentum and had a number of patrons, Mughal paintings continued to survive, but the decline had set in. Some sources however note that a few of the best Mughal paintings were made for Aurangzeb, speculating that the painters may have realized that he was about to close the workshops and thus exceeded themselves in his behalf.

A brief revival was noticed during the reign of Muhammad Shah 'Rangeela' (1719-48), but by the time of Shah Alam II (1759-1806), the art of Mughal painting had lost its glory. By that time, other schools of Indian painting had developed, including, in the royal courts of the Rajput kingdoms of Rajputana, Rajput painting and in the cities ruled by the British East India Company, the Company style under Western influence.

Modern Mughal Art

Mughal miniature paintings are still being created today by a small number of artists in Rajasthan concentrated mainly in Jaipur. Although many of these miniatures are skillful copies of the originals, some artists have produced modern works using classic methods to, at times, remarkable artistic effect.

The skills needed to produce these modern versions of Mughal miniatures are still passed on from generation to generation, although many artisans also employ dozens of workers, often painting under trying working conditions, to produce remarkable works sold under the signature of their modern masters. Of the modern Mughal masters recognized by India, the most prominent remains Rafi Uddin who is the recipient of a large number of artistic honours from India over the last several decades. His younger brother Saif Uddin, who ghost-painted for his famous brother for years, has since become the most recognized modern Mughal painter straying from traditional Indian scenes into themes well away from century old traditions with remarkable effect.

Other masters in Rajasthan include Kaluram Panchal, Ram Gopal Vijayvargiya, Ved Pal Sharma, Kailash Raj, Tilak Gitai, Gopal Kamawat, Mohammed Usman and Mohammed Luqman, Kishan Mali Sharma and the Joshi family.

Hamzanama

The Hamzanama or Dastan-e-Amir Hamza is an important work which narrates the fantastic exploits of Amir Hamza, the uncle of the prophet of Islam. An illustrated manuscript of the *Hamzanama,* an artistic masterpiece was created about 1558–1573 under the Mughal emperor Akbar.

The *Hamzanama* was designed to augment a storytelling performance. This romance originated more than 1,000 years ago, probably in Persia, and subsequently spread throughout the Islamic world in oral and written forms.

Manuscripts of the Hamzanama

The illustrated manuscript created during the Akbar's reign originally comprised 1,400 canvas folios. On one side of most of the folios is a painting, about 54cm x 69cm in area, done in a fusion of Persian and Indian styles. On the other side of most of the folios is Persian text in Nasta'liq script. The folios are ordered, and the text on the back of one folio accompanies the painting on the subsequent folio.

The bulk of these folios are to be found in the Victoria and Albert Museum and the British Museum in London. Further the Austrian Museum of Applied Art (MAK) in Vienna possesses another bulk of these folios and organized in 2009 the exhibition *Global: Lab, Art as a Message. Asia and Europe 1500-1700,* which showed the whole collection of the *Hamzanama* of the museum.

The colophon of this manuscript is still missing. None of the folios of this manuscript so far found is signed. According to

Badauni and Shahnawaz Khan the work of preparing the illustrations was supervised initially by Mir Sayyid Ali and subsequently by Abdus Samad. It took fifteen years to complete the work.

The *Dastan-e-Amir Hamza* existed in several manuscript versions. One version by Navab Mirza Aman Ali Khan Ghalib Lakhnavi was printed in 1855 and published by the Hakim Sahib Press, Calcutta, India. This version was later embellished by Abdullah Bilgrami and published from the Naval Kishore Press, Lucknow, in 1871.

2

Mughal Painting

Mughal painting reflects an exclusive combination of Indian, Persian and Islamic styles. As the name suggests, these paintings evolved as well as developed during the rule of Mughal Emperors in India, between 16th to 19th century. The Mughal paintings of India revolved around themes, like battles, court scenes, receptions, legendary stories, hunting scenes, wildlife, portraits, etc. The Victoria and Albert Museums of London house a large and impressive collection of Mughal paintings.

History of Mughal Painting

Indian Mughal paintings originated during the rule of Mughal Emperor, Humayun (1530-1540). When he came back to India from the exile, he also brought along two excellent Persian artists, Mir-Sayyid Ali and Abd-us-samad. With time, their art got influenced by the local styles and gradually; it gave rise to the Mughal painting of India. The earliest example of the Mughal style is the Tutinama ('Tales of a Parrot') Painting, now in the Cleveland Museum of Art. Then, there is the 'Princess of the House of Timur', a painting redone numerous times.

Growth of Mughal Painting

Mughal paintings of India developed as well as prospered under the rule of Mughal Emperors, Akbar, Jahangir and Shah Jahan.

Under Akbar

Mughal painting experienced large-scale growth under the reign of Emperor Akbar. During that time, hundreds of artists used to paint under the direction of the two Persian artists. Since the Emperor was fond of tales, one can see the paintings mainly being based on the Mahabharata, Ramayana and Persian epics. Mughal paintings also started illustrating an enhanced naturalism, with animal tales, landscape, portraits, etc.

Under Jahangir

Emperor Jahangir reigned from 1605 to 1627 and extended great support to various art forms, especially paintings. This period saw more and more refinement in brushwork, along with the use of much lighter and subdued colors. The main themes of the Mughal paintings revolved around the events from Jahangir's own life, along with portraits, birds, flowers, animals, etc. One of the most popular examples of Mughal paintings of this time include the pictorial illustrations of the Jehangir-nama, the biography of Emperor Jahangir.

Under Shah Jahan

The grace and refinement of the Jahangir period was seen at the time of Emperor Shah Jahan (1628-1658). However, the sensitivity of the paintings was replaced by coldness and rigidity. The themes of that time revolved around musical parties, lovers on terraces and gardens, ascetics gathered around a fire, etc.

Decline of Mughal Painting

The trend that was seen during the time of Shah Jahan was also found under the rule of Aurangzeb (1658-1707). However, the emperor did not pay too much attention on the growth of the Mughal paintings. Still, the art form continued to survive with the support received from its other patrons. However, gradually, because of diminishing support, a declining trend set in. The time of Muhammad Shah, (1719-1748), did experience a brief revival of the Mughal paintings. Nonetheless, with the arrival of Shah Alam II (1759-1806), the art almost became extinct and another school of painting, known as Rajput paintings, started evolving.

Mughal Miniatures and Rajasthan Paintings Representing Parallal History of Medieval India

Baburnama

Mughal Period: When we talk about Mughal Paintings; we talk about Miniature Paintings. The term Mughal paintings refers to the Miniature Paintings done during the reign of Mughal emperors who ruled over India from 1920 to the 1957 when the British Army finally took over the reigns. The Mughal era of miniature paintings owns a noteworthy page in the history of art of paintings in India. The Mughals-descendants of Timur and Genghiz Khan felt strong cultural ties to the Persian world and imported the same with their rule over Indiawhen they conquered most of the north India. After Babur won the war of Panipat against Rajput Kings, the Mughal became the most important artistically active Muslim dynasty on the subcontinent.

After death of Babur, who was a poet and an artist himself, his heirs carried the artistic journey. The following Emperors Mumayun, Akbar, Jahangir and Shah Jahan added their vision and transported the car of the art ahead. Mughal miniature paintings put India's medieval cultures into the colours; the miniature artists injected history into the paintings, through their skill and the indigenous colours. Mughal Emperors and Rajaput kings explored the undefined aspects of the art of paintings, through their patronage and help provided to the artists.

Mughal Art: The miniature style of paintings practiced during this period was clearly influenced by the Persian style of paintings. The Persian painters of miniature style used upright format and general setting with emphasis on flat aerial perspective. The Mighal era artists, especially in the time of King Akbar (1556-1605), maintained that qualities of the Persian style in their work. But they added their vision and took some freedom. They applied naturalism and the tried the depiction of the detailed observation of the world in immediate surround.

Subjects Depicted: Capturing the vitality and luxurious sensuality of the life of Emperors, Rajput kings and their prices and princesses, the miniature artists had tried narrating the medieval culture of India through their art. The characters of the court of Mughal Emperors and Rajput kings were recorded in an informal and engaging style. Many of the paintings narrated the characteristics of the warriors and the elephants and horses they used during war. These miniatures are done in with brilliant colours and dynamic line work depicting the essence of the scene painted.

Govardhan (17th Century) was a noted Indian painter of the Mughal school of painting. He was the son of another painter, Bhavani Das. He joined the imperial service during the reign of Akbar and he continued his work till the reign of Shah Jahan. The examples of his work survived till date show that he was fond of rich, sensuous colour and softly modeled forms.

Govardhan was one of the illustrators of the *Baburnama* presently located in the British Museum, London. The *Jahangir celebrating the festival of Ab-Pashi* (1615), presently kept in the Raza Library in Rampur, India is one of his significant creations. The portraits created by him in the Jahangir albums are presently in the collections of various American and European museums. He depicted the different human physiques of the Indians with much accuracy. An excellent portrait of him was prepared by one of his contemporary painter, Daulat.

Basawan

Basawan, or Basavan (flourished 1580-1600), was an Indian miniature painter in the Mughal style. He was known by his contemporaries as a skilled colourist and keen observer of human nature, and for his use of portraiture in the illustrations of *Akbarnama,* Mughal Emperor, Akbar's official Biography, which is seen as an innovation in Indian art.

Biography

Little is known about his life, although his name suggests that he may have been part of the Ahir (cow-herding caste) in what is now Uttar Pradesh. He became a court painter for Akbar the Great, where he came under the influence of Khwaja Abd-us-Samad.

He had a son, Manohar, who was also a famous artist, noted for his animal studies and portraits.

Work

Over 100 paintings are attributed to Basawan. Most of them are illustrations for manuscripts. In many of them, Basawan was the designer, in collaboration with a second artist who supplied the colour. Among the works that can definitely be attributed to Basawan are illustrations for the *Razmnama,* the *Akbar-nama,* the *Darab-nama,* the *Bahararistan of Jami,* and the *Timur-nama.*

Basawan was one of the first Indian artists to be interested in western techniques, inspired by the European paintings brought to Akbar's court by Jesuit missionaries. It can be seen in his use of strong contrasts of light and shade, although Western influence is never predominant in his work. Basawan was also noted for his exploration of space, the delineation of his backgrounds, the strength of his colors, and his strong, moving characterizations of his subjects. Abu al-Fadl 'Allami, historiographer for Akbar the Great, wrote about Basawan: "In designing and portrait painting and colouring and painting illusi

Ustad Mansur

Ustad Mansur was a seventeenth century Mughal painter and court artist of Jehangir who specialised in depicting plants and animals.

Life and Works

Ustad Mansur started his career during the last few years of Akbar's reign as a minor painter. But during the reign of Jahangir, he created his masterpieces. Jahangir bestowed on him the title of *Nadir-ul-Asar*. His two signed works, one of a rare Siberian Crane and the other of a Bengal Florican are in the Indian Museum, Kolkata. His other works are in the National Museum, Delhi, the Maharaja Sawai Man Singh II Museum, Jaipur and the Chhatrapati Sivaji Vastu Sangrahalaya, Mumbai.

He was the first artist to paint both the Siberian Crane and the Dodo. The Dodo was brought to Jehangir's court via Portuguese controlled Goa and a painting of it is found in the Hermitage in St. Petersburg and unsigned but attributed to Mansur.

Abu al-Hasan (Mughal Painter)

Abu al-Hasan (b. 1589, d. c. 1630), from Delhi, India, was a Mughal painter under the reign of Jahangir.

Abu al-Hasan was the son of Aqa Reza of Herat in western Afghanistan, a city with an artistic tradition. Aqa Reza had taken up employment with Jahangir before the latter's accession to the throne of the Mughal empire.

Abu al-Hasan was initially trained by the emperor himself in his large studios and workshops but soon surpassed his father and his employer. Jahangir siad of him that he had no equal and bestowed the title *Nadir-uz-Saman* ("Wonder of the Age") on him.

Abu al-Hasan's main task was the documentation of events at the imperial court, which resulted in many superb portraits. Not many of Abu al-Hasan's paintings survived, but those that identify him as the artist show that he also worked on a range of subjects including some everyday scenes.

The most famous painting associated with his name, "Squirrels in a Plane Tree" held in the British Library is a masterful depiction of animal posture and movement that could only have been derived from direct observation. Since the painting depicts European squirrels unknown in India his work suggests that Jahangir's zoo may have held a few of these animals. Alternatively Abu al-Hasan may have accompanied Jahangir on one of his travels. The signature on the painting is confusing;*Nadir al-Asr* ("Miracle of the Age") is the title of Ustad Mansur, not of Abu al-Hasan, but the painting is definitely not Ustad Mansur's style. It is possible that both painters collaborated on this painting.

This illustration by the Mughal court artists Miskin and Shankar depicts Adham Khan, foster brother of the Mughal emperor Akbar (r.1556–1605), being thrown from the palace walls at Agra, north-west India. This was his punishment for having burst into the private apartments of the palace with his companions, one of whom had stabbed the emperor's prime minister to death. The different episodes of the incident are shown concurrently. Akbar emerges from his sleeping quarters, sword in hand, having been awoken by the commotion. He orders the immediate death of Adham Khan, who is thrown from the terrace.

The painting is from the Akbarnama (Book of Akbar), commissioned by Akbar as the official chronicle of his reign. The Akbarnama was written in Persian by his court historian and biographer, Abul Fazal, between 1590 and 1596, and the V&A's partial copy of the manuscript is thought to have been illustrated between about 1592 and 1595. This is thought to be the earliest illustrated version of the text, and drew upon the expertise of some of the best royal artists of the time. Many of these are listed by Abul Fazal in the third volume of the text, the A'in-i Akbari, and some of these names appear in the V&A illustrations, written in red ink beneath the pictures, showing that this was a royal copy made for Akbar himself. After his death, the manuscript remained in the library of his son Jahangir, from whom it was inherited by Shah Jahan.

The V&A purchased the manuscript in 1896 from Frances Clarke, the widow of Major General John Clarke, who bought it in India while serving as Commissioner of Oudh between 1858 and 1862.

Farrukh Beg

Farrukh Beg (ca. 1545 — ca. 1615) was a Persian born Mughal painter who served in the court of Muhammad Hakim before working directly for Mughal emperor Akbar.

Bishandas was a 17th-century portrait painter at the court of the Mughal emperor Jahangir. Jahangir praised him as "unrivalled in the art of portraiture". Though little is known of Bishandas' life, his name can indicate that he was a Hindu. In 1613 he was sent on a diplomatic mission to Persia, to paint the Shah's portrait. Here he was so successful that he remained until 1620, when he returned with the gift of an elephant.

Jahangir's Love of Painting

Mughal Emperor Jahangir was a great patron of painting from the days of his Viceroyalty. He patronised many great painters of the time including Mansoor, Abul Hasan, Daswant and Basawan. He acknowledged that his liking for painting was so strong that he was able to judge which painter had executed which work. He also stated that if there was a picture containing many portraits drawn by different artists he was able to identify the artists from the stroke of the brushes.

Once, British Ambassador Thomas Roe arrived in the court of Jahangir and the Emperor asked him to identify the original European Painting placed alongside five copies of it, made by the Indians. This completely foxed the Ambassador much to the delight of the Emperor highlighting the artistic merit of the Indian painters.

Khwaja Abdus Samad

Khwaja Abdus Samad (16th century) was an Iranian painter and one of the founders of the Mughal school of painting in India. He was born in Shiraz.

Early in life, Samad became known for his painting and

calligraphy. Samad met the Mughal emperor Humayun in Tabriz, where he was invited to come with the emperor, though he was unable to accompany the emperor at that time. In 1548, he came to the temporary Mughal capital, Kabul where he was hired by Humayun to teach himself and his son Akbar, how to draw. Samad was thus one of the first to become a member of the imperial atelier (imperial art studio) of India.

A few of his works executed during this period is located in the Royal Library of the Golestan palace in Tehran. One such miniature painting created by Samad depicts Akbar giving a miniature painting to his father Humayun. This painting looks very typical of Persian paintings of that time, but it also contains aspects that would go on to influence future Indian painting.

While at the atelier, Samad supervised (along with Mir Sayyid Ali) the illustrations that were done for the Hamzanama-about 1,400 large paintings (although it is uncertain whether Samad himself painted any of them). Also in the course of teaching at the atelier, Samad taught Dasvant and Basavan, two Hindu men who went on to become famous Mughal painters.

In 1576, Akbar put Samad in charge of the Fatehpur Sikri mint. In 1584, Akbar made him dewan of Multan. He was given a *mansab* of 400 and honoured with the title of *Shirin Qalam* (sweet pen).

More of Samad's work can be seen in the illustrations found in the 1595 manuscript of the Khamseh of Nezami, today located in the British Museum.

Notes

Mushfiq was a sub-imperial Mughal painter who worked in the atelier of Abd-ur-Rahim Khan-i-Khanan (also called Abdul Rahim Khan-I-Khana), commander-in-chief of the Mughal army in the late 16th/early 17th century.

Sahibdin

Sahibdin (fl. 17th century) was an Indian miniature painter of the Mewar school of Rajasthan painting. He was one of the dominant painters of the era, and one of the few whose name is still known today. Sahibdin was a Muslim, but that kept neither his Hindu patrons from employing him, nor him from composing Hindu-themed works of great value.

Among his surviving works are a series of musically themed "*ragamala*" from 1628; a series on the scriptural text Bhagavata Purana from 1648; and illustrations to the sixth book of the Hindu epic Ramayana – the *Yuddha Kanda* – from 1652. His style can be seen to continue the figure style of the Gujarati era, while also incorporating new elements, like mountainous terrains, from Mughal art.

The Mughal School of Painting is taken as a style par excellence in the history of illustrated manuscripts within subcontinent. Two great patrons of art were the two gorgeous emperors, happened to be the father and son in relationship; Akbar the Great and Jahangir. Akbar considered artists as god-like figures who, through their creations, could embark on a stage where they could make others happy or sad. It is enough to understand that why the great King had managed to have *Navratana* (the nine jewels), a group of nine outstanding people comprised of geniuses of diverse art-forms, skills and branches of knowledge.

Tansen, Abu al-Fazal, Birbal, Faizy are well known figures of the group of nine other than those who are not much famous but are equal in status. The *Mughals* are considered to be "the torch bearer" of colossal architecture with ornate and floral motives, attributed to the basic concept of paradise with only sacred fauna and flora to be found there. Contrary to the rock-cut narrow style of architecture which, Hindus were obsessed with in erecting temples of monstrous height and abundance of figurative sculptures, in and around these sanctuaries; showing great level of devotion and fervor towards iconographic nature of religious doctrine, the *Mughals* introduced wide, fortified, ventilated and naturally illumine structures with special cooling system accomplished by virtue of water.

The home-grown attitude of figurative representation, accredited to Hindus, was also voguish in painting in this part of the world. The Jains in compassionate relation with *Tirthankaras,* of which Mahavira was the last one, painted their figures in order to elaborate the religious texts like *Kalpasutra.* This sort of painting was famous in *Gujarat* and *Karnataka,* but the main issue was to publish the scripture as the intention was to elaborate the writings; pictures of religious figures were crafted at the border of the page which, with the passage of time strengthened its place at the centre, after receiving popularity and acceptance from elites and commons. This tradition was later adopted by the Hindus in rendering of their pictorial scriptures like, *Mahabharata, Ramayana, Gita Govinda* and *Bhagvatgita Purana.*

Other than religious librettos, some secular stories also got proper place in this illustrative convention, *Ragmalas,* royal love-stories and adventurous lives of travelers and knights were also in fashion by the time when the great *Mughals* occupied this terra firma. The *Mughals* were already possessing, the ritual of recording sacred characters and events owing to the great Persian tradition of miniature painting which in *Saved* period, got its zenith. The south Asians never stopped anyone to come to this land for taking it up and rule.

The Aryans, Greeks, Persians, Muslims and Britons, all enjoyed the fertility of this soil that lately became their eternal shroud. Babur, the first of the *Mughals,* entered from the western side and after defeating Ibrahim Lodhi, captured Delhi to make this area a crucible of diverse influences. In painting, already existing miniature tradition got blended with the influences, the *Mughals* brought with them from the rich lands of Persia. The dynasty was known for their liberal and secular approach especially during and after the regime of Akbar till Shahjahan.

Akbar was a great admirer of indigenous music, dance, cuisine and costumes. He even honoured a *Rajput* lady *Jodha Bai* as his queen, although this act had its unique place in history as diplomatic ploy by the great emperor. During the epoch of the *Mughals; Ragmalas,* Mythologies and anecdotes of *Rama* and *Sita* and *Krishna* were painted in an approach which, was persuaded by the Persian style of painting, introduced to this part of the world by *Bihzad* and *Abd al-Samad,* two mammoth icons of the art of illustration who accompanied *Humayun* when he recaptured South Asia on his return from exile in Persia. Other than indigenous stories, the royal patrons also commissioned the illustrations depicting their own court-life, battle scenes and hunt-expeditions. *Babur Nama, Akbar Nama, Tuzk-e Jahangiri* and *Padshanama* are few of this series which were painted repeatedly.

On the other hand, famous fables like *Kalila-o Dimna* and *Anwar-e Sahili* were also illustrated time and again in different periods; *Hamza Nama, Tuti Nama, Razm Nama* and *Bustan-i Sa'di* were also amongst the popular collection, commissioned by the dynasty. Critically speaking, what the *Mughals* brought to the South Asia was not just the Persian influence, but there could be found traces of Chinese and Japanese technique and sway the *Mughals* were acquainted with. These influences are obvious in *Hamzanama,* furnished under the *Mughals,* where one could find very colorful rendering of Dragons, an imaginary character of Chinese Mythology.

The making of rocks in the back or fore grounds also reminds the Japanese style adopted years ago in their woodcuts. In addition to rocks, the depiction of whirling waves of river or sea also takes one back to those woodcuts which, even inspired Vincent Van Gogh at Netherlands, especially in his whirling-brush technique. The *Mughals* were successors of the *Mongols;* the Chinese influence could be ascribed to them as an indispensable disposition of their genetics. But the interesting thing was that the local schools of painting, that were on hype in *Rajasthan* and *Gujarat* got enriched by the *Mughal* style when the detail of the green flora and grass was put against the blazing reds of *Gujarat* and soothing blues of *Rajasthan.* Akbar, who was in close relations with the *Rajputs* of *Vijaynagar,* condescended this blend in order to promote his doctrine of secular ideology.

The *Mughal* court was rich and stable in terms of economic condition during Akbar's era after acquiring most of the land, that was available to rule over, so the royal activity regarding music, dance, literature and painting was on full swing; an atelier including renowned painters and craftsmen was always found accompanying the emperor through thick and thin to perform artistic duties.

That atelier worked as a team even on one painting, causing the reason that we could not find the name or signature of one artist on most of the paintings, what you may discover is only anonymity. During the *Mughal* period, the aim of art, besides traditional and religious epics, was basically to record events of political, social and royal nature, therefore, the *Mughal* art was often called of photographic nature.

The lavish royal life was to be portrayed and the already existing art of illustrative manuscripts suited this longing of the Persian blue blood of the *Mughal* Royals resulting into profusion at a large scale of that style of art. When Britons discovered the golden land of India, western style of painting was one of the effects, what they delivered at the *Mughal* court. The crucible got more enriched with court-scenes composed in triangular compositions with raised eye level.

Although the cutout and perspective techniques were already there in the aboriginal style but it was not as precise as the western world was, in their approach towards paining. So we could have a profound look into the tradition of Mughal Painting getting evolved from the early illustrated manuscripts, carrying the influence of the *Persian Saved* tradition, to the modern techniques of composition, especially with reference to perspective and outlook, which allowed the *Mughal* painting to accomplish a native style by giving a picture of the Indian flora and fauna like the Mango, Banyan, and *Pipal* trees and the portrayal of the black bear found only in Kashmir, pictures of birds, cows and monkeys rather than portraying blossoming plums, peaches and amber foliage of Persia.

Mansur, a distinguished painter of Jahangir's court, put the art of illustrating animal, birds and flowers at cloud nine owing to his detailed and meticulous expose of natural world, a rare, perhaps the first wildlife venture in the south Asia in terms of record and depiction of plant and animal kingdoms. No doubt that the *Mughal* painting style is seen absorbing local and far-off influences, but this phenomenon applies on each and every style around the globe and is considered as the essential part of any great evolution. The *Mughal* painting is one example of alteration and evolution, especially in the field of illustrated manuscripts, this part of the world would be remembered for.

Rajput Painting

Rajput painting originated in the royal states of Rajasthan, somewhere around the late 16th and early 17th century. The Mughals ruled almost all the princely states of Rajasthan at that time and because of this; most of the schools of Rajput Painting in India reflect strong Mughal influence. Each of the Rajput kingdoms evolved a distinctive style. However, similarities and common features can still be found in the paintings of different territories.

One can also observe the dominance of Chaurapanchasika group style in Indian Rajasthani Paintings. The main themes around which Rajasthani Paintings of India revolved include the Great epics of Ramayana and the Mahabharata, the life of Lord Krishna, landscapes and humans. Rajput paintings of India were also done on the walls of palaces, inner chambers of the forts, havelis, etc. Colors used for the painting were derived from minerals, plant sources, conch shells, precious stones, gold and silver, etc.

Schools of Rajput Painting

Starting from the 16th century, when the Rajput Painting originated, numerous schools emerged, including:

- Bikaner School
- Bundi-Kota Kalam School
- Jaipur School
- Kishengarh School
- Marwar School
- Mewar School
- Raagamala School.

Amber and Jaipur

The paintings of Amber and Jaipur show strong Mughal influence. However, at the same time, the bold compositions and use of abstractions reflected regional characteristics. The 18th and early 19th century saw Rajput paintings illustrating episodes from the life of Krishna. The other popular themes of the 19th century were Ragamala and devotional subjects.

Bikaner

Rajasthani paintings of Bikaner were also based on Mughal tradition. Apart from the Mughal style, the paintings of Bikaner also reflect marked influence of Deccan paintings. During the late 18th century, the city started showing conservative Rajput styles with smoothness and abstractions. However, they were devoid of any pomposity and flamboyance.

Bundi

Rajput paintings started originating in Bundi around the late 16th century and reflected heavy Mughal influence. Wall paintings, dating back to the reign of Rao Ratan Singh (1607-1631), are good examples of Bundi style of paintings. The time of Rao Chattar Sal (1631-1658) and Bhao Singh (1658-1681) saw great emphasis on court scenes as themes. Other themes include those based on the lives of nobles, lovers and ladies.

Kota

Kota paintings look very natural in their appearance and are calligraphic in their execution. The reign of Jagat Singh (1658-1684) saw vivacious colors and bold lines being used in portraitures. With the arrival of Arjun Singh (1720-1723), the painting started depicting males with a long hooked nose. 18th century was also the time for hunting scenes, Ragamalas, and portraits as the themes. Ram Singh II (1827-1866) ordered the depiction of worship, hunting, Darbar and processions in paintings.

Kishangarh

Kishangarh style of painting was basically a fusion of Mughal and regional style. The most common theme of this style consisted of the depiction of the love between Krishna and Radha. Other popular themes included the poetry of Sawant Singh, Shahnama and court scenes, etc. Kishangarh School is best known for its Bani Thani paintings. With the demise of Savant Singh and his leading painters, this school lost its glory and started breaking down.

Malwa

One of the most conservative Rajput Painting Schools of the 17th century, Malwa was highly influenced by Chaurpanchasika style. The emphasis was laid on strong colors and bold lines. At times, one can also observe a remote Mughal influence on these paintings.

Marwar

The earliest example of the Rajasthani paintings of Marwar is that of Ragamala, which was painted in Pali in 1623. In the 18th century, the most common themes included, the portraitures of nobles on horses and Darbar scenes. With the arrival of artists like Dalchand, Marwar paintings also started reflecting Mughal influence.

Mewar

Mewar school of Rajput paintings concentrated on its conservative style, trying to avoid the dominance of the Mughals. The earliest example of the Mewar School is that of Chawand

Ragamala, dating back to 1605. One can observe heavy similarity with the Chaurapanchasika style, especially the flatness, the bright colors, and even common motifs. Towards the end of the 17th century and the early 18th century, Mewar style saw revival and late 18th century again witnessed its decline. From mid 19th century to mid 20th century, it continued as a court art.

Mughal Miniatures Reveal the Big Picture

In the world of the visual arts of India, Robert Skelton needs no introduction. As one of the foremost postwar authorities on Indian painting and fine objects, he started as a young and enthusiastic scholar in the 1950s at the Victoria and Albert Museum under William G. Archer, who had been in the Indian Civil Service before the war. Until this time, Western scholarship on India was expected to be in the hands of those who had served there, but times were changing and a new breed of scholar with a fresh viewpoint was emerging.

Archer soon recognised Skelton's sharp and critical powers of observation, which led to a thorough re-evaluation of the museum's Mughal miniatures. Skelton was later in charge of the Indian collections and nurtured many young scholars, not just in the museum, but worldwide. It is not surprising that he is admired by all those involved with Indian art.

Arts of Mughal India is a finely produced volume presenting a number of essays, mainly, but not exclusively, on Indian painting, written by Skelton's eminent friends and colleagues. The book opens with reminiscences by three old friends, Pramod Chandra, Simon Digby and Stuart Cary Welch, and is followed by a select bibliography of Skelton's publications that may not appear extensive but shows his wide knowledge of all aspects of Indian art and includes a paper on Shah Jahan's wine cup, one of the V&A's finest Mughal jade objects, obtained through his efforts. The essays follow. Daniel Ehnbom discusses a single painting from the *Hamzanama,* a magical and heroic tale of the legendary Persian hero Amir Hamza. The work, apparently painted in the early days of Akbar's court, is almost entirely Persian in style and detail, and Ehnbom recalls the formative influence of Persian artists, in this case the celebrated Mir Sayyid 'Ali, on Mughal court painting.

In the next essay, Welch demonstrates a similar influence through the illustrations of the *Shahnama,* the great Persian epic that was at the time also regarded as history, illustrated by Mir Sayyid 'Ali. Welch compares the *Shahnama* illustration with another painting attributed to Mir Sayyid 'Ali and comments on the extent of the influence on Indian art of the older Persian masters at the height of their powers. This paper should have perhaps been the opening essay.

Linda York Leach's essay is on the illustrations of a royal copy of the *Akbarnama,* an official history of the Emperor Akbar, many illustrated copies of which were produced in the Mughal court in the late 16th century and given to princes and courtiers. Persian influence is still present in this example, but elements such as costumes and architectural features are Indian.

In spite of the early Mughals' leanings towards Persia, book illustration had long antecedents in pre-Mughal India, for both Hindu and Muslim works.

The influence of such illustrations on Mughal works is explored in essays by B. N. Goswamy on a series of paintings of the time of Akbar depicting the Hindu goddess Devi Mahatmya, and by Asok Kumar Das on paintings related to a number of copies of the *Razmnama,* a Persian translation of the *Mahabharata* epic. Non-Muslim regional book illustration is presented in essays by Shridhar Andhare and Catherine Glynn, while Joachim K. Bautze studies the Rajput wall-paintings at Karwar, Rajasthan. This is a pioneering work on the subject because Rajasthan is a region where there are many Rajput palaces with fine wall paintings awaiting investigation, among them the private rooms of the palace at the fort of Nagaur.

For Mughal painting in its maturity, we should turn to studies presented by Terence McInerney, John Seyller and Milo Cleveland Beach. Friedericke Weis introduces yet another influence on later Mughal art, European imports to India through Portuguese trade; and Barbara Brend writes on the possible influence of European botanical illustration.

Europeans and Mughal India are also represented in a number of essays. Nuno Vassallo e Silva goes back a step and discusses the treasures presented by the Portuguese to the Sultan of Gujarat even before the appearance of the Mughals. None of these well-documented treasures has survived, but the records are of considerable interest for understanding the initial attitude of the

Portuguese towards the local powers. Gauvin Alexander Bailey, on the other hand, discusses the Catholic churches founded by Portuguese Jesuit missions in Mughal India. Ebba Koch, in turn, looks at the influence of Mughal painting in Europe, not just through Rembrandt's well-known version of a Mughal miniature, but through a detailed study of the Mughal-style wall paintings at the Schonbrunn Palace at Vienna. These paintings, although Europeanised, are clearly based on specific Mughal miniatures.

Other aspects of the arts are not neglected. Manuel Keene studies Mughal jewellery, and Rai Anand Krishna a group of Rajasthani painted panels from Jaisalmer. Navina N. Haidar Haykel writes on painted and lacquered papier-mache objects, mainly pen boxes, of the late 17th and early 18th century that are closely linked with Iranian traditions of the same period.

There is much to study here, particularly on the Iranian side. If Mughal painting originally owes much to the earlier Persian masters, at the end of the Mughal period and after their fall there seems to have been a migration of Indian artists to Iran, but little attention has been paid to their influence, evident in pen box decoration and miniature painting. The book ends with essays by Debra Diamond and J. P. Losty on late-Mughal cartography, a subject that provides a wealth of material for those interested in the architecture and urban planning of the period.

Credit for the production of this attractive volume should go to the editors, colleagues of Skelton who have also each contributed a paper.

Rosemary Crill writes on a piece of 17th or early 18th-century chintz (*qalamkari*) painted and dyed with floral borders and animal and birds surrounding a medallion in the middle. Through comparative material, she demonstrates how far textile design in India benefited from the international textile trade, which spread patterns and design worldwide.

What could have perhaps been added is the close similarity of the treatment of the birds and even the background colours of this textile with those of the wall paintings of Ali Qapu at Isfahan.

Susan Stronge's contribution is on Robert Hughes, a merchant and amateur artist in India during the reign of the Emperor Jahangir. With the help of an Armenian, who apparently knew English and Persian, Hughes produced a little-known Persian dictionary with

Persian words transliterated in Roman letters. For philologists, this book could be a mine of information on how Persian was pronounced in Mughal India.

Finally, Andrew Topsfield discusses the representation of court musicians in the paintings of the Udaipur Rajputs in the late 17th and early 18th century. Through a number of paintings, he surveys court traditions concerning music and musicians. His work is a rare attempt to reinvestigate cultural history not just through written material but through physical evidence-a useful model for young scholars to begin looking at Indian miniatures not only as art objects but in a wider perspective, as documents of social and cultural history.

Admirers of Indian visual arts will find this book an up-to-date and informative work with finely produced illustrations. It will serve as a reference tool for scholars for years to come.

3

The Synthesis of European and Mughal Art

The European engravings brought to India in the sixteenth century by the Jesuits to help communicate Christian doctrines to the Mughals are well documented. Prints of non-religious subjects and topographical materials, which need not have necessarily found their way into Mughal possession by way of the Jesuit missionaries is a subject that has been dealt with to a far lesser extent. Individual travelers and merchants took engravings of classical nudes and mythical subjects to the East; this would explain the presence in Mughal albums of prints of nude, mythological and classical subjects, and motifs from maps in background landscapes.

What has also been neglected is a study of how the Mughal artists synthesized aspects of these prints and maps to create a new painting style. Perhaps the best example of the synthesis of Mughal and European art in any one manuscript may be seen in an illustrated *Khamsa,* or collection of epic poems by the Persian poet Nizami now in the British Library, dating between 1593-1595. While some scholars of Indian and Islamic art have dealt with this famous manuscript, the use of European painting techniques and the exact European origins of the paintings of this *Khamsa* have so far been largely ignored.

The purpose of this article is to examine the adoption of the European techniques of *sfumato,* modeling and stereoscopic perspective in the *Khamsa* illustrations and then to trace the European sources for the motifs of some the key miniatures. In this regard, it is necessary also to look at the use of motifs taken from European maps for Mughal background landscapes, which is a subject that has not been dealt with in Mughal art history.

This article also demonstrates that the use of these European elements in the *Khamsa* was not the sign of a passive acceptance of 'superior' painting techniques but a creative and meaningful response by the Mughal artists in the form of articulating their own ideas. Indeed, to use the language of modern technology, the *Khamsa* is a fine example of the Mughal artists' ingenuity in "uploading" these foreign elements into their own aesthetic and semantic structures.

We begin with subject of artistic techniques. "*Sfumato*" may be defined as the deliberate blurring of a line or contour to make an object seem to disappear in the distance, or to add a soft-focus effect to a face or body in the foreground. In the *Khamsa,* this technique is used in conjunction with another technique, that of painting distant landscape in pale blue in order to create the appearance of distance through gradual shifts of colour from dark to pale tones towards the horizon.

Such a technique has its origins in European book illustration, as a folio depicting the *Martyrdom of St. Sebastian* clearly shows. This is by Simon Bening from a book of hours painted around 1520-30 in Bruges. It is unlikely that an original page from a treasured Book of Hours found its way to Mughal India, as these folios were avidly collected by the rich and powerful in Europe. However, there were single folios in wide circulation, which were meant as samples for potential buyers.

In the *Khamsa,* several pictures feature the same technique used for the background scenes. One of the best examples is in the background of a picture of Mary the Copt, the legendary founder of alchemy. Here, behind a distant city, hills and mountains have been painted with faint blue tones to add an idyllic atmosphere to the scene. Such deliberate blurring of forms is also uncharacteristic of the sharper linearity of forms and the use of flat, gold leaf backgrounds in Persian and earlier Mughal art.

Many of the engravings found in Mughal possession excel in the technique of modeling – using light and dark tones to depict the direction of light in order to conjure up the illusion of three dimensions. This is seen best in the modeling of cloth. European engravings provided clear models of the principle of establishing the direction of light. In an engraving of a man and a woman by Jacob Golzius, which was undoubtedly in Mughal possession, as it was eventually to be copied by a Mughal painter in the Gulshan Album, almost all the surface of this print is a spectacle of the engraver's skill in rendering the play of light on the folds of silk garments and curtains.

The other major European technique utilized by the Mughal artists was the depiction of perspective. One of the most remarkable illustrations in the *Khamsa* is *The King is Carried Away by a Giant Bird – The Story of the Princess of the Black Pavilion*, f.195a. It is rich in incidental detail and rural vignettes on a minute scale. Most of all, however, this miniature is an opportunity to show off the new technique of perspective, not to mention a new aerial viewpoint. The is here shown soaring above the earth, over farms, towns and figures absorbed in the minutiae of everyday life, all oblivious to the, except for the spectators in the castle who raise their hands in wonder and bewilderment.

The King of Black Carried Away by a Giant Bird – The Story of the Princess of the Black Pavilion is a complex exercise in rendering of the illusion of distance: there are no fewer than seven receding planes and several rustic vignettes. This miniaturisation accentuates the feeling of distance and dizzying height. There is also a play on contrasts of scale: the tiny figure in the talons of the monstrous bird and the diminution of objects in the distance. The use of this form of stereoscopic perspective is a decisive break with the earlier techniques of Persian painting where figures near the horizon differ little in size from those in the foreground and where objects appear stacked, one upon another.

This miniature is remarkable not only for demonstrating the Mughal adoption and mastery of techniques of European art but it also shows the Mughal artists adapting aspects of European maps and paintings as subordinate aspects of an overall composition and to support their visual storytelling techniques.

An example of this is *The Fall of Icarus* (Staedtel, Frankfurt-am-Main, no.1689), by the Antwerp painter, Tobias Verhaecht (1561-1631). When considering the landscape and main subject together, the colouring and composition of this painting compare favourably to the *Khamsa* illustration, which also synthesizes landscape elements and deep perspective. Also comparable are prints and paintings of the story of Ganymede, seized by Jupiter in the form of a great eagle.

At least in these works, it is a bird carrying off a figure rather than a man with wings. In a charming reversal, the Europeans were influenced by Indian imagery in a print by Stradanus (Jan van der Straet, 1523-1605) of *Magellan's Discovery of the Straits,* which features a large bird, this time carrying an elephant in its talons across the sky. The image first appears as a description of the *Garuda* in the *Mahabharata* (I, 1353) and (III, 39) and in Europe from Marco Polo's description of Madagascar. There is also a related picture from a manuscript of the *Katha-Sacrit-Sagara* of *A Man Hiding in an Elephant Skin Carried Off by a Giant* c.1590-1600.

In Arabic literature, the great bird appears in the *Arabian Nights* as a rescuer of the stranded travelling merchant in one of the tales; in, it appears as a protector and substitute parent of but also, as an evil bird to be conquered by Iskandar. The is the divine entity encompassing all others in ᶜ's *Mantiq al-Tayr.* Any of these sentiments may have attached to the image of the in *The King of Black Carried Away by a Giant Bird – The Story of the Princess of the Black Pavilion* in the Emperor Akbar's *Khamsa.* Further motivation for choosing to illustrate the subject besides the deliberately conspicuous manipulation of European painting techniques to execute the image, may have arisen from knowledge of the great bird as a powerful universal symbol in both the Indian, Chinese, Iranian and European cultural traditions.

Other symbolic associations available to the Mughals may be found in some verses from the *Mantiq al-Tayr,* where ᶜ describes the dropping one of its magic feathers in China:

Everybody procured himself an image of that feather... This feather is, thus, in the picture gallery of China....All these works of creation are there because of its radiance. All images stem from the image of her feather.

The was thus also known as the inspirational spirit of painting and the inclusion of its image in Akbar's *Khamsa* of puts the illustrated manuscript on a par with the picture gallery of China mentioned in the verse above.

Many European maps and topographical views of the sixteenth century may be seen as the sources for figural elements and views of ships and distant cities on hills found in the *Khamsa* pages, these connexions have so far remained unknown. Whether these were brought to India by merchants or by the Jesuits is not known but the Jesuits had certainly brought over maps to their other missions in Japan. One Japanese copy of a map for a screen is from the *Civitates Orbis Terrarum* published in Antwerp in 1572 and 1581. One of the most significant gifts to Akbar from the first Jesuit mission was an atlas of the world. The Jesuit father Monserrate reports that on one occasion, while the Jesuits were before Akbar, the emperor called for an atlas and asked where Portugal was in relation to his own kingdom.

In the *Khamsa,* motifs from maps may be seen in the form of the figure playing bagpipes accompanied by a greyhound dog in *The King of Black Carried Away by a Giant Bird – The Story of the Princess of the Black Pavilion* described above. There is a strikingly similar figure found in a map of 1584, printed by Gottfried von Kempen in an edition of Ptolemy's *Geographiae Libri Octo.*

Scenes of boats and figures pulling in nets from the sea are found in the *Civitates Orbis Terrarum,* mentioned above, in the *Urbium praecipuarum mundi theatrum quintam* and in Abraham Ortelius's atlas, the *Theatrum Orbis Terrarum* (Antwerp, 1570). These are scenes that may be found also in so many Mughal miniatures of the late sixteenth century and in the *Khamsa's Mourning the Death of His Father* in particular. One can perhaps understand the consistent use of this motif as recognition of the expansionism of the Portuguese fleet in real life, invading the outer reaches of the Mughal artist's psyche.

Other pictures reinforce the view that the Mughals used European illustrations and maps as a source of imagery for their book illustrations. A Flemish seascape may be identified in the background to the illustration of *and the Gazelle,* f.19a. The seascape with a European boat and a farmer ploughing the land immediately in front of this bears a remarkable resemblance to a page representing a calendar scene of *February* from a Flemish Book of Hours c.1535. The archaic boat with shields and oars found in the background of this Mughal miniature may also be seen as an incidental detail taken from the *Geographiae Libri Octo* mentioned above.

Another aspect indebted to European prints in the *Khamsa* is that of a bridge over a river with tiny figures walking over it. This may be seen in the background of *and the Gazelle.* The motif can be traced back to a print after Maarten van Heemskerk of *Heraclitus and Democritus,* 1557, which in turn, was revived in the topographical views such as those published by Plantin in the 1570s.

European imagery was also used in the *Khamsa* for the picture of *The Disputing Physicians (or Philosophers)* folio 23b. The picture features a series of wall paintings in the background; one rectangular panel with another beneath it is situated in an architectural niche with curtains at the centre. To the left is an arch under which is painted a scene with a background of its own, as if to appear as a window view on to a landscape. In the spandrel of the arch is an angel, painted to appear as a relief.

These features in the composition can be compared to a sixteenth-century European print of the *Visitation* from the *Evangclicae Historiae Imagines*. This has the same organization of space: an arch to the left in where there is a subsidiary scene, the *Birth of St. John the Baptist,* and a central panel (the *Journey to Nazareth*), in front of which the main 'real' scene takes place, the *Visitation*., who painted *The Disputing Physicians,* must have adapted the basic composition from this original and added to it a rather conventional Persian scene in the foreground.

The central panel in the background of folio 23b may be identified as *St. Luke and the Angel* or a *St. Matthew and the Angel.* It is clear that the wall painting is based on a version of a very similar scene by c.1590. There is an even earlier copy by, dated 1587-8, now at the Bodleian Library. This is of St. Matthew writing in a book held by an angel. The original European engraving of c.1565, with the kind of boats and far-off townscapes typical of the *Khamsa,* is by Philip Galle, based on a work by Maarten van Heemskerk the *Khamsa* is obviously related to this although this connection has never before been made explicit.

The only difference in the *Khamsa* painting is that the angel writes on a scroll of paper, while in the other versions, the angel holds open the page of the book for the saint to write on. Another version of this image is a folio from the Plantin *Humanae Salutis Monumenta* c. 1571, which shows an angel encouraging the saint to write. The smaller inset below this in *The Disputing Physicians* picture represents a female reading from a scroll with an attendant standing nearby. This may be an *Annunciation*: several European engravings by the Wierix family depict the Virgin in bed, receiving an angel with a scroll, bearing good tidings.

The scene depicted on the left of the *Disputing Physicians* features several bathers in a tub. The picture is obviously European in origin, as nudity in Islamic art is extremely rare. The panel to the left appears as a real opening onto a background landscape under a painted arch. It presents itself as problematic: either this is an obvious illusion, or the nude scene is taking place in the same room as the encounter between the disputing physicians.

In contemporary Europe, nude scenes such as *Diana and Actaeon,* or *David Surprising Bathsheba* were becoming popular in paintings and prints. *Susannah and the Elders,* a biblical story, which contains a bathing scene, was frequently represented in the form of prints and tapestries in the sixteenth century. But in these images, the elders are always shown fully clothed.

The scene in the *Khamsa* appears not to be based on a bible story, or on Ovid, but is in fact, related to an entirely different pictorial tradition. The image is copied from a print from a fifteenth-century genre depicting women's bathhouses, common in the Northern Renaissance. The central motif that runs through several of these prints is a tub with scantily clad or nude bathers in it.

By the sixteenth century, the tradition of representing bath-houses was carried on by Durer in such drawings as *Im Turspalt ein Voyeur,* which was copied later in that century by Hans Springinklee. H. S. Beham also executed several prints of women bathing in tubs comparable to the scene in the *Khamsa.* The reason for including the bathtub scene in this picture was perhaps to cast an aspersion on the consistent nudity found in European art, in contradiction to the rather more sacred imagery found in the painting next to it.

Although the painting illustrates 's story of the disputing physicians, the presence of the Christian pictures in the background can only be explained as an elaboration meant to allude to the theological debates held between the Jesuits and the Mughals. The, the chronicle of the Emperor's reign, describes an invitation to scholars and theologians of all religions, heralded by the foundation of the (or debating chamber), opened at Akbar's splendid palace at Fatehpur Sikri:

The doors of the treasury of secrets were opened out without fear of hostile seekers after battle. The just and truth-perceiving ones of each sect emerged from haughtiness and conceit and began their search anew.

Many of the debates that took place between Akbar's Islamic theologians and the Jesuits are recorded in Father Monserrate's *Commentary* and tell of the theological debates about the Trinity, the Immaculate conception and the Art of the Covenant, for example.

Thus, *The Disputing Physicians* may be seen to have a dual nature: it illustrates a legendary story and a real life event, so that each appears to reflect the other. The painting illustrates the episode in the text and is this is the outer meaning of the painting (known as the by the Mughals) but also, its inner meaning refers to the Mughal and Jesuits' theological debates *and* the artistic contest between the Mughal artists and the European.

Akbar asked his artists to copy European works (as one of them has done in the *Disputing Physicians* miniature) to see if they could do better than the Europeans. The 'inner picture' is about the inspirational sources of painting: the prime mover of the scene is God who has given the saint a vision in the form of the angel; secondly, the angel prompts the painter to paint, or write; the result is a painting which itself has inspired several copies by other artists, one of them, the painter of the *Disputing Physicians.*

It is also possible to see the picture of a painting within a painting in the *Disputing Physicians* as a representation of one of the physician's visionary experiences (revealed by the curtain being drawn to one side), hence the physician swooning to the right. St. Luke (or St. Matthew) has a vision of the angel in the European painting on the wall, which in turn is portrayed as the vision of one of the physicians. In parallel with a common compositional scheme in Counter-Reformation Europe, the *Disputing Physicians* is a Mughal example of an artistic device that consists of the representation of a visionary experience, by placing the visionary in the lower part of the picture with the vision in the upper part.

With the kind of synthesis of European and Mughal Indian painting seen in the *Khamsa's Disputing Physicians; and The Gazelle* and *The King of the Black is Carried Off by a Giant Bird,* it may be said that the Mughals' use of European art had moved beyond simple copying to the application of *sfumato,* perspective and the illusion of volume to articulate their own storytelling. European techniques of modeling and creating the illusion of light and shade created a new interest in textures and surface effects.

In all of the pictures mentioned here, the artists of Akbar's *Khamsa* took details from Western works and painted them in different and innovative landscape environments and contexts for subtle evocations of mood and atmosphere. The so-called European elements in the *Khamsa* are thus selected carefully and are used in a balanced and sophisticated manner. Moreover, in the case of the *Disputing Physicians* in particular, European art was manipulated to add allegorical meaning to the narrative structure.

Thus, the Mughal painting repertoire was expanded to include European techniques and motifs and utilized in complex compositional and semantic structures. The Mughal response to European art was not slavish imitation but creative reinvention.

The Mughal Literature

There was tremendous literary activity during the Mughal period, because with the return of a stable and prosperous empire, there was once again patronage for their work. Languages like Persian, Sanskrit, Hindi and Urdu saw tremendous creative activity as did many vernacular languages.

Persian literature received a lot of attention as it was the court language. A vast number of works were written during the period of the Mughals. Broadly one can divide them into three categories, historical works, translations, poetry and novels. Our understanding of the Mughal period was greatly enhanced by these books, and most of the historical works of this period provide us with a fairly reliable source of information.

The important historical works written in this time were *Ain-I-Akbari,* and *Akbarnamath* by Abul Fazal, the *Tarikh-I-Alfi* by Mulla Daud. Jehangir possessed a keen interest in literature, and his autobiography is one of the finest amongst the Mughal emperors. During his reign important historical works like *Maasir-I-Jahangir,* the *Igbalnamah-I-Jahangiri* and the *Zubud-ut-Tawaikh* were written.

Many important works in translation were also written during this period, with the translation of the epics, the Mahabharata and the Ramayana taking place. Many of the Vedas were also translated and several previous historical books were also translated. All this translation added to the wealth of Indian literature and spread ancient knowledge to a greater audience. This renewed interest in Indian literature would be an important tool used by the social reformers of the eighteenth century to educate the people about what the ancient texts really said as opposed to the distorted interpretations that were being followed.

The Mughal empire had a large number of poets and writers and hence there was a lot of work published in this era. Especially during the reign of Akbar, Jehangir and Shah Jahan they had tremendous patronage and many remarkable works were composed. Since the Mughal emperors had integrated themselves into Indian society, they patronized many Indian languages leading to some good quality literature being developed for these languages.

The main themes of the period were essentially religious, covering most of the major religions of the period. One of the fine Hindu works composed during this time was *Ramcharitmanasa* (the pool of Rama's life) by Tulsidasa, which was a simplified version of the Ramayana. In Bengal there was a lot of work being created in Vaishnava literature. Writers like *Krishnada* and *Kaviraj* were popular authors of the time. Many biographies were written, especially of the great saint Chaitanya Deya.

The keen interest in literature that the Mughal emperors had led to the establishment of many great libraries which became repositories of tremendous knowledge. The works were properly filed and locating information was very easy. The art of calligraphy also reached a level of excellence. Literary activity did not decline with the Mughal empire and flourished even in the twilight years of the Mughal empire, in fact some of the later Mughals were better poets and writers than they were capable emperors.

Literature in Mughal Empire

The Mughal period saw great developments in the field of literature. Many Mughal emperors and members of the royal family were great men of letters. Babar the first Mughal emperor was one of the pioneers of Turkish poetry and also the author of a very valuable autobiography in Turkish Babar Nama which was later translated into Persian. Gulbadan Begum sister of Humayun wrote the Humayun Nama. Jahangir the great connoisseur of painting wrote his autobiography the Tuzuk-i-Jahangiri. Aurangzeb also was a prolific writer and the last Mughal emperor Bahadur Shah Zafar was a notable Urdu poet.

Hindi literature made significant progress during Akbar's reign. Tulsidas and the Surdas wrote in this period. Keshavdas a great poet wrote on themes of love. Rahim's dohas or couplets are extremely popular. It was also in Akbar's time that the great Sanskrit work on styles of writing, the Alankarashekhara by Keshava Misra appeared. This was the period of many notable writings in the Persian language.

Abul Fazal wrote the Ain-i-Akbari and Akbar Nama. Abul Fazal's brother Faizi was a great poet of Persian and was responsible for the translation of many Sanskrit works into Persian. Akbar had started a whole dept for translation of works like Mahabharata, the Ramayana, the Atharva –Veda, the Bhagvad Gita and the Panchatantra.

Many important historical works were produced under the emperors after Akbar. Some of the important historians were Abdul Hamid Lahori, Khafi Khan, Muhammad Kazim and Sujan Rai Bhandari. Literature in modern Indian languages also continued to grow. The famous book of Bihari called the Satsai in Hindi belongs to this period. One of the most significant developments during the medieval period was the birth of the Urdu language. This new language soon developed one of the richest literatures as a modern Indian language. It produced great poets like Wali, Mir Dard, Mir Taqi Mir. Nazir Akbarabadi, Asadullah Khan Ghalib.

Many original prose works in Urdu were written like Muhammad Hussain Azad's Darbar-i-Akbari. The Urdu novel was one of the earliest development in the Indian languages. Urdu became the language of the urban people of northern India and the Deccan.

Abul-Fazal ibn Mubarak

Shaikh Abu al-Fazal ibn Mubarak also known as Abul-Fazal, Abul Fadl and Abul-Fadl 'Allami (January 14, 1551- August 12, 1602) was the vizier of the great Mughal emperor Akbar, and author of the *Akbarnama,* the official history of Akbar's reign in three volumes, the third volume is known as the *Ain-i-Akbari* and a Persian translation of the Bible. He was also the brother of Faizi, the poet laureate of emperor Akbar.

Biography

Abul Fazal was the fifth descendant of Shaikh Musa who lived in Rel Sindh. His grandfather, Shaikh Khizr settled at Nagaur, where his father Shaikh Mubarak was born. Initially Shaikh Mubarak studied in Nagaur under Khwaja Ahrar. Later he went to Ahmedabad and studied under Shaikh Abul Fazal, Shaikh Umar and Shaikh Yusuf. Finally, he settled in Agra, where his eldest son, poet Abul Faizi and his second son Abul Fazal were born He came to Akbar's court in 1575 and was influential in Akbar's religious views becoming more liberal into the 1580s and 1590s. He also led the Mughal imperial army in its wars in the Deccan.

He was assassinated by Vir Singh Bundela (who later became the ruler of Orchha) between Sarai Vir and Antri (near Narwar) in a plot contrived by the Mughal Prince Salim, who later became the Emperor Jahangir in 1602, because Abul Fazal was known to oppose the accession of Prince Salim to the throne. His severed head was sent to Salim at Allahabad. Abul Fazal was buried at Antri. Abul Fazal's son Shaikh Abdur Rahman Afzal Khan (December 29, 1571-1613) was later appointed governor of Bihar in 1608 by Jahangir.

His Own Account of the First Twenty Years

As I have now recounted somewhat of my ancestors, I proceed to say a few words regarding myself and thus unburden my mind, in order to refresh this narrative and loosen the bonds of my tongue. In the year 473 of the Jalali era, corresponding to the night of Sunday, the 6th of Muharram 958 of the lunar reckoning (14 January 1551), my pure spirit joined to this elemental body came forth from the womb into this fair expanse of the world. At a little over one year I had the miraculous gift of fluent speech and at five years of age I had acquired an unusual stock of information and could both read and write.

At the age of seven I became the treasurer of my father's stores of knowledge and a trusty keeper of the jewels of hidden meaning and as a serpent, guarded the treasure. And it was strange that by a freak of fortune my heart was disinclined, my will ever averse, and my disposition repugnant to conventional learning and the ordinary courses of instruction. Generally I could not understand them. My father in his way conjured with the spell of knowledge and taught me a little of every branch of science, and although my intelligence grew, I gained no deep impressions from the school of learning.

Sometimes I understood nothing at all, at others doubts suggested themselves which my tongue was incapable of explaining. Either shame made me hesitate or I had not the power of expression. I used to weep in public and put all the blame upon myself. In this state of things I came into fellowship of mind with a congenial helper and my spirit recovered from that ignorance and incomprehension. Not many days had elapsed before his conversation and society induced me to go to college and there they restored to rest my bewildered and dissipated mind and by the wondrous working of destiny they took me away and brought another back.

The temple as I entered, drew they nigh
And brought their gift, a wine-cup brimming high.
Its strength snatched all my senses, self from self,
Wherein some other entered and not I.

The truths of philosophy and the subtleties of the schools now appeared plain, and a book which I had never before seen gave me a clearer insight than any thing I could read. Although I had a special gift which came down upon me from the throne of holiness, yet the inspirations of my venerable father and his making me commit to memory the essential elements of every branch of science, together with the unbroken continuity of this chain, were of immense help, and became one of the most important causes of my enlightenment.

For ten years longer I made no distinction between night and day, teaching and learning, and recognized no difference between satiety and hunger, nor discriminated between privacy and society, nor had I the power to dissever pain from pleasure. I acknowledged nothing else but the bond of demonstration and the tie of knowledge. Those who had a regard for my constitution, from seeing that two and sometimes three days passed without my taking food, and that my studious spirit had no inclination therefore, were amazed, and stood out strongly against it.

I answered that my withdrawal, was now a matter of habit and custom, and how was it that no one was astonished when the natural inclination of a sick man on an attack of illness was averse from food. If therefore my love of study induced forgetfulness, where was the wonder? Most of the current arguments of the schools, frequently misquoted and misunderstood when heard, and abstruse questions from ancient works, had been presented to the fresh tablet of my mind.

Before these points had been elucidated and the attribution to me of extreme ignorance had passed to that of transcendent knowledge, I had taken objection to ancient writers, and men learning my youth, dissented, and my mind was troubled and my inexperienced heart was in agitation. Once in the early part of my career they brought the gloss of Khwajah Abul Qasim, on the Mutawwal.

All that I had stated before learned doctors and divines of which some of my friends had taken notes, was there found, and those present were astounded and withdrew their dissent, and began to regard me with other eyes and to raise the wicket of misunderstanding and to open the gate of comprehension. In my early days of study, the gloss of Isfahani more than half of which had been eaten by white ants, came under my observation. The public being in despair at profiting by it, I removed the parts that had been eaten and joined blank paper to the rest.

In the serene hours of morning, with a little reflection, I discovered the beginnings and endings of each fragment and conjecturally penned a draft text which I transcribed on the paper. In the meanwhile the entire work was discovered, and when both were compared, in two or three places only were there found differences of words, though synonymous in meaning; and in three or four others, (differing) citations but approximate in sense. All were astounded.

The more my will was engaged, the more my mind was illumined. At the age of twenty the good tidings of my independence reached me. My mind cast off its former bonds and my early bewilderment recurred. With a parade of much learning, the intoxication of youth effervescing, the skirts of pretension spread wide, and the world-displaying cup of wisdom in my hand, the ringings of delirium began to sound in my ears, and suggested a total withdrawal from the world.

Meanwhile the wise prince-regnant called me to mind and drew me from my obscurity, somewhat of which I have in its entirety and somewhat but approximately suggested and acknowledged. Here my coin has been tested and its full weight passed into currency. Men now view me with a different regard, and many effusive speeches have been made amid felicitous congratulations evoked.

On this day which is the last of the 42nd year of His Majesty's reign (A.D. 1598), my spirit again breaks away from its yoke and a new solicitude arises within me.

My songster heart knows not King David's strains:
Let it go free—'its no bird for a cage.

I know not how it will all end nor in what resting-place my last journey will have to be made, but from the beginning of my existence until now the grace of God has continuously kept me under its protection. It is my firm hope that my last moments may be spent in doing His will and that I may pass unburdened to eternal rest.

The Akbarnama

The Akbarnama is a document of history of Akbar's reign and his ancestors spread over three volumes. It contains the history of Akbar's ancestors from Timur to Humayun, Akbar's reign up to the 46th regnal year (1602), and an administrative report of Akbar's empire, the Ain-i-Akbari, which itself is in three volumes. The third volume of Ain-i-Akbari gives an account of the ancestry and life of the author. The Ain-i-Akbari was completed in the 42nd regnal year, but a slight addition was made to it in the 43rd regnal year on the account of the conquest of Berar.

Akbarnama

The Akbarnma, which literally means *Book of Akbar*, is a official biographical account of Akbar, the third Mughal Emperor (r. 1556–1605), written in Persian. It includes vivid and detailed descriptions of his life and times.

The work was commissioned by Akbar, and written by Abul Fazal, one of the *Nine Jewels* (Hindi: Navaratnas) of Akbar's royal court. It is stated that the book took seven years to be completed and the original manuscripts contained a number of paintings supporting the texts, and all the paintings represented the Mughal school of painting, and work of masters of the imperial workshop, including Basawan, whose use of portraiture in its illustrations was an innovation in Indian art.

Contents of the Volumes I and II

The Akbarnama consists of three volumes or parts. The first volume deals with the genealogy of the descendants of Timur, and detailed information from the birth of Akbar, his accession to the throne, and the first seventeen years of his reign. The second volume narrates the reign of Akbar from the eighteenth year of his reign to the forty sixth year of his reign.

It stops there because Abul Fazal was assassinated at the order of Jahangir, Akbar's son and heir on August 12, 1602. The account of Akbar's reign from the 46th regnal year, where Abul Fazal's work stops till his death in October, 1605 was later added to the second volume by Inayat Ullah or Muhammad Salih. This work is known as *Takmil-i-Akbarnama*. This work omits many happenings between 1602 and 1605.

Besides recording Akbar's life and reign, the Akbarnama also includes many descriptions of the social order of India. Both Abul Fazal and Akbar had very tolerant religious ideas, and Fazal used his writing to show Hinduism in a good light to the Muslims of the Mughal ruling class.

Volume III: The Ain-i-Akbari

Ain-i-Akbari

The Ain-i-Akbari or the "Institutes of Akbar", is a 16th century, detailed document recording the administration of emperor Akbar's empire, written by his vizier, Abul-Fazal ibn Mubarak. It makes the Volume III and the final part of the much larger document, the Akbarnama, the Book of Akbar, also by Abul Fazal, and it itself is in three volumes.

Contents

The Ain-i-Akbari is the third volume of the Akbarnama contains information regarding Akbar's reign in the form of, what would be called in modern times, administration reports, statistical compilations, or gazetteers. It contains the ain (i.e., mode of governing) of Akbar, and is, in fact, the administration report and statistical Return of his government. The first volume of the Akbarnama contains the history of Timur's family and the reigns of Babar, the Sur kings, and Humayun. The second volume is devoted to the detailed history of the nearly forty-six years of the Akbar's reign. Since it was written around 1590, it also contains details of Hindu beliefs and practices as well as a history of India.

The Ain-i-Akbari is itself divided into five books. The first book deals with the imperial household, and the second with the servants of the emperor, the military and civil services. The third book deals with the imperial administration, containing the regulations for the judicial and executive departments. The fourth book contains information about Hindu philosophy, science, social customs and literature. The fifth book contains sayings of Akbar, along with an account of the ancestry and biography of the author.

Translations

The original Persian text was translated into English in three volumes. The first volume, translated by H. Blochmann (1873) consisted of Books I and II. The second volume, translated by Colonel H.S. Jarrett (1891), consisted of Book III. The third volume, also translated by Colonel H.S. Jarrett (1896), consisted of Books IV and V. These three volumes were published by the Asiatic Society of Bengal, Calcutta as a part of their *Bibliotheca Indica* series.

Faizi

Shaikh Abu al-Faiz ibn Mubarak, popularly known by his pen-name, Faizi (24 September, 1547, Agra–5 October, 1595, Lahore) was a Persian poet of late medieval India. In 1588, he became the *Malik-ush-Shuara* (poet laureate) of Akbar's Court. He was the elder brother of Akbar's historian Abul Fazal. Akbar highly recognized the genius in him and appointed him tutor for his sons and gave place to him among his decorative 'Nav Ratnas'.

Life

Faizi was the eldest son of Shaikh Mubarak of Nagaur. He was born at Agra on 5 Sha'ban, AH 954 (24 September, 1547). His father, Shaikh Mubarak was a scholar in the philosophy and literature of Greece as well as in Islamic theology. He was educated mostly by his father. In AH 974 (1566-7), he reached Akbar's court. Akbar successively appointed him tutor for his princes, Salim, Murad and Daniyal. In AH 990 (1581), he was appointed *sadr* of

Agra, Kalpi and Kalinjar. In AH 999 (1591-2), he was sent to Khandesh and Ahmednagar as Mughal envoy. In AH 1003 (1594), a few years after his return from Deccan, Faizi suffered from Asthma and died on 10 Safar, AH 1004 (5 October, 1595) at Lahore. Initially, he was buried in the Ram Bagh at Agra but his body was later transferred to another family mausoleum near Sikandara.

Works

He composed significant poetic works in Persian and is ascribed by Bada'uni and his other contemporaries to have composed over a hundered poetic works, but all the titles are not known to us. His *Divan* (collection of poems), was entitled *Tabashir al-Subh*. His *Divan* comprises qasidas, ghazals, ruba'is and elegies. In pursuance of the literary practice then in vogue, Faizi planned to produce a *Panj Ganj* (literally five treasures) or *Khamsa* in imitation of the Persian poet Nezami Ganjavi. At the age of 30, he started writing five works: the *Nal o Daman*, the *Markaz ul-Advar*, the *Sulaiman o Bilqis*, the *Haft Kishvar* and the *Akbarnama*.

His two completed works, the *Markaz ul-Advar* and the *Nal o Daman* (completed in 1594) was the *javab* (imitation) of Nezami's the *Makhzan ul-Asrar*and the *Layla o Majnun*. His other three incomplete works, the *Sulaiman o Bilqis*, the *Haft Kishvar* and the *Akbarnama* were the imitations of the *Khusraw o Shirin*, the *Haft Paykar* and the *Sikandarnama* respectively. During his stay in Deccan from 1591-3, he wrote a celebrated series of reports on political and cultural conditions of Deccan, as well as contemporary Iran. He also wrote a commentary on the Quran.

Faizi translated Bhaskaracharya's celebrated Sanskrit work on mathematics, *Lilavati* in to Persian. According to its preface, this work was completed in AH 995 (1587).

Abd al-Qadir Bada'uni

Mulla ¿Abd-ul-Qadir Bada'uni (1540, Toda, India – c. 1615, India) was an Indo-Persian historian and translator living during the Mughal period in India.. He was son of Muluk Shah. He lived in Basavar as a boy studying in Sambhal and Agra. He moved to Badaun, the town of his name, in 1562 before moving on to enter the service of prince Husayn Khan for the next nine years in Patiala. His later years of study were governed by Muslim mystics. Jalaluddin Muhammad Akbar appointed him to the religious office in the royal courts in 1574 where he spent much of his career. He translated the Hindu works, the Ramayana and the Mahabharata. However, as an Orthodox Muslim, he strongly resented the reforms of Akbar, and the elevation of Hindus to high offices. He was also renowned for his rivalry with Abul Fazal.

Major Works

The most notable work of Bada'uni is *Muntakhab-ut-Tawarikh* (Selection of Chronicles) or *Tarikh-i-Bada'uni* (Bada'uni's History) composed in 1004 AH (1595). This work in three volumes is a general History of the Muslims of India. The first volume contains an account of Babur and Humayun. The second volume exclusively deals with Akbar's reign up to 1595. This volume is an unusually frank and critical account of Akbar's administrative measures, particularly religious and his conduct.

This volume was kept concealed till Akbar's death and was published after Jahangir's accession this book is written from the point of view of an orthodox Sunni Muslim and gives a biased view regarding the development of Akbar's views on religion and his religious policy. The third volume describes the lives and works of Muslim religious figures, scholars, physicians and poets.

The first printed edition of the text of this work was published by the College Press, Calcutta in 1865 and later this work was translated into English by G.S.A. Ranking (Vol.I), W.H. Lowe (Vol.II) and T.W. Haig (Vol.III) (published by the Asiatic Society, Calcutta between 1884-1925 as a part of their Bibliotheca Indiaca series). Other works by Bada'uni include the *Bahr-ul-Asmar*, a work on *Kitab al-Hadith* "book of sayings [of Muhammad]", (lost), a chapter in the *Tarikh-i-Alfi* (History of the Millennium), commissioned by Akbar to celebrate the millenary of the Hijrah, and the *Najat-ur-Rashid* (1581), a summary of the *Jami al-Tawarikh*, the "Universal History" of

Keshavdas

Keshavdas (Keshvdas) (1555-1617) was a Sanskrit scholar and Hindi poet, best known for his Rasik Priya, a pioneering work of the *riti kaal* (procedure period) of Hindi literature.

Life

He was born in Orchha in a Sanadhya Brahmin family. His

father Kashinath and the elder brother Balabhadra Mishra were both Sanskrit scholars. Initially he was in the court of Indrajit Singh, the brother of the Bundela ruler Ram Singh. In 1608, when Vir Singh Dev came to power, he joined his court. He was granted a jaageer of 21 villages.

Major Works

His first work is *Ratan Bavani* (c.1581). Three anthology of poems are attributed to him, *Rasikpriya* (1591), *Ramchandrika* (1600), and *Kavipriya* (1601). The *Ramchandrika* is an abridged translation of the Ramayana in 30 sections. His other works include *Rakhshikh* (1600), *Chhandamala* (1602), *Virsinghdev Charit* (1607), *Vijnangita* (1610) and *Jahangirjas Chandrika* (1612). He wrote in Brij Bhasha, though with a heavy mixture of Bundelkhandi dialect.

He praised the Betwa and Orchha as the most beautiful things on earth. More so because it was he, Keshav Das, who had made them famous. Greyed by years he rued the day when pretty girls he eyed on the Betwa addressed him as Baba—old man.

Bihari Lal

Bihari Lal Chaube or Bihari, (1595 – 1663, was a Hindi poet, who is famous for writing the *Satasai* (Seven Hundred Verses) in Brajbhasha, a collection of approximately seven hundred distichs, which is perhaps the most celebrated Hindi work of poetic art, as distinguished from narrative and simpler styles. Today it is considered the most well known book of the Ritikavya Kaal or 'Riti Kaal' of Hindi literature.

The language is the form of Hindi called *Brajbhasha,* spoken in the country about Mathura, where the poet lived. The couplets are inspired by the Krishna side of Vishnu-worship, and the majority of them take the shape of amorous utterances of Radha, the chief of the Gopis or cowherd maidens of Braj, and her divine lover, the son of Vasudeva. Each couplet is independent and complete in itself, and is a triumph of skill in compression of language, felicity of description. and rhetorical artifice. The distichs, in their collected form, are arranged, not in any sequence of narrative or dialogue, but according to the technical classification of the sentiments which they convey as set forth in the treatises on Indian rhetoric. Bihari was born in Govindpur near Gwalior in 1595, and spent his boyhood in Orchha in the Bundelkhand region, where his father, Keshav Rai lived. After marriage he settled with in-law's in Mathura.

His father, Kesav Rai, was a twiceborn (*Dwija*) by caste, which is generally means an offspring of a Brahman father by a Kshatriya mother.

Early in his life, he studied ancient Sanskrit texts. In Orchha state, he met the famous poet Keshavdas from whom he took lessons in poetry. Later, when he had shifted to Mathura, he got an opportunity to present his in court of visiting Mughal Emperor Shah Jahan, who immediately got impressed by his work and invited him to stay in Agra.

Once at Agra, he learnt Persian language and came into contact with Rahim, another famous poet. It was also at Agra that Raja Jai Singh I (ruled. 1611-1667), of Amber, near Jaipur, happened to hear him, and invited him over to Jaipur, and it was here that he composed his greatest work, Satasai.

Career

Bihari wrote in Brajbhasha. His poetry is in *shringar* ras, depicting the divine love of Krishna and Radha.

A couplet in the *Sat-sai* states that it was completed in A.D. 1662. It is certain that his patron, whom he calls Jai Shah, Raja Jai Singh I (1611-1667), of Amber, near Jaipur, during the reigns of the emperors Jahangir, Shah Jahan and Aurangzeb. A couplet (No. 705) appears to refer to an event which occurred in 1665, and in which Raja Jai Singh was concerned. For this prince the couplets were composed, and for each Doha or couplet, the poet is said to have received a gold piece worth sixteen rupees.

Though Bihari 'Satasai' is only known work of Bihari, an estimation in which the work is held may be measured by the number of commentators who have devoted themselves to its elucidation, of whom Dr. G. A. Grierson mentions seventeen. The collection has also twice been translated into Sanskrit.

The best-known commentary is that of Lallu ji-Lal, entitled the *Lala-chandrika*. The author was employed by Dr. Gilchrist in the College of Fort William, where he finished his commentary in 1818. A critical edition of it has been published by Dr. G. A. Grierson. The Mughals established a mighty empire that dominated India for more than two centuries. Their passion for literature and knowledge commissioned excellent literary works. They add luster and wealth to the literatures of India.

India is a rich mine of hidden literatures! The vast wealth of literature still in palm leaves has to be brought out for open studies which surely will have a great impact on history as well as the knowledge of so many sciences. Tamil, Sanskrit, Urdu and other languages have contributed unimaginable wealth to the Indian literatures. When the countries enjoyed a peaceful life, literature and arts were flourishing well. That we can see in the history of India, especially during the Sangam periods, the Guptas and the Mughals.

Printing in India

Most of the Indian literatures were in palm leaves till the arrival of the printing technology in the sixteenth century. Printing was a turning point in the Indian history. It came with the missionary movement of the Portuguese and others. Fifty-nine years after the landing of Vasco da Gama in India, the printing press opened its account at Goa, a few decades after the beginning of the 16th century. Within a hundred years of the printing of Gutenberg's Bible in Germany, India initiated its groping towards fashioning of types for the many Indian languages.

Mughal Empire which was established in the north in the sixteenth century and the Vijayanagara Empire in the south witnessed the changes that were brought by the printing technology in India.

Mughal Contribution To Literature

There was tremendous literary activity during the Mughal period, because with the return of a stable and prosperous empire. There was once again patronage for the literary works. Languages like Persian, Sanskrit, Hindi and Urdu saw tremendous creative activity as did many vernacular languages. The Mughal Emperors, themselves interested in literature, encouraged literary contributions. Vast number of works were written during the period of the Mughals.

The Three Categories of Contributions

We can easily divide the contributions of the Mughals into three categories: historical works, translations, poetry and novels.

Our understanding of the Mughal period was greatly enhanced by these books, and most of the historical works of this period provide us with a fairly reliable source of information.

The important historical works written in this time were Ain-I-Akbari, and Akbarnama by Abul Fazal, the Tarikh-I-Alfi by Mulla Daud. Akbar, though was not educated in any formal educational institution, could contribute much to literature. Jehangir possessed a keen interest in literature, and his autobiography is one of the finest amongst the Mughal emperors. During his reign important historical works like Maasir-I-Jahangir, the Igbalnamah-I-Jahangiri and the Zubud-ut-Tawaikh were written.

Great Translations

Many important works in translation were also written during this period, with the translation of the epics, the Mahabharata and the Ramayana taking place.

Many of the Vedas were also translated and several previous historical books were also translated. All this translation added to the wealth of Indian literature and spread ancient knowledge to a greater audience. This renewed interest in Indian literature would be an important tool used by the social reformers of the eighteenth century to educate the people about what the ancient texts really said as opposed to the distorted interpretations that were being followed.

New Contributions

The Mughal empire encouraged a large number of poets and writers and hence there were a lot of new contributions published in this era. During the reign of Akbar, Jehangir and Shah Jahan the literary people had tremendous patronage and many remarkable works were composed. Since the Mughal emperors had integrated themselves into Indian society, they patronized many Indian languages leading to some good quality literature being developed for these languages.

The main themes of the period were essentially religious, covering most of the major religions of the period. One of the fine Hindu works composed during this time was Ramcharitmanasa (the life of Rama) by Tulsidasa, which was a simplified version of the Ramayana. In Bengal there was a lot of work being created in Vaishnava literature. Writers like Krishnada and Kaviraj were popular authors of the time. Many biographies were also written during this period.

Valuable Contributions

The Mughals established a mighty empire that dominated India for more than two centuries. Their passion for nature and literature contributed much for the Indian literature. Books were very precious to the Mughal kings. Expensive and laborious contributions were as marked the symbols of royal wealth, power and intelligence. At the height of the Mughal power, the imperial studios hummed with the activity of hundreds papermakers, printers and business people of books. Today we can see and enjoy the books and manuscripts illustrated with exquisite miniature paintings of the Mughal Emperors treasured by museums around the world. The Mughal contribution to the Indian literatures is really great

4

Mughal Contribution to Indian Literature

The Mughals established a mighty empire that dominated India for more than two centuries. Their passion for literature and knowledge commissioned excellent literary works. They add luster and wealth to the literatures of India.

India is a rich mine of hidden literatures! The vast wealth of literature still in palm leaves has to be brought out for open studies which surely will have a great impact on history as well as the knowledge of so many sciences. Tamil, Sanskrit, Urdu and other languages have contributed unimaginable wealth to the Indian literatures. When the countries enjoyed a peaceful life, literature and arts were flourishing well. That we can see in the history of India, especially during the Sangam periods, the Guptas and the Mughals.

Printing in India

Most of the Indian literatures were in palm leaves till the arrival of the printing technology in the sixteenth century. Printing was a turning point in the Indian history. It came with the missionary movement of the Portuguese and others. Fifty-nine years after the landing of Vasco da Gama in India, the printing press opened its account at Goa, a few decades after the beginning of the 16th century. Within a hundred years of the printing of Gutenberg's Bible in Germany, India initiated its groping towards fashioning of types for the many Indian languages.

Mughal Empire which was established in the north in the sixteenth century and the Vijayanagara Empire in the south witnessed the changes that were brought by the printing technology in India.

Mughal Contribution To Literature

There was tremendous literary activity during the Mughal period, because with the return of a stable and prosperous empire. There was once again patronage for the literary works. Languages like Persian, Sanskrit, Hindi and Urdu saw tremendous creative activity as did many vernacular languages. The Mughal Emperors, themselves interested in literature, encouraged literary contributions. Vast number of works were written during the period of the Mughals.

The Three Categories of Contributions

We can easily divide the contributions of the Mughals into three categories: historical works, translations, poetry and novels. Our understanding of the Mughal period was greatly enhanced by these books, and most of the historical works of this period provide us with a fairly reliable source of information.

The important historical works written in this time were Ain-I-Akbari, and Akbarnama by Abul Fazal, the Tarikh-I-Alfi by Mulla Daud.

Akbar, though was not educated in any formal educational institution, could contribute much to literature. Jehangir possessed a keen interest in literature, and his autobiography is one of the finest amongst the Mughal emperors. During his reign important historical works like Maasir-I-Jahangir, the Igbalnamah-I-Jahangiri and the Zubud-ut-Tawaikh were written.

Great Translations

Many important works in translation were also written during this period, with the translation of the epics, the Mahabharata and the Ramayana taking place. Many of the Vedas were also translated and several previous historical books were also translated. All this translation added to the wealth of Indian literature and spread ancient knowledge to a greater audience. This renewed interest in Indian literature would be an important tool used by the social reformers of the eighteenth century to educate the people about what the ancient texts really said as opposed to the distorted interpretations that were being followed.

New Contributions

The Mughal empire encouraged a large number of poets and writers and hence there were a lot of new contributions published in this era. During the reign of Akbar, Jehangir and Shah Jahan the literary people had tremendous patronage and many remarkable works were composed. Since the Mughal emperors had integrated themselves into Indian society, they patronized many Indian languages leading to some good quality literature being developed for these languages. The main themes of the period were essentially religious, covering most of the major religions of the period. One of the fine Hindu works composed during this time was Ramcharitmanasa (the life of Rama) by Tulsidasa, which was a simplified version of the Ramayana. In Bengal there was a lot of work being created in Vaishnava literature. Writers like Krishnada and Kaviraj were popular authors of the time. Many biographies were also written during this period.

Valuable Contributions

The Mughals established a mighty empire that dominated India for more than two centuries. Their passion for nature and literature contributed much for the Indian literature. Books were very precious to the Mughal kings. Expensive and laborious contributions were as marked the symbols of royal wealth, power and intelligence. At the height of the Mughal power, the imperial studios hummed with the activity of hundreds papermakers, printers and business people of books. Today we can see and enjoy the books and manuscripts illustrated with exquisite miniature paintings of the Mughal Emperors treasured by museums around the world. The Mughal contribution to the Indian literatures is really great.

1. Tawarikh-E-Khandan-E-Tamuria:-History of Tamur raised upto 22years of Akbar region painted during 1582 to 1585 the main painters of this book was Daswant.
2. Razmanama (Mahabharat): -Razmanama completed in 3 volumes in 1588 a painting translation of Mahabharat.
3. Ramayana:-Ramayana translated in Persian and painted
4. Bakat Babri:-Bakat Babri a biography of Babar translated from Jurkish Language to Persian written by Khan-E-Khana painted in 1589.

5. Akbar Nama:-Akbar Nama completed in 1602 had more than 100 of paintings.
6. Anwar Sohely (1610):- Anwar Sohely was a illustrated translation of Panch Tantra Story.
7. Ayar Danish:-It was also one of the collections of panch Tantara story.

Other menu script of this period Katha Sarit Sagar, Nal Damyanti, Kalia Daman, Changez Nama, Zafar Nama, Shakuntala or Ain-E-Akbari etc.

Bahadur Shah Zafar

The last Mughal emperor of India, Bahadur Shah Zafar II (1775-1862) was born Abu Zafar Sirajuddin Muhammad Bahadur Shah Zafar and was a very famous Urdu poet in his times. His poems are still read with much enthusiasm and admiration among the numerous Urdu poetry fans. The life history of Bahadur Shah Zafar is very interesting and is read with much enthusiasm by all. Read on further about Bahadur Shah Zafar biography and learn more about this Mughal emperor who was a genius poet.

Regarded as one of the greatest Urdu poets in the history of India, Bahadur Shah Zafar wrote a large number of Urdu Ghazals most of which were lost during wars fought in the year 1857. Yet, many of them were saved and were later on compiled as Kulliyat-I-Zafar. His Ghazals are a beautiful collection of words that spell magic and are read with awe and admiration even today. Bahadur Shah Zafar was the last and the weakest Mughal emperor. Even then he was considered a hero and was portrayed like one in many Hindi films. A road has been named in his honor in New Delhi, India. His valuable contribution in the Indian freedom struggle is very much acknowledged and he is known as a nationalist in modern India.

He was not a very able emperor and his empire had a lot of chaos and unrest. He was defeated and was sent on an exile in Rangoon. He died over there in the year 1862 and a tomb was built in his honor, which exists even today.

Tuzk-e-Jahangiri

Tuzk-e-Jahangiri or *Tuzk-i-Jahangiri* is the autobiography of Mughal Emperor Nor-u-Din Muhammad Jahangir (1569-1609).

Also referred to as *Jahangirnama,* Tuzk-e-Jahangiri is written in Persian, and follows the tradition of his great-grandfather, Babur (1487-1530), who had written the Baburnama; though Jahangir went a step further and besides the history of his reign, he includes details like his reflections on art, politics, and also information about his family.

The Writer

Jahangir was a good writer and loved nature. Jahangir recorded detailed description about wildlife in his autobiography. Jahangir admired paintings and collected them in his palace. Many of them survived and are found in museums around

The text details the first nineteen years of his reign, but gave up the writing of his Memoirs in the seventeenth year of his reign. He then entrusted the task to Mu'tamad Khan, the author of the Iqbal-nama, who continued the Memoirs to the beginning of the nineteenth year. From where, it was taken up by Muhammad Hadi, who continued it to Jahangir's death. It forms an important reference point for the era along with his father, Akbar's, Akbarnama. First important printed version of 'Jahangirnama', was by, Sayyid Ahmad printed at Ghazipur in 1863 and at Aligarh in 1864

Jahangir's autobiography also reflects the royal ideology of Jahangir's views on various political, religious and social issues. Within the memory, he noted many of his local level legislative policies in his large empire consisting of all of modern day India. Among them were his decrees to manage and regulate the jagirdars.

Jagirdars were holders of the jagir, the emperor's land grant title. The jagirdars were to take the income of the land and use it mainly to finance the maintenance of the troops and to address the town needs.

Jahangir made various attempts to halt corruption within the jagirdars. He prohibited each of them from using the money for personal profit by ordering that part of the land income to go to hospitals and infirmaries and for each town to be equipped with religious buildings according to the religion of that area. Jahangir also kept the jagirdars from gaining interest in family or land riches by ordering for jagirdars to seek his approval before marrying someone from the town they ruled in.

Baburnama

Baburnama is the name given to the memoirs of Zahir ud-Din Mohammad Babur (1483-1530), founder of the Mughal Empire and a great-great-great-grandson of Timur.

It is an autobiographical work, originally written in the Chagatai language, known to Babur as "Turki" (meaning *Turkic*), the spoken language of the Andijan-Timurids.

Because of Babur's cultural origin, his prose is highly Persianized in its sentence structure, morphology, and vocabulary, and also contains many phrases and smaller poems in Persian. During Emperor Akbar's reign, the work was completely translated to Persian by a Mughal courtier, Abdul Rahim, in AH 998 (1589-90).

Overview

Babur was an educated Central Asian Muslim and his observations and comments in his memoirs reflect an interest in nature, society, politics and economics. His vivid account of events covers not just his life, but the history and geography of the areas he lived in, and their flora and fauna, as well as the people with whom he came into contact.

The Baburnama begins with these plain words:

> *"In the province of Fergana, in the year 1494, when I was twelve years old, I became king."*

After some background, Babur describes his fluctuating fortunes as a minor ruler in Central Asia-in which he took and lost Samarkand twice-and his move to Kabul in 1504.

There is a break in the manuscript between 1508 and 1519. By the latter date Babur is established in Kabul, now in Afghanistan, and is campaigning in northwestern India. The final section of the Baburnama covers the years 1525 to 1529 and the establishment of the Mughal empire in South Asia, which Babur's descendants would rule for three centuries.

Babur also writes about his homeland, Fergana:

> *"The Domain of Fergana has seven towns, five on the south and two on the north of the Syr river. Of those on the south, one is Andijan. It has a central position and is the capital of the Fergana Domain."*

He also wrote:

> *"A man took aim at Ibrahim Beg. But then Ibrahim Beg yelled," Hai! Hai!"; and he let him pass, and by mistake shot me in an armpit from as near as a man on guard at the Gate stands from another. Two plates of my armour cracked. I shot at a man running away along the ramparts, adjusting his cap against the battlements. He abandoned his cap, nailed to the wall and went off, gathering his turban sash together in his hand."*

The Baburnama is widely translated and is part of text books in no less than 25 countries mostly in Central, Western, and Southern Asia. It was first translated into English by John Leyden and William Erskine as *Memoirs of Zehir-Ed-Din Muhammed Baber: Emperor of Hindustan* and later by the British orientalist scholar Annette Akroyd.

Urdu Literature History

One the sweetest language in the world, the history and origin of Urdu literature is vivid, colorful and harmoniously conjoined that has led to the development of this language. The style of writing the Urdu language has developed tremendously with the domination of Ghazals and nazms, the most dominant forms of verses. The evolution of Urdu literature history has been slow yet steady and today, it is still one of the preferred languages for writing poetry and songs that express true meaning and feelings. Read on further to know about Urdu literature origin.

The Urdu literature has a heavy domination of poetry. It is this domination that has led to the expansion and development of writing style in literature. In the contemporary world, Urdu is still popular in India and Pakistan and other south Asian countries. The origin of Urdu literature can be traced to the 14th century in India during the Mughal rule. It was very much prevalent among the urbane Persians in the elite Muslim classes. The origin of the Urdu literature struck a fine balance between the new cultural amalgamation of a vocabulary of Sanskrit and Persian words and firm retention of the best of Persia and Afghanistan.

One of the most influential people who initiated the growth and development of Urdu literature is undoubtedly, the famous Amir Khusro. He is credited with categorizing of north Indian classical music, which is popularly known as Hindustani music. He frequently wrote in both Persian and Hindi and often mixed the two ingeniously. His influence was so vast that even a century after his death, the famous Quli Qutub Shah took an immense liking to this language that was called Urdu.

Causes of Decline of Mughal Empire

Although the Mughal Empire began breaking –up in the 18th century, the causes of its decline can be traced back much earlier. Aurangzeb's long reign of constant and uninterrupted fighting was not only a big drain on the exchequer but it also led to the negligence of administration. Politically he made number of mistakes which undermined the strength of the Mughal Empire.

The empire was also met with financial troubles. There was neither enough money nor jagirs to assign to various officers. This led to rivalry among the nobles for the possessing the existing jagirs. They tried to extort the maximum income from their jagirs at the cost of the peasantry. Attempts were made to transform existing offices and jagirs into hereditary ones.

The officers invariably reduced their expenditure by not maintaining their full quota of troops thus weakening the empire's armed strength. The condition of the peasant had also gradually worsened. Higher revenue demands, a greater level of exploitation by jagirdars because of frequent transfers tried to extract as much as possible during their tenure as Jagirdar.

The practice of farming the land revenue to the highest bidder after the death of Aurangzeb increased peasant discontentment. The rebellions of the Satnamis, Jats, and the Sikhs were indicative of this. The Zamindars too became rebellious and withheld revenue. The Mughal Empire might have continued to exist for a long time if its administration and armed power had not broken down.

Mughal Empire

The English had been trading their woollen cloth at Bantam market, but it soon became clear that they would do better to barter with other Asian goods, especially Indian textiles. For this reason they needed to dispose of their broadcloth and to find other Asian goods for barter. India, with its rich textiles, seemed to offer the answer.

The Mughal Empire covered northern and central India. It was perhaps the world's most civilised centre of power. Its glittering court at Agra, Delhi and Lahore, was filled with all the magnificence and luxury that Asia could supply.

The Portuguese had traded directly with India for over 100 years before the first Fnglish East India Company ships reached Surat. The Company was not welcome, and in 1611 it asked King James to send an ambassador, Sir Thomas Roe, to visit the Mughal Emperor, Jahangir. The Emperor ruled over a prosperous civilisation that produced many goods, and had many different religions (the Mughals were Muslim).

In 1608, William Hawkins, commander of the Hector, was sent to ask the Mughal Emperor about trade with England. He impressed Jahangir with his grasp of Turkish and ability to drink copious amounts of wine, but he failed to get an agreement for an English factory. It took the arrival of a proper amabassador, Sir Thomas Roe, sent by King James I in 1615, before the Company was able to set up a base in India. From Surat the Company could send Indian textiles to the market at Bantam.

Highly skilled dyers and weavers in India produced cloth with beautiful colour-fast designs. This successful industry created an enormous amount of cloth for markets throughout Asia. In England, demand for Indian textiles grew fast, and many patterns for the new English textile industry came from India. By 1750, Indian silks, cottons and calicoes made up 60 per cent of the company's sales.

By 1750, the Mughal Empire was in a state of collapse. Regional states emerged in India and the Company began to get involved in power politics. It raised its own armies and prepared for war.

Having seen off the rival French in the Carnatic, in 1765 the Company assumed the Diwani of Bengal. A trading company from England was now responsible for the civil, judicial and revenue administration of India's richest province, with some 20 million inhabitants. It was now a regional state in India.

The Rise and Fall of the Mughals

A Revaluation of their Role in Indian History

No period in Indian history has drawn as much attention and scholarly research as has the period in Indian history that corresponds with Mughal rule. Western and many Indian historians alike have focused on the reign of the Mughals almost to the point of total neglect and exclusion of other periods in Indian history. In-depth investigation of other ruling dynasties whether subordinate to the Mughals (such as the lesser-known Rajputs or Bundelkhandis) or preceding them (such as the Parmars, Kakathiyas, or Sharqis) or their southern contemporaries (such as Tamil Nadu's Pandyas) has rarely attracted the scholarly attention of influential historians, and often their role in Indian history has been seen as peripheral to that of the Mughals, or their contribution to Indian civilization seen as tangential and marginal.

Journalists, art critics and popular historians have been particularly infected by such biases, and even highly respected art critics and social scientists have written quite dismissively of India's regional kingdoms that preceded Mughal rule or rose in the wake of it's precipitous decline.

While the romance of the Taj Mahal (and other such grand monuments) and the extraordinary brilliance of Mughal artifacts might partially justify and explain the special attention Western and Indian scholars have paid to the Mughal courts, it cannot be denied that at least some of this interest echoes colonially motivated biases leading to slanted interpretations of Indian history. It is also motivated by the tendency to view history from the perspective of the most powerful rulers and elites rather than from the perspective of the masses or intermediate categories.

While the Indianness or foreignness of the Mughals has been quite hotly debated in recent years, one aspect of the history of the Mughals that has largely escaped scholarly attention-(even by subaltern scholars) has been the role of expansionist militarism in shaping the reign of virtually every Mughal ruler up to Aurangzeb (with the possible exclusion of Jehangir).

Although war-making was not a uniquely Mughal practice, the centrality of the military campaigns in Mughal decision-making and administration does stand out. In the frequency, scale and intensity of their military campaigns, the Mughals had more in common with the ruling heads of the Delhi Sultanate than is commonly acknowledged.

This is not to say that there weren't important distinctions. Unlike many of the earlier invaders, the Mughals were relatively more conscious of being in a foreign land, andin his memoirs Babar spoke very deliberately of the need for conducting a secular policy in a country that was predominantly non-Islamic. In this respect, the Mughals were much more aware of the need to gain legitimacy and to win political allies in an alien land.

Their taste for the fine things in life-for beautifully designed artifacts and the enjoyment and appreciation of cultural activities also distinguished them from other interlopers who were skilled at war-making and little else. But it should be noted that the reigns of Akbar and Aurangzeb in particular, were marked by a shrewd (and sometimes ruthless) approach in the conduct of their political and military strategies.

Several aspects of their policy illustrate the importance of their military campaigns. Capitals were frequently moved to centres more suited to the conduct of specific military campaigns. Alliances with Rajput rulers were sought based on their ability to contribute to the Mughal war efforts. Investments were made in upgrading the weapons of war and ensuring that Mughal military technology maintained it's edge. Every Mughal prince was groomed in the battle arts not only through early training but through hands-on experience in real battles. So entrenched was the culture of war that it pit brother against brother in battles of succession.

This concentration on war efforts emerges quite vividly from court chronicles and surviving correspondence between Shahjahan and the young Aurangzeb where almost nothing else is discussed but the progress of the latest war effort. War scenes and gory depictions of battles were also common themes in the miniatures commissioned during the reign of Akbar.

The militarist character of the Mughals was not entirely unexpected since had they not been seeped in the tradition of warfare, they would have never attempted to conquer Northern India and extend their control over the rest of the Indian subcontinent in the first place.

In this respect, the Mughals were very much in the tradition of the nomadic warrior clans that periodically swooped down from the grasslands and deserts of Central Asia and either plundered and raided the settled agricultural civilizations or succeeded in conquering them. Not only India, but China, Eastern Europe, and the fertile crescents of the Middle East also experienced such attacks and invasions. Since the nomadic hunter clans lacked agricultural territories that could be tapped for their surplus, the only means to wealth in such parts of the globe were raids on settled civilizations or looting or taxation of trade caravans. Trading in slaves was another source of income. Seasoned and practised in the art of warfare, the nomadic warrior clans often prevailed with considerable ease over the armies of the settled civilizations who were usually taken by surprise and were inexperienced at handling the unconventional (and terrorist-like) tactics of the invaders.

Over time, in settled civilizations, the cost to both sides of protracted battles and the potential destruction of vital crop-lands and urban settlements created a natural resistance to internecine warfare. When the combatants were roughly evenly matched (as was often the case) decisive victories were virtually impossible. Even if one side finally prevailed, the cost of victory would be very high. (Ashoka's conversion to Buddhism, in part, came about as a result of the massive loss of life that took place on both sides in the Kalingan battles).

In India, this led not only to critiques of war from Jains and Buddhists but also from followers of the various Bhakti streams that drew the artisans and the peasantry. Even Kautilya's Arthashastra (which did not call for eschewing war) counseled kings in approaching war with shrewd caution and foresight. Kings were advised to make peace and offer diplomatic treaties in exchange for war whenever decisive victories were deemed unlikely. While such pragmatism did not eliminate wars, it did help in limiting their frequency and length. And since agricultural taxes were the primary source of income for both the warring factions, it was in the mutual interest of both parties to enforce a culture of chivalry and ethics in war that prevented civilian casualties and avoided the destruction of farmland, orchards and irrigation works.

When the Arab armies invaded Sindh, the local populations were caught completely off guard when their irrigation systems were destroyed and all the rules of chivalry considered customary in the subcontinent appeared to have little relevance for the invaders who sought victory at any cost. Of course, by the time the Mughals arrived in the Indian subcontinent, Northern India was no longer ruled by Hindu kings. But the Islamic rulers were no more adept at preventing conquests from new invaders. Once victorious, no Islamic conqueror was able to establish a stable dynastic reign for any length of time. New invaders arrived on the scene with regularity, and defeated previous rulers, many of whom were hated and despised by the local populace. Lacking popular support, none were able to establish kingdoms of any size.

Thus the initial victory of Babar over the Lodhis was not a particularly remarkable event. An event of far greater consequence was the defeat of Humayun at the hands of Sher Shah Suri-the Narnaul (Haryana) born son of a regional Mughal administrator. Born and raised in India, Sher Shah Suri was much more familiar with Indian conditions and keenly aware of how Humayun's hold on power was extremely tenuous. Taking advantage of the hollowness of support for the second Mughal, he succeeded in subduing Mughal holdouts and unifying Punjab and the Gangetic plain. The construction of the Grand Trunk Road and the launching of new (and specialized) manufacturing towns in the plains facilitated in the expansion of trade and industry. Administrative changes and social reforms that helped in creating a stable tax base and a modicum of legitimacy for the kingdom were also introduced. When Humayun returned to the throne in Delhi, he thus inherited the foundations of a potentially larger and more wealthy empire.

During Akbar's reign (and to a much greater extent during the reign of Jehangir), trade activities were further facilitated by the construction of numerous *caravansarais* (inns) and hospitals along the Grand Trunk Road, especially in Punjab. State-owned *karkhanas* (factories) were commissioned so as to produce high-quality luxury goods for use in the courts and for export. Income from agriculture and trade filled the Mughal treasuries and was used to fund the series of war campaigns that took the Mughal armies deep into the Deccan plateau and as far east as Assam, and westwards to the Afghan border with Iran. These war campaigns depended in large measure on the collaboration of the Rajput and Bundelkhand armies, who were won over through a combination of incentives and political coercion.

The sizeable tax base of the fertile plain of the Ganges enabled Akbar to entice the allegiance of the most powerful Rajput chiefs (such as those of Jaipur and Bikaner), who were granted tax rights on parts of the Gangetic plain. Marriage alliances cemented the relationships, and some of the most decisive Mughal victories were achieved under the military leadership of Jaipur's Raja Man Singh. Others were coerced into accepting Mughal "partnership" on unequal terms through a combination of military threats and by holding members of the royal clans hostage in Delhi. The hill Rajputs, the kingdoms of Datia, Jhansi and Orchha, were all required to pay tribute, and provide soldiers for the Mughal expeditions. Those who resisted such coercive collaboration (such as Gwalior) were suitably punished so as to warn others of what may befall them if they rebelled.

In this manner, the Mughal empire expanded to cover almost the entire length and breadth of the Indian subcontinent (excluding only the deep South). But military success did not guarantee stability or popular acceptance. While initially, income from agricultural taxes and trade exceeded the cost of the incessant war campaigns (and the lavish expenditure on locally procured and imported luxury goods), by the time Aurangzeb took over the throne, the Mughal treasuries had been virtually depleted.

The earliest of the Islamic invasions into the Indian subcontinent had paid for themselves through the pillage and plunder of temple wealth and jewelry and other savings of the defeated populations (which may have been accumulated over several generations). The invading armies also profited from the sale of captured soldiers and civilians taken as slaves. However, by the time the Mughals arrived on the Indian scene, all the temples with any wealth had already been plundered, and considerable resistance had developed to the practice of taking slaves through warfare. As a result, these avenues of wealth were no longer available to the Mughals who had to rely mainly on agricultural taxes. Trade was not heavily taxed because like their predecessors, the Mughals depended on the support of the mercantile classes in legitimizing their rule. Agricultural taxes thus reached an all-time high in India during Mughal rule (and were exceeded only by the British colonisers).

This naturally led to constant rebellions in large parts of the Mughal territories. The hill Rajputs, the Mewar Rajputs and the Central Indian kings resisted paying tribute, while many local nobles reneged on passing on the taxes to Delhi. Many local officials (in attempting to emulate the luxurious lifestyles of the Mughal courts) spent all the tax income locally, and got away by bribing Mughal officials in Delhi. During the reign of Shah Jahan, a new problem appeared. Even though the demand for Indian manufactures and exports had reached unprecedented levels, little of that wealth reached the Mughal treasuries since traders outside India began to hold on to most of the profits. A series of unsuccessful military campaigns were initiated in an attempt to achieve greater control over India's export trade, but these efforts came to naught. At the same time, Shah Jehan's appetite for grand building projects and luxury imports remained undiminished.

Fearing the bankruptcy of the Mughal state, Aurangzeb staged a military coup against his father and put an end to all lavish spending. But without the ability to dole out expensive gifts and tax rights, Aurangzeb relied more and more on the orthodox clergy to legitimize his rule (a trend initiated by Shah Jahan). But this was hardly the solution for the Mughal state's diminishing credibility. Although Aurangzeb managed to keep up the outward appearance of invincibility, the Mughal state was in fact in severe crisis. After Aurangzeb's death, centrifugal forces quickly spun out of control, and only some of the plains close to Delhi eventually remained in Mughal hands.

The peasantry almost throughout the Mughal territories had been chafing under the burden of high taxes. In Punjab, the peasants and artisans had been radicalized under the influence of Guru Gobind Singh who encouraged the equal participation of women-both in matters of religion and on the battlefield. In Haryana, Jat and Yadav allies declared their independence. In the Marathwada region, a multi-caste alliance of Brahmins, Kshatriyas, volunteers from peasant and artisan castes, along with disaffected Muslims joined hands in the Maratha rebellions. Regional administrators declared their independence in the Afghan region, and in Kashmir, Awadh and Bengal. The hill Rajputs, the Bundelkhandis and the Adivasi-origin rulers of the Jabalpur/Nagpur belt-all refused to pay tribute. Some historians have attempted to lay the blame for this Mughal collapse entirely on Aurangzeb's zealotry, contrasting Aurangzeb's religious conservatism with Akbar's eclectic tolerance which led to architectural innovations and cultural synthesis. Admirers of the syncretic traditions that developed in Akbar's court point to the stylistic fusion that took place in Fatehpur Sikri, and how some talented Hindus played an important role in his administration.

But even as Aurangzeb's sectarian messianic tendencies may have been the immediate catalyst for some of the rebellions that triggered the downfall of the Mughal empire, they should not be seen as the sole explanation for the disintegration of the Mughal empire. Challenges to Mughal rule had already begun right after Akbar's military successes. And although Aurangzeb identified closely with Islamic orthodoxy-the employment of Hindus in Aurangzeb's court was at a higher level than what prevailed in the court of Akbar. Like his predecessors, Aurangzeb also continued with the practice of seeking alliances with Hindu rulers, but abandoned the practice of developing marital ties with them. Without the bonds of inter-marriage, and with a tax base that was becoming less stable, the motivations for the Rajputs to fight Mughal battles was waning, and coercion was becoming less effective.

But even more fundamental factors were also in play. The high rate of taxation on the peasantry was simply unsustainable. Another important reason for the unraveling of Mughal power was that beyond Sindh, Punjab, Kashmir and the Yamuna and Gangetic plains, Mughal rule had simply not made enough of a positive contribution to justify its continuance.

It is therefore ironic how some of the most ardent fans of economic and political decentralization in modern India have written admiringly of the "unified" Mughal empire, as though centralization was an end in itself. It is important to note that the "unification" of India that Akbar had achieved was almost entirely through war and coercion. But more important, the benefits of this centralization did not flow throughout the empire. Some territories paid tribute but received no tangible gains in exchange. In particular, the regions corresponding to present-day Gujarat, Chhatisgarh, Chota Nagpur and Vidarbha, Eastern Madhya Pradesh, Jharkhand and much of North Bihar were starved of investment, and experienced stagnation or decline.

Beyond the main trade routes that linked Northern India to the rest of the world, the Mughal state invested neither in agricultural expansion nor in manufacturing or infrastructure to promote trade. Since the bulk of the Mughal manufacturing towns were located either along the Yamuna and Gangetic plains (or along the Indus), it is no coincidence that Mughal legitimacy survived primarily only in these regions of India.

Historians who write admiringly and uncritically about Akbar's "secularism" and eclectic tastes, and draw too sharp a distinction between Akbar and Aurangzeb miss such crucial points. It should be clarified that although most of the Mughals were consciously "secular"-at no point during their rule did the Mughals allot administrative posts in proportion to the actual population of Hindus and Muslims. Muslims were always over-represented. And in their support of the arts and music, the tastes of the early Mughals remained strongly biased towards Central Asian, Persian and Chinese traditions. Miniatures sponsored by Babar were entirely in the Samarqand/Bukhara tradition, while during the reign of Akbar, Persian and Western imitations also became popular. Only with Jehangir did the Mughal arts lose their hotchpotch and uneven character and begin to develop into a distinctive and more consistent style.

Jehangir (born of a Rajput mother) was considerably influenced by Rajput tastes, and rewarded skilled Hindu artisans with prominent positions in his court. With a remarkable eye for excellence in design and execution in the arts and crafts, he encouraged talent and promoted merit without discrimination. He also took an interest in local flora and fauna, and like his father, had an interest in philosophy. Dara Shukoh and Shah Jahan were inheritors of this taste for creative sophistication and ornamental exuberance. With Shah Jahan, a refined delicacy came to define courtly tastes, but there was also a trend towards rarified formalism, which prevented the Mughal tradition from imbibing popular and folk influences in the manner of the Rajput or Bundelkhand rulers.

Mughal courtly culture also remained somewhat apart from the folk traditions of the Indian masses through the promotion of Persian as the language of culture, and Urdu as the language of administration. Although popular with urban intellectuals and the cultural elite, Urdu with it's plethora of Persian and Arabic words, and non-Indian script could not have gained mass acceptance, and remained a language primarily of the elite. Outside the Hindi belt, this was an even bigger problem. Considering the steady drain of wealth from areas further away from the Mughal capitals and urban centres, it was almost inevitable that alienation from Mughal rule would set in very quickly. The plateau regions of Central India (and other outlying regions) had simply no stake in a unified Mughal empire and that is why a broad and secular coalition of forces arose in defiance of Mughal authority in such areas.

A grave drawback of Mughal rule was the failure of the Mughal rulers to devote even a fraction of their treasuries on anything resembling modern education. Aurangzeb was especially skeptical about the relevance of modern science and technology. Whereas the European nations had begun to invest in printed books and public universities, the Mughal rulers demonstrated at best a passing interest in the sciences. As a result, even though the Mughal empire under Aurangzeb had successfully fended off the expansion of European trading settlements in India, no durable foundation for the unity and scientific advancement of India had been laid by the Mughals. Mughal rule had left India largely incapable of dealing with the challenge of European military and cultural ascendance.

Unfortunately, such shortcomings of Mughal rule have largely escaped the attention of serious historians in India. And those who have been critical have focused almost exclusively on the communal angle (on the repression of Hindu religion and culture), ignoring socio-economic and political factors that may have been equally, or far more germane. Communally focused critics of Mughal rule have often ignored how particular caste categories offered their services and allegiance to Mughal rule, and received tangible benefits in exchange. Kayasthas in particular experienced upward mobility as they rose from being scribes and junior record-keepers to hold important administrative posts, and achieved a social rank comparable to court Brahmins. Mercantile caste categories also had a stake in the success of Mughal rule. Hindu money-lenders and shop-keepers did quite well in the prosperous Mughal towns, and a majority of the top revenue administrators under the Mughals (even during the reign of Aurangzeb) were either Hindu Banias or Brahmins.

Bihar's Maithil Brahmins had been promoted by earlier Islamic rulers, and their regional and local authority was not challenged by the Mughals. And while other regional Hindu rulers (such as the Mewar and Hill Rajputs, or the Bundelkhandis) often felt oppressed by Mughal rule, they lived lives of considerable comfort and leisure, and this restrained them from organizing collectively and mounting any serious challenge to Mughal rule.

On the other hand, the fascination for the Mughals amongst British (or British-influenced) historians, art critics and Indologists is not too hard to explain. By treating Mughal rule as the high point of Indian civilization and by over-emphasizing its Persian inspiration, British scholars of Indian civilization have tried to create the false impression that all great things in India have required external stimulus.

Their interest in Mughal rule has also stemmed from the subconscious desire to represent colonial rule in India as not too different from that of the Mughals. The fact that the Mughals came as alien conquerors and created a vast empire on the basis of shrewdly conceived coercive political strategies and military victories gives apologists for British colonial rule almost an excuse to ignore the uniquely devastating consequences of colonization. That the Mughals increased the taxes on the peasantry, introduced a language that was laden with foreign words and written in a foreign script, that in certain respects they remained aloof and apart from indigenous cultural trends-all this made British rule appear more as continuation than sharp departure from the Indian experience.

But in spite of such parallels, there are vital and important distinctions that separate Mughal rule in India from British rule in India. Firstly, at no point during Mughal rule was the impoverishment of the peasantry and the broad masses as extreme as it was during the period of British colonization. It should also be noted that whereas Indian manufactures acquired a well-deserved reputation for outstanding quality, and were in great demand during the reigns of Jehangir and Shahjahan, India became a dumping ground for European exports and manufacturing suffered a precipitous decline after the defeat at Plassey.

For all their flaws, and their alien instincts, the Mughals came to settle in India. Over time, they became steadily indigenized, and that is why the last Mughals resisted the British during the rebellion of 1857. Akbar's policy of inter-marriage with Rajput princesses not only served a tactical purpose in the realm of military policy, it also had the effect of indigenizing Mughal tastes. Although British historians and art critics have written at great length on how Akbar drew from the courts in Herat (now Afghanistan) and Shiraz or Tabriz (now Iran)-Jehangir's encouragement of bold colors and creative naturalist designs in the artifacts he commissioned owed much to Rajput traditions. Local influences rubbed off on the Mughals to a much greater extent than on the British rulers who virtually destroyed the cultural traditions of the areas they ruled directly. But more importantly, even as the Mughals frittered away the wealth they extracted from the peasantry-their legacy of fine arts and architecture remained in India. India's wealth was not systematically transferred to another country. In the aftermath of their collapse, regional forces with greater popular acceptance took over and some indigenous cultural traditions reasserted themselves fairly quickly and easily. But the legacy of colonial plunder and cultural indoctrination has been much harder to reverse and erase. It continues to have an insidious effect on many aspects of Indian life.

Thus no matter how artfully British intellectuals have used their representations of Mughal rule to rationalize the immiserization of India during British rule, the colossal drain of wealth and psychic destruction that took place simply has no parallels in Indian history. For that reason, Mughal rule cannot and should not be equated to European colonization.

At the same time, for Indian (or Pakistani, Bangladeshi or Afghan) historians and social scientists interested in expanding democratic rights and furthering the process of social equity in the subcontinent, it is critical that Mughal rule be subject to greater scrutiny. The romance and mystique surrounding the Mughal era in India needs to be overcome but without falling into the communal trap where Mughal rule is seen as an even greater evil than colonization.

The Mughal Empire reached its greatest extent in the time of Aurangzeb Alamgir, but it collapsed with dramatic suddenness within a few decades after his death. The Mughal Empire owes its decline and ultimate downfall to a combination of factors; firstly Aurangzeb's religious policy is regarded as a cause for the decline of the Mughal Empire as it led to disunity among the people. Although the policy did lead to weakening of the empire but the major cause of decline was the lack of worthy and competent successors after him. The character of Mughal kings had deteriorated over a period of time. The successive rulers after Aurangzeb were weak and lacked the character, motivation and commitment to rule the empire strongly. They had become ease loving and cowardly. They totally disregarded their state duties and were unable to detain the declining empire from its fall.

The absence of any definite law of accession was another important factor. The war of successions not only led to bitterness, bloodshed, and loss of money and prestige of the empire over a period of time, but to its eventual fall. The degeneration of the rulers had also led to the moral degeneration of the nobility. Under the early Mughals, the nobles performed useful functions and distinguished themselves both in war and peace. But the elite under the later Mughals was more interested in worldly pursuit and self-enhancement. The nobles who had once been talented men with integrity, honesty, and loyalty, turned selfish and deceitful. Growth of hostile and rival clique in the court also undermined the strength of the government. Widespread corruption in the administration started and taking bribes became common.

The weakened Mughal Empire invited havoc in the form of the Persian king Nadir Shah, in 1738-39. On his orders a general massacre of the citizens of Delhi was carried out, resulting in the death of 30,000 people. Another threat to the Mughal Empire came from the Afghans of Rohilkhand, lying northeast of Delhi. By the middle of 18th century, the Rohillas became independent of the Mughal rule. At the same time the Jats also raised their heads against the central rule.

Taking advantage of this chaotic situation, the East India Company began strengthening its military capabilities. They conspired with Hindu traders and moneylenders against Nawab Sirajuddullah of Bengal to take over his principality. The Battle of Plassey of 1757 is considered a major breakthrough for the British in the Sub-continent. It paved the way for the company's rule in Bengal, and hence the whole of India ultimately came under the company's rule.

In the 19th century, Muslims like Syed Ahmad Brailvi and Shah Ismail carried out Jihad against the Sikhs, as did Haider Ali and Tipu Sultan in Deccan against the British. However, they failed in their efforts to stop the downfall of the Muslim rule. The final crunch came after the war of 1857 when the Mughal rule officially came to an end and India came under the direct rule of the British crown.

The Mughal Empire reached its greatest extent in the time of Aurangzeb Alamgir, but it collapsed with dramatic suddenness within a few decades after his death. The Mughal Empire owes its decline and ultimate downfall to a combination of factors; firstly Aurangzeb's religious policy is regarded as a cause for the decline of the Mughal Empire as it led to disunity among the people. Although the policy did lead to weakening of the empire but the major cause of decline was the lack of worthy and competent successors after him. The character of Mughal kings had deteriorated over a period of time. The successive rulers after Aurangzeb were weak and lacked the character, motivation and commitment to rule the empire strongly. They had become ease loving and cowardly. They totally disregarded their state duties and were unable to detain the declining empire from its fall.

The absence of any definite law of accession was another important factor. The war of successions not only led to bitterness, bloodshed, and loss of money and prestige of the empire over a period of time, but to its eventual fall. The degeneration of the rulers had also led to the moral degeneration of the nobility. Under the early Mughals, the nobles performed useful functions and distinguished themselves both in war and peace. But the elite under the later Mughals was more interested in worldly pursuit and self-enhancement. The nobles who had once been talented men with integrity, honesty, and loyalty, turned selfish and deceitful. Growth of hostile and rival clique in the court also undermined the strength of the government. Widespread corruption in the administration started and taking bribes became common.

One of the most potent causes of the fall of the Mughal Empire was the deterioration and demoralization of the army. The military had not only become inefficient but also lacked in training, discipline and cohesion. The army was out-dated in regard to equipment. It consisted of contingents maintained by various nobles, which was the main source of Army's weakness. As the weakening of the nobles occurred, so did the army. This was because of the soldiers, instead of identifying and uniting as Mughal Indians, identified themselves with different ethnic groups like Persian, Afghans and Central Asians. The Mughals had no navy and only maintained small ships that were no match for the well-equipped ships of the foreign traders. It was this weakness that the French and the British used to their advantage, and were eventually able to establish their control over India.

The war of successions, rebellions and luxurious style of living had depleted the once enormous treasury and had led to financial bankruptcy. During the time of Aurangzeb, the Mughal Empire had expanded to reach its maximum size. This vast area had become impossible for one ruler to control and govern from one centre. It was during the later Mughals that Deccan, Bengal, Bihar and Orrisa declared their independence. The raids by Nadir Shah, and repeated invasions of Ahmad Shah Abdali, resulted in further weakening of the empire. The already weakened empire faced further encroachment by the British and the French, which proved to be the last nail in the already drowning empire's coffin. The British and French, who had initially come as traders, took full advantage of the weakening empire and soon became masters of the whole of India.

The Causes That Leads To Decline And Fall of Mighty Mughal Dynasty

Descended from both Genghis Khan and Tamerlane, the Mughal dynasty originated in Central Asia.

It became the strongest dynasty to rule India, lasting from 1526 to 1858. The Mughal dynasty reached its height under Akbar, who encouraged reconciliation among his subjects by encouraging intermarriage between Hindus and Muslims and appointed competent administrators. His empire stretched from the Himalayas to the Hindu Kush and included present-day India, Bangladesh, Afghanistan, and Pakistan. The Mughal Empire passed its zenith after Akbar.

Shah Jahan, although famous for the construction of the Taj Mahal, was an unsuccessful military leader. He launched three failed campaigns against the ruler of southern Afghanistan, was defeated in his attempt to regain the ancient Mughal patrimony in Central Asia, was repulsed four times in his efforts to extend rule from northern to southern Deccan, and lost an effort to oust the Portuguese from its coast. The cumulative effect of these campaigns was the imposition of higher taxes on the peasantry, whose loyalty to the Mughals began to diminish. This became more evident under Aurangzeb. The fortunes of both the empire and the dynasty decreased in the last half of Aurangzeb's reign. Overwhelmingly ambitious, he spent the last 28 years of his reign campaigning in the south to conquer and unite the subcontinent from the south tip to the northern Himalayas and Hindu Kush. Although initially successful, many areas quickly revolted.

Aurangzeb's wars took a toll on the empire's resources, which became strained. This led to peasant resistance and flight, thereby increasing the burden on the remaining peasants. Aurangzeb's strict Islam and intolerance toward other religions also roused opposition. He destroyed Hindu temples and schools, dismissed Hindu officials from government, and reimposed the tax on non-Muslims. These policies led to the rise of the greatest military opponents of the Mughals—the Marathas and the Sikhs. Under the leadership of Shivaji, the Marathas in the northwest Deccan carried out resistance and by 1750 controlled large sections of central and northern India. The Sikhs, originally a peaceful sect that attempted to synthesize Hindu and Muslim beliefs, became militarized by persecution and by 1750 controlled much of the Punjab in northeast India. The Hindu Rajputs in north central India, initially won over by Akbar's policies, became hostile and began to attack the Mughals. Even within the Delhi area, Hindu peasants called the Jats became radicalized and also revolted.

After Aurangzeb's death in 1707, most of the 10 Mughal emperors who followed him between 1707 and 1857 were little more than figureheads for one of the contending parties for power in India. Court feuds and civil wars also led to disintegration as Muslim dynasties arose in south Deccan, the eastern province of Oudh, and northeast Bengal between 1704 and 1720. One Mughal emperor, Muhammad Shah, attempted to repair some of the damage by placating the Hindus but with little success, partly due to his own indolence and foreign invasions. Mughal power never recovered from the invasion of the Persian ruler Nadir Shah, who sacked Delhi in 1739, carried away the fabled peacock throne, symbol of the dynasty, and plundered northern India. Even more devastating was the invasion of Ahmed Khan, ruler of eastern Persia, Afghanistan, Uzbekistan, and portions of northern India. He sacked Delhi, defeating the Marathas and Rajputs, but his empire disintegrated after his death in 1772.

Mughal power also suffered with the rise of European merchants, especially the British and French who replaced the earlier Portuguese and Dutch. In 1691 the British East India Company received a charter from the Mughal government not only to trade but to collect taxes in what is now Calcutta. In time, it became progressively more involved in politics; by 1765, the Company controlled all Bengal, the richest province of India. By 1800 Britain had ousted the French from India. By 1818 the Company either directly or indirectly ruled most of India. By the 19th century, Mughal emperors had become mere pensioners of the Company. The last Mughal emperor was deposed and exiled to Burma after the Indian Mutiny in 1857.

There were many causes for the decline and fall of the Mughal dynasty. First, the lack of tolerance shown to the non-Islamic majority by later Mughal emperors; second, the imperial overreach by emperors in terms of military expeditions which strained resources after 1680; third, the diversity of India's ethnic and religious groups as well as strong traditions of regionalism which served to weaken the centre; and fourth, the superior technological and financial expertise which the West, including England, enjoyed after 1500 gave it an advantage dealing with Islamic emperors who had fallen behind. Finally, and perhaps most important, the Mughal dynasty remained a minority in India, distinct in religion, culture, and language from the majority of subjects. Given the circumstances, its was Mughal decline inevitable? Discuss the view that Indian society and economy was 'divided but buoyant' in the eighteenth century

Traditionally the great Mughal Empire which, at its height, covered over four million square kilometres of land was thought to have fallen into irreversible decline in the eighteenth century. Early histories, such as that by Sir Jadunath Sarkar, pointed to the breakdown of centralised administration, claiming the result was a descent into political chaos and confusion. This in turn was said to have created economic and social problems as individuals vied for power. In more recent years however this view has been strongly challenged. The increasing focus on regional studies has led to a reassessment of the buoyancy of the pre-colonial economy, and stability of social structures. Commercialisation is no longer seen as an innovation of the Europeans, with evidence of a move towards private ownership in many areas. Primarily what has been proven is that there is no easy summary that can be applied to the whole of the India; the eighteenth century experience was far from uniform.

At the very beginning of the eighteenth century the Mughal Empire was widely understood to be as strong – if not stronger – than it had ever been. Huge swathes of land were under Mughal control covering most of present day India, Pakistan and Afghanistan. Early signs of change became evident however following the death of Aurangzeb, the sixth Mughal Emperor, in 1707. Bahadur Shah, Aurangzeb's successor, not only was forced to fight off rival claims to the throne from his brothers Azum Shah and Muhammad Kam Baksh, he also inherited the task of trying to stamp out elite factionalism and overcoming hostility from the provinces over his father's strict enforcement of Sharia law. Upon Bahadur Shah's death in 1712 another bitter succession struggle broke out between his sons. The short and unpopular reign of Jahandar Shah was brought to an end in battle with Farrukhisyar in 1713, who then began his own reign, dominated by his advisers such as the self serving Syed brothers. This tumultuous overview provides insight into the sudden instability within the official administration. Without strong leadership from the centre it is unsurprising that local figures of authority should try and consolidate their own power.

This certainly seemed to be the case in some areas of the empire. Om Prakash highlights the example of Murshid Quli Khan in Bengal. Maintaining the level of revenue collection expected by the central Mughal administration, Khan proved himself capable and was made Subedar in 1716, giving him and Bengal effective autonomy. This kind of arrangement, whilst a sign of weakening central control, could be said to support the idea that Indian society and economy was 'divided but buoyant'. Clearly, sufficient revenue was still being raised in Bengal and the official recognition of Khan from the centre suggests that this division was not overly problematic.

Perhaps this is a misleadingly optimistic view however. In other parts of India the situation was not so favourable. Muzaffar Alam describes how in northern India the Mughal forces struggled to defend territory from local competitors. In 1708 for example the governor of Awadh resigned, citing his insufficient authority to deal with the threat from 'recalcitrant' zamindars (officials employed to collect taxes from peasants) as a significant part of his reasoning. In 1709 Daruban Singh and his clansmen invaded and held Ghazipur, defeating the Mughal forces sent to remove him. This hints at the extent of the threat such individuals could cause. They often had charge of large private armies and cavalries; the Gaur Rajput rebels of Sarkar Khairbad had control over no less than 25 fortresses for example. Aside from being unable to defend territory from rebels Mughal forces were also faced with fighting between rival factions. In 1715 for example the zamindars of Samanpur and Pargana Bhagwant fought and killed the zamindar of the riaya of Bahramganj. In such conditions it is difficult to believe social and economic 'buoyancy' could have been maintained.

Traditional accounts of this period of Indian history have assumed that the impact of the late seventeenth-century economic crisis was hugely damaging. Faced with internal succession disputes and unfeasibly high taxation demands from the new local elites, it was believed that the Indian economy was failing and therefore in desperate need of European commercialism, such as that imposed by the British from the late eighteenth century. Work by the likes of Alam and Bayly has gone a long way to disproving this assumption.

The scope of the so called 'crisis' is now questioned, and its affects are thought to have been, in many instances, negligible. In the early eighteenth century, far from being a stagnating economy, India actually possessed upwards of a quarter of the world's total manufacturing capacity and was a major player in the world economy. Accountancy skills, formerly thought to be introduced to India by Europeans in this period, had in fact been flourishing since the sixteenth century, particularly in western India. In more social terms there is increasing evidence that the caste system was not as restrictive as has previously been believed, and that there was in fact a relatively high level of worker mobility.

The 'modernity' of the economy of eighteenth century India can be seen in the high level of market dependence, even amongst the peasantry. Trade was an incredibly important part of the economy, and not just with the Europeans. Large amounts of trade were also done with other parts of Asia and, of course, internally for the domestic market. Washbrook quotes for example that in a single salt season between 70,000 and 120,000 bullocks laden with goods were expected to visit each of the eight major salt trading centres along the southeast coast of India.

Prakash and Chaudry maintain that economy of Bengal was prosperous throughout the first half of the eighteenth century and that, in fact, it is only in light of increasing interference from the European trading companies, the British East India Trading Company in particular, that real problems emerged. Sivakumar and Sivakumar argue for instance that real earnings from agricultural work in Chingleput were three times higher in 1795 than 1796 after the land settlement.

A case study demonstrating this model of the Indian economy can be seen in Prasannan Parthasarathi's work on the cloth industry in South India. In the early eighteenth century cloth was already a massive business interest; in Awadh trade with the Europeans actually only represented a very small percentage of the entire cloth trade. Weavers held a lot of power within the workforce, dictating whom they worked for, for example. This situation rested on custom, the ability to negate contracts for work by weavers giving back the advance payment for instance, but also on newer trade developments.

Merchants competed in the marketplace to sell cloth to the Europeans at a profit. Oppression of the weavers then was not something that had always been there as was once believed. Instead it was a situation which was created by ever tighter controls on manufacture from the British. The policy of direct advances – cutting out the merchant middlemen – from the 1760s was unpopular because up to 2/3 of the advance was paid in yarn. In addition the clause whereby a contract could be annulled by repaying this advance was soon eroded. In this way the weavers, a group of independent workers, were reduced to dependency on the Company because of its growing monopoly. This suggests that, were it not for outside forces, the Indian economy could have indeed been 'divided but buoyant'.

The main obstacle to this interpretation comes, as does its main support, from regional studies. Contemporary Dean Mahomet devotes page after page of his travel journal to describing the differences between the regions he passes through on his journey. The Mughal Empire stretched over millions of square kilometres and, so, it stands to reason that the regional experience was not uniform. Some areas were prosperous, revenue collection in Bengal rose from around £2million in 1765-6 to £3.33million in 1770-1, the fact it was paid in full suggesting its inhabitants were well off enough to do so, even after a transfer of authority away from the central Mughal courts.

Other areas struggled, for example those with unscrupulous individuals in charge and a heavy reliance on the jajmani system (whereby families of different castes were expected to perform certain services for each other.) In some areas European intervention might be welcomed, in others it would be vehemently resisted. The point is that it is hard to generalise when considering such a massive expanse of land, populated by such a wide variety of peoples.

This might seem to suggest that Mughal decline was inevitable in that the Empire had been too centralised, too determined to enforce top-down policies such as Sharia law, even in areas where it would inevitably be resented such as the Sikh majority Punjab. This has long been seen as the secret of British success in obtaining power in India. By working with local elites and seeming to be sympathetic to regional conditions, the British could gain support from the ground roots. Stein points to the practice of 'military fiscalism' that grew in the eighteenth century. Standing armies were maintained by the Company to protect their interests which, at the same time, provided employment in the army, or in providing supplies for it. Although, again, the success of this policy was often linked with local circumstances.

For a long time study into this area has been swamped by expectations formed from the big overarching theories of history. Washbrook suggests that because India's story had not terminated in the creation of a modern industrial society, historians were disinclined to look at the eighteenth century Indian economy through a capitalist or commercial lens. Such developments were assumed to be European impositions, although we now have evidence for the development of an industrialist class structure before the Raj for example. Some regions such as Mysore were already controlling production in the early eighteenth century, and monopolies on goods controlled by local elites were actually fairly common.

In societal terms again there is no coherent general overview. Many areas had maintained their own character throughout the period of Mughal rule. The jajmani system had never been widespread in Bengal for example, and was close to dying out in Maharashtra and Gujerat by the eighteenth century. In many areas there was continuity, for example by the 1770s artisans in Banaras were being supported by the patronage of the new great merchant families, taking over the role traditionally held by the Mughal nobility. In this way Mughal culture and societal expectations were being preserved. ...

In conclusion Mughal decline was not necessarily inevitable. Had there been more competent successors to follow Aurangzeb perhaps the decentralisation of power could have been curbed.

Even if it had not, greater co-operation between the rising local elites and the central power could have helped to maintain Mughal cultural dominance at the very least. What was most likely inevitable was continued regional diversity, which is what we see throughout the eighteenth century. This supports the suggestion that the Indian economy and Indian society were, to a certain extent, always 'divided'.

Whether or not it was 'buoyant' is a more difficult issue. In some areas economic prosperity continued, such as the south Indian cloth industry, throughout much of the eighteenth century. Yet other areas struggled; for example the older port towns which were losing out to the new European centres of trade. Above all the question should be considered in a regional context, rather than in the terms of overarching historiographical theories which have framed the study of Indian history for so long.

5

Position of Women in Mughal Period

The Indian woman's position in the society further deteriorated during the medieval period when Sati, child marriages and a ban on widow remarriages became part of social life in India. The Muslim conquest in the Indian subcontinent brought the purdah practice in the Indian society. Among the Rajputs of Rajasthan, the Jauhar was practised. In some parts of India, the Devadasis or the temple women were sexually exploited. Polygamy was widely practised esp. among Hindu Kshatriya rulers. In many Muslim families, women were restricted to Zenana areas.

In spite of these conditions, some women execeled in the fields of politics, literature, education and religion. Razia Sultana became the only woman monarch to have ever ruled Delhi. The Gond queen Durgavati ruled for fifteen years, before she lost her life in a battle with Mughal emperor Akbar's general Asaf Khan in 1564. Chand Bibi defended Ahmednagar against the mighty Mughal forces of Akbar in 1590s. Jehangir's wife Nur Jehan effectively wielded imperial power and was recognized as the real force behind the Mughal throne. The Mughal princesses Jahanara and Zebunnissa were well-known poets, and also influenced the ruling administration Shivaji's mother, Jijabai was deputed as queen regent, because of her ability as a warrior and an administrator. In South India, many women administered villages, towns, divisions and heralded social and religious institutions.

The Bhakti movements tried to restore women's status and questioned some of the forms of oppression. Mirabai, a female saint-poet, was one of the most important Bhakti movement figures.

Some other female saint-poets from this period include Akka Mahadevi, Rami Janabai and Lal Ded. Bhakti sects within Hinduism such as the Mahanubhav, Varkari and many others were principle movements within the Hindu fold to openly advocate social justice and equality between men and women.

Shortly after the Bhakti movement, Guru Nanak, the first Guru of Sikhs also preached the message of equality between men and women. He advocated that women be allowed to lead religious assemblies; to perform and lead congregational hymn singing called Kirtan or Bhajan; become members of religious management committees; to lead armies on the battlefield; have equality in marriage, and equality in Amrit (Baptism). Other Sikh Gurus also preached against the discrimination against women.

Chand Bibi

Chand Bibi (1550-1599), also known as Chand Khatun or Chand Sultana, was an Indian Muslim woman warrior. She acted as the Regent of Bijapur (1580-90) and Regent of Ahmednagar (1596-99). Chand Bibi is best known for defending Ahmednagar against the Mughal forces of Emperor Akbar.

Biography

Chand Bibi was the daughter of Hussain Nizam Shah I of Ahmednagar, and the sister of Burhan-ul-Mulk, the Sultan of Ahmednagar. She knew many languages including Arabic, Persian, Turkish, Marathi and Kannada. She played sitar, and painting flowers was her hobby.

Bijapur Sultanate

Following an alliance policy, Chand Bibi was married to Ali Adil Shah I of the Bijapur Sultanate. Her husband had a stepwell (bawdi) constructed near the eastern boundary of Bijapur and named it *Chand Bawdi* after her.

Ali Adil Shah's father, Ibrahim Adil Shah I had divided power between the Sunni nobles, the Habshis and the Deccanis. However, Ali Adil Shah favoured Shias. After his death in 1580, the Shia nobles proclaimed his nine-year old nephew Ibrahim Adil Shah II as the ruler.

A Deccani general called Kamal Khan sieged the power and became the regent. Kamal Khan showed disrespect to Chand Bibi, who felt that he had ambitions to usurp the throne. Chand Bibi plotted an attack against Kamal Khan, with help from another general, Haji Kishvar Khan. Kamal Khan was captured while fleeing and was beheaded in the fort.

Kishvar Khan became the second regent of Ibrhaim. He defeated the Ahmednagar Sultan at Dharaseo, capturing all the artillery and elephants of the enemy army. He then ordered other Bijapur generals to surrender all captured elephants to him. The elephants were highly valued and the generals took great offense. The generals, along with Chand Bibi, hatched a plan to eliminate Kishvar Khan with help from General Mustafa Khan of Bankapur. Kishvar Khan's spies informed him of the conspiracy. Kishvar Khan sent troops against Mustafa Khan, who was captured and killed in the battle.

Chand Bibi challenged Kishvar Khan, who got her imprisoned at the Satara fort and tried to declare himself the king. However, Kishvar Khan was already unpopular among rest of the generals. He was forced to flee, when a joint army led by a Habshi general called Ikhlas Khan marched to Bijapur. The army consisted of forces of three Habshi nobles: Ikhlas Khan, Hamid Khan and Dilavar Khan. Kishvar Khan tried his luck at Ahmednagar unsuccessfully, and then fled to Golconda. He was killed in exile by a relative of Mustafa Khan. Chand Bibi was then declared the regent.

Ikhlas Khan then became the regent, but he was dismissed by Chand Bibi shortly afterwards. Later, he resumed his dictatorship, which was soon challenged by the other Habshi generals. Taking advantage of the situation in Bijapur, Ahmednagar's Nizam Shahi sultan allied with the Qutb Shahi of Golconda to attack Bijapur. The troops available at Bijapur were not sufficient to repulse the joint attack. The Habshi generals realized that they could not defend the city alone, and tended their resignation to Chand Bibi. Abu-ul-Hassan, a Shia general appointed by Chand Bibi, called for the Maratha forces in Carnatic. The Marathas attacked the invaders' supply lines. Finally, the Ahmednagar-Golconda allied army had to retreat,

Ikhlas Khan then attacked Dilavar Khan to seize the control of Bijapur. However, he was defeated and Dilavar Khan became the regent from 1582 to 1591. When order was restored in Bijapur kingdom, Chand Bibi returned to Ahmednagar.

Ahmednagar Sultanate

In 1591, the Mughal emperor Akbar had asked all the four Deccan sultanates to acknowledge his supremacy. All the sultanates evaded compliance, and Akbar's ambassadors returned in 1593. In 1595, Ibrahim Shah, the ruler of Bijapur was killed in a severe general action about 40 miles from Ahmednagar. After his death, most nobles felt that his infant son Bahadur Shah should be proclaimed the King under the regency of Chand Bibi (his father's aunt).

However, the Deccani minister Mian Manju proclaimed the twelve-year old son of Shah Tahir, Ahmad Shah II, as the ruler on August 6, 1594. The Habshi nobles of Ahmednagar, led by Ikhlas Khan, were opposed to this plan. The rising dissent among the nobles prompted Mian Manju to invite Akbar's son Shah Murad (who was in Gujarat) to march his army to Ahmednagar. Murad came to Malwa, where he joined Mughal forces led by Abdul Rahim Khan-I-Khana. Raja Ali Khan joined them at Mandu, and the united army advanced on Ahmednagar.

However, while Murad was on march to Ahmednagar, many noblemen left Ikhlas Khan and joined Mian Manju. Mian Manju defeated Ikhlas Khan and other opponents. Now, he regretted having invited the Mughals, but it was too late. He requested Chand Bibi to accept the regency, and marched out of Ahmednagar, with Ahmed Shah II. Ikhlas Khan also escaped to Paithan, where he was attacked and defeated by the Mughals.

Chand Bibi accepted the regency and proclaimed Bahadur Shah king of Ahmednagar.

Defence of Ahmednagar

Ahmednagar was invaded by the Mughals in November 1595. Chand Bibi took the leadership in Ahmednagar and defended the Ahmednagar fort successfully. Later, Shah Murad sent an envoy to Chand Bibi, offering to raise the siege in return for the cession of Berar. Chand Bibi's troops were suffering from famine. In 1596, she decided to make peace by ceding Berar to Murad, who retreated.

Chand Bibi appealed to her nephews Ibrahim Adil Shah II of Bijapur and Muhammad Quli Qutb Shah of Golconda, asking them to unite against the Mughal forces. Ibrahim Adil Shah II sent a contingent of 25,000 men under Sohil Khan, which was joined by the remainder of Yekhlas Khan's force at Naldurg. Later, it was joined by a contingent of 6,000 men from Golconda.

Chand Bibi had appointed Muhammad Khan as the minister, but he proved treacherous. He made overtures to the Khan Khanan, offering to surrender the whole Sultanate to the Mughals. Meanwhile, Khan Khanan started taking possession of districts that were not included in the cession of Berar. Sohil Khan, who was returning to Bijapur, was ordered to come back and attack Khan Khanan's Mughal forces. The Mughal forces under Khan Khanan and Mirza Shah Rukh left Murad's camp at Sahpur in Berar and encountered the combined forces of Bijapur, Ahmadnagar, and Golconda under Sohil Khan, near Sonpet (or Supa) on the banks of Godavari River. In a fierce battle on February 8-9, 1597, the Mughals won.

In spite of their victory, the Mughal forces were too weak to pursue their attack and returned to Sahpur. One of their commanders, Raja Ali Khan was killed in the battle and there were frequent disputes between other commanders. Due to these disputes, Khan Khanan was recalled by Akbar in 1597. Prince Murad died shortly thereafter. Akbar then sent his son Daniyal and Khan Khanan with fresh troops. Akbar himself followed and encamped at Barhanpur.

In Ahmednagar, Chand Bibi's authority was being resisted by the newly-appointed minister Nehang Khan. Nehang Khan had recaptured the town of Bid, taking advantage of Khan Khanan's absence and of the rainy season. In 1599, Akbar dispatched Daniyal, Mirza Yusuf Khan and Khan Khanan to relieve the governor of Bid. Nehang Khan also marched to seize the Jaipur Kotli pass, expecting the Mughals to meet him there. However, Daniyal avoided the pass and reached Ahmednagar fort. His forces laid siege to the fort.

Chand Bibi's Tomb, Ahmednagar

Chand Bibi again defended the fort bravely. However, she could not bring about an effective resistance, and decided to negotiate terms with Daniyal. Hamid Khan, a nobleman, exaggerated and spread the news that Chand Bibi was in treaty with the Mughals. According to another version, Jita Khan, an eunuch valet of Chand Bibi thought that her decision to negotiate with Mughals was treacherous and spread the news that Chand

Bibi was a quisling.. Chand Bibi was then killed by an enraged mob of her own troops.

After her death, and a siege of four months and four days, Ahmednagar was captured by the Mughal forces of Daniyal and Mirza Yusuf Khan.

Nur Jahan

Begum Nur Jahan (alternative spelling Noor Jahan, Nur Jehan, Nor Jahan, etc.) (1577– 1645) also known as Mehr-un-Nisaa was an Indian Empress of the Mughal Dynasty, of Persian origin whose tomb lies in Lahore, Pakistan.

Begum Nur Jahan was the twentieth and favourite wife of Mughal Emperor Jahangir, who was her second husband-and the most famous Empress of the Mughal Empire. The story of the couple's infatuation for each other and the relationship that abided between them is the stuff of many (often apocryphal) legends. She remains historically significant for the sheer amount of imperial authority she wielded-the true "power behind the throne," as Jehangir was battling serious addictions to alcohol and opium throughout his reign-and is known as one of the most powerful women who ruled India with an iron fist.

Birth

Begum Nur Jahan was born in 1577 in Kandahar (now in Afghanistan) to travelling Persians from Tehran (now in Iran). Her Persian-born grandfather, who was in the service of Shah Tahmasp I, died in Yazd, laden with honours. His heirs, however, soon fell upon hard times. His son Mirza Ghias Beg (known as *Itmad-ud-Daulah*, "Pillar of the State", a title conferred on him by Akbar) travelled to India with his family where he rose to become an administrative official in the Mughal court. For their journey, Ghias Beg and his wife, Asmat Begum, joined a caravan travelling southward under the leadership of a merchant noble named Malik Masud.

While still in Persian territory, less than half the way to their destination, Ghias Beg's party was attacked by robbers and the family lost almost everything it owned. Left with only two mules, Ghias Beg, his expectant wife, their children, Muhammad Sharif, Abdul Hasan Asaf Khan, and one daughter, took turns riding on the backs of the animals. When the group reached Kandahar,

Asmat Begum gave birth to her fourth child and second daughter, Mehr-un-Nisaa.

Marriage with Sher Afghan

Mehr-Un-Nisaa was married to Sher Afghan Quli Khan when she was seventeen in 1594, the marriage arranged by Akbar. In 1605, Mehr-Un-Nisaa gave birth to a daughter, also called Mehr-Un-Nisaa (later at court she was named Ladli), Mehr-Un-Nisaa one and only child she ever had. In 1607, Sher Afghan Quli Khan was killed during a misunderstanding. During this time Sher Afghan Quli Khan had held the title of Sher Afghan, granted to him by Jahangir. Also notice, during this time, Jahangir may have been asking Sher Afghan Quli Khan to give Mehr-Un-Nisaa to him, for his harem, although the truth of this is incertain, as Jahangir married her in 1611, after she had been at court for four years.

Marriage with Jahangir

The emperor Akbar died in 1605 and was succeeded by prince Salim, who took the regal name *Jahangir.* After her husband Sher Afghan (who was appointed as jagirdar of Bardhaman, a city in Bengal) was killed in 1607, Mehr-un-Nisaa became a lady-in-waiting to one of the Jahangir's stepmothers, Ruqayya Sultana Begum. Ruqayya was the most senior woman in the harem and had been Akbar's first and principal wife and was also the daughter of Mirza Hindal. The father of Mehr-un-Nisaa was, at that time, a diwan to an amir-ul-umra, decidedly not a very high post.

The year 1607 had not been particularly good for Mehr-un-Nisaa. Her family had fallen into disgrace. Her father, who had been holding important posts under Akbar and Jahangir, had succumbed to his only weakness, money, and had been charged with embezzlement. Moreover, due to possible involvement in the pro-Khusrau assassination attempt on Jahangir in 1607, two of Mehr-un-Nisaa's family members (one brother named Muhammad Sharif and her mother's cousin) were executed on the orders of the Emperor.

In march 1611, her fortune took a turn for the better. She met the emperor Jehangir at the palace *meena bazaar* during the spring festival Nowruz new year. Jahangir grew so infatuated by her beauty that he proposed immediately and they were married on

May 25 of the same year becoming his twentieth wife. Mehr-un-Nisaa received the name Nur Mahal (Light of the Palace), upon her marriage in 1611 and was conferred the title *Nur Jahan* (Light of the world) in 1616. Jahangir's actual name was Nur-ud-din Muhammad, and thus the name that he gave to his wife was his own first name combined with the first part of his regal name.

Mughal empress: For Mehr-un-Nisaa's own immediate family, marriage to Jahangir became a great boon with several members receiving sizeable endowments and promotions as a result. This affection led to Nur Jahan wielding a great deal of actual power in affairs of state. The Mughal state gave absolute power to the emperor, and those who exercised influence over the emperor gained immense influence and prestige.

Jahangir's addiction to opium and alcohol made it easier for Nur Jahan to exert her influence. For many years, she effectively wielded imperial power and was recognized as the real force behind the Mughal throne. She even gave audiences at her palace and the ministers consulted with her on most matters. Indeed, Jahangir even permitted coinage to be struck in her name, something that traditionally defined sovereignty.

Through Nur Jahan's influence, her family, including her brother Asaf Khan, consolidated their position at court. Asaf Khan was appointed grand Wazir (minister) to Jahangir, and his daughter Arjumand Banu Begum (later known as Mumtaz Mahal) was wed to Prince Khurram (the future Shah Jahan), the third son of Jahangir, born by a Rajput princess, Jagat Gosaini. Jahangir's eldest son Khusrau had rebelled against the Emperor and was blinded as a result. The second son, Parviz, was weak and addicted to alcohol.

The fourth son was Prince Shahryar, born by a royal concubine. Khurram rebelled against his father and a war of succession broke out. Due to Khurram's intransigence, Nur Jahan shifted her support to his younger brother, Shahryar. She arranged the marriage of her own daughter Ladli Begum, born of her first marriage, to her stepson Shahryar. The two weddings ensured that one way or another, the influence of Nur Jahan's family would extend over the Mughal Empire for at least another generation.

Jahangir was captured by rebels in 1626 while he was on his way to Kashmir. Nur Jahan intervened to get her husband released. Jahangir was rescued but died on October 28, 1627. After Jahangir's death, Nur Jahan devoted some of her life to the making of perfume, an art form her mother had passed down.

Death

When Jahangir died in 1628, Nur Jahan's brother Asaf Khan took the side of his son-in-law Khurrum against his sister. It was Khurram who became the new Mughal emperor under the regal name Shah Jahan. Nur Jahan was confined to a comfortable mansion for the rest of her life.

During this period, she paid for and oversaw the construction of her father's mausoleum in Agra, known now as Itmad-Ud-Daulah's Tomb, and occasionally composed Persian poems under the assumed name of *Makhfi*.

Nur Jahan died in 1645 at age 68, and is buried at Shahdara Bagh in Lahore Pakistan in a tomb she had built herself, near the tomb of Jahangir. Her brother Asaf Khan's tomb is also located nearby. The tomb attracts many visitors, both Pakistani and foreign, who come to enjoy pleasant walks in its beautiful gardens. All had been personally laid out and designed by Nur Jahan herself.

Meera

Mirabai was an aristocratic Hindu mystical singer and devotee of Krishna from Rajasthan and one of the most significant figures of the Sant tradition of the Vaishnava bhakti movement. Some 12-1300 prayerful songs or *bhajans* attributed to her are popular throughout India and have been published in several translations worldwide. In the *bhakti* tradition, they are in passionate praise of Krishna.

Details of her life, which has been the subject of several films, are pieced together from her poetry and stories recounted by her community and are of debatable historical authenticity, particularly those that connect her with the later Tansen. On the other hand, the traditions that make her a disciple of Ravidas who disputed with Rupa Goswami are consonant with the usual account of her life.

Meera, a Rajput princess was born in Kudki (Kurki), a little village near Merta, which is presently in the Nagaur district of Rajasthan in northwest India. Her father, Ratan Singh Rathore, was a warrior of the Rathore clan, the son of Rao Jodha of Mandore (1416-1489 CE), founder of the city of Jodhpur in 1459.

As an infant Meera became deeply enamoured of an iconic doll of Krishna owned by a visiting holy man she was inconsolable until she possessed it and probably kept it all her life. Her mother was supportive of her religious tendencies but she died early and went to heaven.

Meera's marriage was arranged at an early age, traditionally to Prince Bhoj Raj, the eldest son of Rana Sanga of Chittor. However her new family did not approve of her piety and devotion when she refused to worship their family deity and maintained that she was only truly married to Krishna.

The Rajputana had remained fiercely independent of the Delhi Sultanate, the Islamic regime that otherwise ruled Hindustan after the conquests of Timur. But in the early 16th century CE the central Asian warlord Babur laid claim to the Sultanate and some Rajputs supported him while others ended their lives in battle with him. Her husband's death in battle (in 1527 CE?) was only one of a series of losses Meera experienced in her twenties, including the death of her mother. She appears to have despaired of loving anything temporal and turned to the eternal, transforming her grief into a passionate spiritual devotion that inspired in her countless songs drenched with eroticism and separation.

Meera's devotion to Krishna was at first a private thing but at some moment it overflowed into an ecstasy that led her to dance in the streets of the city. Her brother-in-law, the new ruler of Chittorgarh, was Vikramaaditya, an ill-natured youth who strongly objected to Meera's fame, her mixing with commoners and carelessness of feminine modesty. There were several attempts to poison her. Her sister-in-law Udabai is said to have spread defamatory gossip.

At some time Meera declared herself a disciple of the guru Ravidas ("guru miliyaa raidasjee") and left for the centre of Krishnaism, Vrindavan. She considered herself to be a reborn gopi, Lalita, mad with love for Krishna. Folklore informs us of a particular incident where she expressed her desire to engage in a discussion about spiritual matters with Rupa Goswami, a direct disciple of Chaitanya and one of the foremost saint of Vrindavan that time who, being a renunciate celibate, refused to meet a woman. Meera replied that the only true man (purusha) in this universe is lord Krishna. She continued her pilgrimage, "danced from one village to another village, almost covering the whole north of India". One story has her appearing in the company of Kabir in Kashi, once again causing affront to social mores. She seems to have spent her last years as a pilgrim in Dwarka, Gujarat.

Jijabai

Jijabai was the mother of Shivaji, founder of the Maratha Empire.

Birth Date and Family Life

Jijabai was born on 12 January, 1598 and a daughter of Lakhuji Jadhav, a prominent grandee of Sindkhed Raja in the present-day Buldhana district of Maharashtra State. As per the customs of that age, she was wed at an early age to Shahaji Bhosale, a nobleman and military commander under the Adil Shahi sultans of Bijapur in present-day Karnataka. She was his second wife.

Jijabai gave birth to eight children, six daughters and two sons. Of these only the two sons, Sambhaji and Shivaji, survived while the rest died in infancy. Shivaji creat Swarajya.

On Mission

She wholeheartedly supported her husband's cause. Shahaji had tried to establish a Maratha state on the ruins of the erstwhile Nizamshahi sultanate. However he was defeated by the combined forces of the Mughals and Adilshahi. As per the treaty he was forced to move south. In order to continue the struggle, he deputed her as queen regent. She was chosen for this because of her ability as a warrior and administrator. This has been the tradition of Maratha women since time immemorial. At that time Shivaji was 14 years old and so accompanied his mother. The elder son Sambhaji remained with their father. Shivaji Maharaj left Banglore along with his mother, a council of ministers and chosen military commanders. Against this background, Shivaji took oath at the temple of lord Raireshwar. The rest of the story is well known.

Jijabai's elder son Sambhaji was killed in a battle with Afzal Khan of the Adil Shahi court. Shivaji killed Afzal Khan to avenge Sambhaji's death. When Shahaji died, Jijabai tried to commit sati-committing suicide by burning oneself in the husband's pyre, but Shivaji stopped her from doing so by his request. Jijabai is widely credited with raising Shivaji in a manner that led to his future greatness. She gave a human touch to Shivaji's personality. His policy towards captured women reflects her influence. She died immediately after the coronation of Shivaji, fulfilling her mission.

It is worth mentioning that apart from her, Rukmini (wife of Krishna), Damayanti (wife of Nala), Lopamudra (wife of sage Agasti) were princesses from Bhoj Yadavas of Vidarbha. All four princesses are well known for their versite personality and character..

Death

Jijabai died after the cooronation of Shivaji Maharaj 17 June 1674. Shivaji was heart-broken during her death.

Mumtaz Mahal

Mumtaz Mahal is the common nickname of Arjumand Banu Begum, an Empress of India during the Mughal Dynasty. She was born in Agra, India. Her father was the Persian noble Abdul Hasan Asaf Khan, the brother of Empress Nur Jehan (who subsequently became the wife of the emperor Jahangir). She was religiously a Shia Muslim. She was married at the age of 19, on 10 May 1612, to Prince Khurram, who would later ascend the Peacock Throne as Mughal Emperor Shah Jahan I. She was his third wife, and became his favourite. She died in Burhanpur in the Deccan (now in Madhya Pradesh) during the birth of their fourteenth child, a daughter named Gauhara Begum. Her body remained at Burhanpur for 23 years until the Taj was completed. Only then was her coffin shifted to Agra. Her body was then buried in the Taj Mahal in Agra.

Biography

In 1607 AD (1016 AH), Prince Khurram was betrothed to Arjumand Banu Begum, who was just 14 years old at the time. She would become the unquestioned love of his life. They would however, have to wait five years before they were married in 1612 AD (1021 AH), on a date selected by the court astrologers as most conducive to ensuring a happy marriage. After their wedding celebrations, Khurram "finding her in appearance and character elect among all the women of the time", gave her the title 'Mumtaz Mahal' Begum (Chosen One of the Palace). 18 AH). The intervening years had seen Khurrum take two other wives.

By all accounts however, Khurram was so taken with Mumtaz, that he showed little interest in exercising his polygamous rights with the two earlier wives, other than dutifully siring a child with each. According to the official court chronicler, Qazwini, the relationship with his other wives "had nothing more than the status of marriage. The intimacy, deep affection, attention and favour which His Majesty had for the Cradle of Excellence (Mumtaz) exceeded by a thousand times what he felt for any other."

Mumtaz Mahal had a very deep and loving marriage with Shah Jahan. Even during her lifetime, poets would extol her beauty, gracefulness and compassion. Mumtaz Mahal was Shah Jahan's trusted companion, travelling with him all over the Mughal Empire. His trust in her was so great that he even gave her his imperial seal, the Muhr Uzah. Mumtaz was portrayed as the perfect wife with no aspirations to political power in contrast to Nur Jehan, the wife of Jahangir who had wielded considerable influence in the previous reign. She was a great influence on him, apparently often intervening on behalf of the poor and destitute. But she also enjoyed watching elephant and combat fights performed for the court. It was quite common for women of noble birth to commission architecture in the Mughal Empire. Mumtaz devoted some time to a riverside garden in Agra.

Despite her frequent pregnancies, Mumtaz travelled with Shah Jahan's entourage throughout his earlier military campaigns and the subsequent rebellion against his father. She was his constant companion and trusted confidant and their relationship was intense. Indeed, the court historians go to unheard lengths to document the intimate and erotic relationship the couple enjoyed. In their nineteen years of marriage, they had fourteen children together, eight of whom died at birth or at a very young age.

Mumtaz died in Burhanpur in 1631 AD (1040 AH), while giving birth to their fourteenth child. She had been accompanying her husband whilst he was fighting a campaign in the Deccan Plateau. Her body was temporarily buried at Burhanpur in a walled pleasure garden known as Zainabad originally constructed by Shah Jahan's uncle Daniyal on the bank of the Tapti River. The contemporary court chroniclers paid an unusual amount of attention to Mumtaz Mahal's death and Shah Jahan's grief at her demise. In the immediate aftermath of his bereavement, the emperor was reportedly inconsolable. Apparently after her death, Shah Jahan went into secluded mourning for a year. When he appeared again, his hair had turned white, his back was bent, and his face worn. Jahan's eldest daughter, the devoted Jahanara Begum, gradually brought him out of grief and took the place of Mumtaz at court.

Her personal fortune valued at 10,000,000 rupees was divided by Shah Jahan between Jahanara Begum, who received half and the rest of her surviving children. Burhanpur was never intended by her husband as his wife's final resting spot. As a result her body was disinterred in December 1631 and transported in a golden casket escorted by her son Shah Shuja and the head lady in waiting of the deceased Empress back to Agra. There it was interred in a small building on the banks of the Yamuna River. Shah Jahan stayed behind in Burhanpur to conclude the military campaign that had originally bought him to the region. While there he began planning the design and construction of a suitable mausoleum and funerary garden in Agra for his wife, a task that would take more than 22 years to complete, the Taj Mahal.

Jahanara Begum Sahib

Shahzadi (Imperial Princess) Jahanara Begum Sahib was the eldest daughter of Shah Jahan and Mumtaz Mahal.

Influence at Court

Upon the death of Mumtaz Mahal in 1631, Jahanara, who was just 17, took the place of her mother as first lady in the country, despite her father having one other wife. As well as caring for her younger brothers and sisters, she is also credited with bringing her father out of mourning and restoring normality to a court darkened by her mother's death and her father's grief. One of her tasks after the death of her mother was to oversee the betrothal and wedding of her brother, Dara Shikoh, to a begum, Nadira Banu which had been originally planned by Mumtaz Mahal but postponed by her death. Jahanara's mother Arjumand Banu Begum, Empress Mumtaz Muhal died while giving birth.

Mumtaz Mahal's personal fortune valued at 10,000,000 rupees was divided by Shah Jahan between Jahanara Begum, who received half and the rest of her surviving children. Her father frequently took her advice and entrusted her with charge of the imperial seal.

Shah Jahan's fondness for his daughter was reflected in the multiple titles he bestowed upon her, which include Sahibat al-Zamani (Lady of the Age) and Padishah Begum (Lady Emperor) or Begum Sahib (*Princess of Princesses*).

Her power was such that, unlike the other royal princesses, she was allowed to live in her own palace, outside the confines of the Agra Fort.

Accident

On the night of the 4 April 1644, while she was heading towards her sleeping quarters her dress brushed against a lamp left burning on the floor. Her garment caught fire and she was enveloped in flames.

Two of the attendants who had tried to help Jahanara died of their burns. Her injuries were such that it was not until late in 1644 that she was deemed to be out of danger and an 8 day festival of thanks celebrated. With the assistance of numerous physicians Shah Jahan himself nursed her back to health.

After her recovery Shah Jahan gifted her rare gems and jewellery and bestowed upon her the revenues of the port of Surat. She made a pilgrimage to Ajmer, following the example set by her great-grandfather Akbar.

Relations with Family

Historians report a deep love and genuine liking between Jahanara and her brother Dara Shikoh, unlike the cool politeness that existed between Aurangzeb and herself. Jahanara had referred to Aurangzeb as the "white serpent" in a kind of diary she had written also calling him a tiger and panther.

Legend says that once when Aurangzeb was severely sick, Jahanara took care of him. Later when he asked her whether she would support him for the throne, she said that he would not be emperor due to which Aurangzeb became very angry with her. When Aurangzeb fell out of favour with his father during the time of Jahanara's convalescence she is credited with using the celebrations of her recovery to encourage her father to restore Aurangzeb to his former positions.

There is record of tensions with her sister Roshanara Begum, three years her junior who resented her elder sister's position as first lady of the empire.

Struggle for Power

Jahanara took the side of Dara Shikoh in the struggle for the throne. Dara had promised her to lift the ban on marriage for Moghul princesses, which Akbar had introduced. Had he triumphed, her power would likely have continued.

Care of her Father

On Aurangzeb's usurpation of the throne, Jahanara joined her father in imprisonment at the Agra Fort where she devoted herself to his care until his death.

Relations with Aurangzeb

After the death of their father Jahanara and Aurangzeb were reconciled. He gave her the title, 'Empress of Princesses' and she replaced Roshanara as first lady. Jahanara's sister Roshanara Begum was reportedly very jealous of her sister's return to power. Jahanara was soon secure enough in her position to occasionally argue with Aurangzeb-something which generally resulted in the death of anyone doing so-and have certain rights other women did not have.

She argued against Aurangzeb's strict regulation of public life in accordance with his conservative religious beliefs and his decision in 1679 to restore the poll tax on non-Muslims, which she said would alienate his Hindu subjects.

Roshanara Begum

Roshanara Begum was the second daughter of the Mughal ruler, Shah Jahan and Mumtaz Mahal. Born on September 3, 1617, Roshanara was a brilliant woman, a talented poetess, the mastermind behind Aurangazeb's accession to the Mughal throne, and by the time of her death in 1671, one of the most notorious women in the Mughal kingdom. Today, however, Roshanara is best known for the Roshanara Bagh, a pleasure garden located in north Delhi, next to Kamala Nagar Road and Grand Trunk Road. The present-day Roshanara Club which was constructed in the late 1800s by the British is a famous country club that was actually originally a part of the Roshanara Bagh.

Of his four sons, his oldest, Dara Shikoh, was Shah Jahan's favourite son, and heir apparent to the Peacock Throne. Shah Shuja, the second son, was the rebellious Governor of Bengal, with open designs on his father's throne. Aurangzeb, the third son, was the nominal Governor of Deccan. Murad, the youngest son, was granted Governorship of Gujarat, at which position he proved so weak and so ineffectual that Shah Jahan had him stripped of his titles, offering them to Dara Shikoh, instead. This precipitated a family struggle between Shah Jahan and his embittered younger sons, who resolved to depose the aging emperor and seize the throne for themselves. During this power struggle, Dara Shikoh received the support of his oldest sister, Jahanara Begum while Roshanara Begum sided with Aurangzeb, instead.

Roshanara's rise to power began when she successfully foiled a plot by her father and Dara Shikoh to kill Aurangazeb. According to history, Shah Jahan sent a letter of invitation to Aurangazeb to visit Delhi, in order to peacefully resolve the family crisis.

In truth, however, Shah Jahan planned to capture, imprison and kill Aurangazeb in prison as he viewed his third son as a serious threat to the throne. When Roshanara got wind of her father's plots, she sent a messenger to Aurangazeb, outlining their father's true intentions, and warning Aurangazeb to stay away from Delhi.

Aurangazeb was extremely grateful to Roshanara for her timely warning. When the war of succession was resolved in favour of Aurangazeb, she quickly became a powerful figure at court. Fearing that Dara Shikoh would kill her for her role in the war of succession if he ever returned to power, Roshanara insisted that Aurangazeb order Dara's execution. Legend has it that Dara was bound in chains, paraded around Chandni Chowk and beheaded. Roshanara then had his bloody head wrapped in a golden turban, packaged neatly and sent to her father as a gift from Aurangazeb and her. Shah Jahan, who opened the package just as he was sitting down to dinner, was so distressed by the sight of his favourite son's head that he fell unconscious to the floor. He remained in a stupor for many days after the incident.

Roshanara's relationship with her older sister, Jahanara, was troubled and tinged by jealousy as the latter was undisputedly their father's favourite daughter. Roshanara scored a major victory against her sister when Aurangazeb, who had been displeased with Jahanara for supporting their father and brother during the war of succession, removed her (Jahanara) from her position as head of the Imperial harem, installing Roshanara in her stead.

Eventually, however, Roshanara and Aurangazeb fell out with each other. Roshanara, who was obliged to remain single, as was the tradition with Mughal princesses, instead took many lovers, some openly, some secretly. In addition, she ruled Aurangazeb's harem with an iron hand and earned the hatred of her brother's many wives. She also had a love of gold and land, and accumulated wealth on a large scale, often by corrupt methods. This resulted in numerous complaints against her, none of which were brought to justice due to her position at Court. In addition, she blatantly misused the sweeping powers Aurangazeb had granted her just before leaving for his long military campaign in the Deccan, to further her own financial ends.

Her enemies soon brought these acts of financial and moral turpitude to Aurangazeb's notice. Himself a very strict Muslim, Aurangazeb frowned on Roshanara's libertine lifestyle and her greed. On his return to Delhi, he stripped Roshanara of her powers, banished her from his court, and ordered her to remain in seclusion and live a pious life in her garden palace outside of Delhi. Finally realizing that Roshanara was fast becoming a dangerous liability and afraid that the scandal following his sister would attach itself to his own name, he actively sought an opportunity to eliminate her from the picture.

That opportunity presented itself in late 1671, when Roshanara was discovered with yet another secret lover in her garden. The incident enraged Aurangazeb and sealed Roshanara's end. At the counsel of his ministers, he had her condemned as a "Kafir" for violating Muslim law and ordered her to be poisoned with her lover. Roshanara died a slow and agonizing death three days later at the age of 54. Aurangazeb had her interred in the Roshanara Bagh, a garden that she had designed and commissioned herself.

Gauhara Begum

Gauhara Begum (June 17, 1631 – 1706) was the fourteenth and final child of the Mughal emperor, Shah Jahan I, and his beloved wife, Mumtaz Mahal. Mumtaz Mahal died giving birth to her. Gauhara, however, survived the tragic birth and lived for another 75 years. Like most Mughal princesses at this time, though, Gauhara probably never married. Little is known about her and whether she was involved in the war of succession for her father's throne.

Gauhara died in 1706, at the age of 75, of unknown causes, but most likely of old age or disease.

Zeb-un-Nisa

Zeb-un-Nissa, daughter of Mughal emperor "Aurangzeb" (known as Alamgeer), was born during the reign of Shah Jahan. Her mother was Delras Banoo, daughter of Shahnawaz Safavid.

Her father Aurangzeb charged Mariam, one of the women of court, with the education of Zeb-un-Nissa. Through her efforts, Zeb-un-Nissa memorized the Quran in three years. Then she learned the sciences of the time with Mohammad Saeed Ashraf Mazandarani. Zeb-un-Nissa learned Philosophy, Astronomy and Literature, and knew Persian, Arabic and Urdu. She had a good reputation in calligraphy as well.

Zeb-un-Nissa started to narrate poems in Persian from the age of 14, but as her father did not like poetry, she used to write secretly. Ustad Bayaz, one of her teachers, found her poems and then encouraged her to continue narrating poems. It is reported that in the court of Aurangzeb, there used to be hidden literary and poetic parties among the great poets like Ghani Kashmiri, Naimatullah Khan and Aqil Khan Razi, and Zeb-un-Nissa participated secretly in these parties.

When Aurangzeb became the emperor after Shah Jahan, Zeb-un-Nissa was 21-years old. Aurangzeb found out about the talent and capacity of his daughter and began to discuss the political affairs of his Empire with her, listening to her opinions. It has been mentioned in some books that Aurangzeb sent all the royal princes for the reception of Zeb-un-Nissa each time she entered the court. Zeb-un-Nissa had four other sisters: Zeenat-un-Nissa, Badr-un-Nissa, Mehr-un-Nissa and Zebdat-un-Nissa. Among them, Zeenat-un-Nissa and Zebdat-un-Nissa wrote poems too.

Zeb-un-Nissa did not get married and remained single until her death, despite the fact she had many suitors. She spent all her life on literary works and poetry, as she herself says:

Oh Makhfi, it is the path of love and alone you must go-No one suits your friendship even if Jesus be though

In some books it has been written that there were secret love relation between Zeb-un-Nissa and Aqil Khan Razi, a poet and the governor of Lahore, but it is far from the truth. Even in her poetic book (Diwan), we cannot find a single Ghazal which supports this point. In fact, all her poems are based on the Sufi concept of *Love of God*.

Zeb-un-Nissa lived in a period when many great poets were at the peak of their reputation; e.g. Mawlana Abdul Qader Bedil, Kalim Kashani, Saaeb Tabrizi and Ghani Kashmiri. We notice the influence of Hafez Sherazi's style on the poetry of Zeb-un-Nissa. However, she is considered as one of the poets of Indian School of Poetry in Persian.

Zeb-un-Nissa selected "Makhfi" (which means *Hidden one* in Persian) as her pen-name in her poetry. In addition to her poetic book or collection of poems, called *Diwan*, which contains approximately 5,000 verses, she has also written the following books: "Monis-ul-Roh", "Zeb-ul Monshaat" and "Zeb-ul-Tafasir". In Maghzan-ul Gharaeb, the author writes that the poetic book of Zeb-un-Nissa contained 15,000 verses. Her poetic book was printed in Delhi in 1929 and in Tehran in 2001. Its manuscripts are in National Library of Paris, Library of the British Museum, Library of Tubingen University in Germany and in the Mota Library in India.

Zeb-un-Nissa died in 1701 in Shahjahanabad (old Delhi), while Aurangzeb was in trip to Deccan. Her tomb was in the garden of "Thirty thousand trees", outside of the Kabuli Gate. But when the railway line was laid out at Delhi, her tomb was shifted to Akbar's mausoleum at Sikandara, Agra.

Mariam-uz-Zamani

Mariam uz-Zamani Begum Sahiba nee Rajkumari Hira Afandi, alias Harkha Bai (often shortened to Mariam-uz-Zamani; October 1, 1542 – 1622), was a Rajput princess who became the Mughal Empress. She was the eldest daughter of Kacchwaha Rajput, Raja Bharmal, Raja of Amber, the older name of the Rajput State of Jaipur.

Her notability arises from her marriage to the Mughal emperor Jalaluddin Muhammad Akbar. She was also the mother of emperor Nuruddin Salim Jahangir, her husband's heir.

Her name as recorded in Mughal chronicles was Mariam-uz-Zamani. This is why the mosque of Mariyam Zamani Begum was constructed in Lahore, Pakistan, in her honour. She has been also referred to as Jodha Bai or Jodhabai in modern times, although she was never known as such during her lifetime. Hira Kunwar, Akbar's first Rajput wife, was the eldest daughter of Raja Bhar Mal of Amer. She was also the sister of Bhagwandas and the aunt of Man Singh I of Amber, who later became one the nine jewels (Navaratnas) in the court of Akbar..

The Mosque of Mariyam Zamani Begum was built by her son Nuruddin Salim Jahangir and is situated in the Walled City of Lahore, Pakistan, while Mariam's Tomb is situated one km away from Tomb of Akbar the Great, at Sikandra, near Agra.

Life

Hira Kunwari (her maiden name) was married to Akbar on January 20, 1562, at Sambhar, near Jaipur. She was Akbar's third wife and one of his three chief queens. She was 22 days older than her husband. Akbar's first queen was the childless Ruqaiyya Begum, and his second wife was Salima Sultan, the widow of his most trusted general, Bairam Khan. After her marriage, Hira Kunwari was given the title Mariam-ul-Zamani ("Mary of the Age").

She is said to have been politically involved in the court until Nur Jahan became empress.

Like few other women at the Mughal court, Maryam-uz-Zamani could issue official documents (singularly called *farman*), which was usually the exclusive privilege of the emperor. Maryam Zamani used her wealth and influence to build gardens, wells, and mosques around the country. In 1586, she arranged a marriage of her son, Prince Salim (later Jahangir), to her niece, Princess Manmati (Manbhawati Bai), who was the mother of Prince Khusrau Mirza.

Maryam Zamani owned and oversaw the ships that carried pilgrims to and from the Islamic holy city Mecca. In 1613, her ship, the *Rahîmî* was seized by Portuguese pirates along with the 600-700 passengers and the cargo. When the Portuguese officially refused to return the ship and the passengers, the outcry at the Moghul court was quite severe. Zamani's son, the Indian emperor Jahangir ordered the seizure of the Portuguese town Daman. This episode is considered to be an example of the struggle for wealth that would later ensue and lead to colonization of India.

Maryam Zamani died in 1622. As per her last wishes, a *vav* or step well was constructed by Jahangir. Her tomb, built in 1611, is on the Tantpur road now known as in Jyoti Nagar. Her tomb is now known as "Jodhabai ki chhatri". She was buried according to Islamic custom.

The Misnomer Jodha Bai

There is popular perception that the Rajput wife of Akbar, mother of Jahangir, was known as "Jodha Bai". In Tuzuk-e-Jahangiri she is referred as Mariam Zamani. Neither the Akbarnama (a biography of Akbar commissioned by Akbar himself), nor any historical text from the period refer to her as Jodha Bai. Tuzk-e-Jahangiri, the autobiography of Jahangir, doesn't mention Jodha Bai either.

According to Professor Shirin Moosvi, a historian of Aligarh Muslim University, the name "Jodha Bai" was first used to refer to Akbar's wife in the 18th and 19th centuries in historical writings. According to the historian Imtiaz Ahmad, the director of the Khuda Baksh Oriental Public Library in Patna, the name "Jodha" was used for Akbar's wife for the first time by Lieutenant-Colonel James Tod, in his book *Annals and Antiquities of Rajasthan.*

According to Professor N R Farooqi, a historian of Allahabad Central University, Jodha Bai was not the name of Akbar's Rajput queen; it was the name of Jahangir's Rajput wife Princess Manmati of Jodhpur, whose real name was Jagat Gosain.

Gulbadan Begum

Gulbadan Begum (c. 1523 – 1603) was a daughter of Zahir ud-Din Mohammad Babur, the first Mughal emperor of India, she is most known as the author of 'Humayun Nama', the account of the life of her brother, Humayun. Her name means literally *princess with a body like roses* in Persian. She was a descendant of the lines of highest Central Asian aristocracy: Timur through his son Miran Shah, and Genghis Khan through his son Chagatai Khan. Her mother was Dildar Begum and she was sister to Humayun, the second Mughal emperor.

She also finds reference throughout, Akbarnama, the Book of Akbar, written by Abul Fazal, and much of her biographical details are accessible through the work.

Biography

When Princess Gulbadan was born her father had been lord

in Kabul for nineteen years; he was master also in Kunduz and Badakhshan, had held Bajaur and Swat since 1519, and Qandahar for a year. During ten of those nineteen years he had been styled "padshah", in token of headship of the house of Timur and of his independent sovereignty. Two years later Babur set out on his last expedition across the Indus to conquer an empire in India. Gulbadan Begum was brought to India at the age of six. Gulbadan was married at 17, and had at least one son.

Humayun and his Sister

In 1540 Humayun lost the kingdom that his Kabul-born father Babur had established in India to Sher Shah Suri, an upstart from Bihar. With only his pregnant wife, one female attendant and a few loyal supporters, Humayun first fled to Lahore, and then later to Kabul. He was in exile for the next fifteen years in Afghanistan and Persia. Gulbadan Begum went to live in Kabul again. Her life, like all the other Mughal women of the harem, was intricately intertwined with three Mughal kings – her father Babur, brother Humayun and nephew Akbar. Two years after Humayun re-established the Delhi Empire, she accompanied other Mughal women of the harem back to Agra at the behest of Akbar, who had begun his rule.

Writing of Humayun Nama

Akbar commissioned Gulbadan Begum to chronicle the story of her brother Humayun. He was fond of his aunt and knew of her storytelling skills. It was fashionable for the Mughals to engage writers to document their own reigns (Akbar's own history, Akbarnama, was written by the well-known Persian scholar Abul Fazal). Akbar asked his aunt to write whatever she remembered about her brother's life. Gulbadan Begum took the challenge and produced a document titled *Ahwal Humayun Padshah Jamah Kardom Gulbadan Begum bint Babur Padshah amma Akbar Padshah.* It came to be known as *Humayun-nama.*

Gulbadan wrote in simple Persian without the erudite language used by better known writers. Her father Babur had written Babur-nama in the same style and she took his cue and wrote down from her memory. Unlike some of her contemporary writers, Gulbadan wrote a factual account of what she remembered, without embellishment. What she produced not only chronicles the trials and tribulations of Humayun's rule, but also gives us a glimpse of life in the Mughal harem. It is the only surviving writing penned by a woman of Mughal royalty in the sixteenth century.

The memory had been lost for several centuries and what has been found is not well preserved, poorly bound with many pages missing. It also appears to be incomplete, with the last chapters missing. There must have been very few copies of the manuscript, and for this reason it did not receive the recognition it deserved.

Translation of Humayun Nama

A battered copy of the manuscript is kept in the British Museum. Originally found by an Englishman, Colonel G. W. Hamilton it was sold to the British Museum by his widow in 1868. Its existence was little known until 1901, when Annette S. Beveridge translated it into English (Beveridge affectionately called her Princess Rosebud).

Historian Dr. Rieu called it one of the most remarkable manuscripts in the collection of Colonel Hamilton (who had collected more than 1,000 manuscripts). A paperback edition of Beveridge's English translation was published in India in 2001.

Pradosh Chattopadhyay has translated Humayun Nama into Bengali in 2006. Chirayata Prokashan published the book.

Content of the Document

Upon being entrusted with the directive by Akbar to write the manuscript, Gulbadan Begum begins thus:

There had been an order issued, 'Write down whatever you know of the doings of Firdous-Makani (Babur) and Jannat-Ashyani (Humayun)'. At this time when his Majesty Firdaus-Makani passed from this perishable world to the everlasting home, I, this lowly one, was eight years old, so it may well be that I do not remember much. However in obedience to the royal command, I set down whatever there is that I have heard and remember.

From her account we know that Gulbadan was married by the age of seventeen to Khizr Khwaja Khan, a Chagtai Mughal by ancestry and her second cousin. She had at least one son. She had moved to Delhi/Agra in 1528 from Kabul with her foster mother. After the defeat of Humayun in 1540 she moved back to Kabul to live with one of her half brothers. She did not return to Agra immediately after Humayun won back his kingdom. Instead, she stayed behind in Kabul until she was brought back to Agra by Akbar, two years after Humayun died in a tragic accident in 1556. Gulbadan Begum lived in Agra and then Sikri for the rest of her life, except for a period of seven years when she undertook a pilgrimage to Mecca.

She appears to have been an educated, pious, and cultured woman of royalty. She was fond of reading and she had enjoyed the confidences of both her brother Humayun and nephew Akbar. From her account it is also apparent that she was an astute observer, well versed with the intricacies of warfare, and the intrigues of royal deal making. The first part of her story deals with Humayun's rule after her father's death and the travails of Humayun after his defeat. She had written little about her father Babur, as she was only aged eight when he died. However, there are anecdotes and stories she had heard about him from her companions in the Mahal (harem) that she included in her account. The latter part also deals with life in the Mughal harem.

She recorded one light-hearted incident about Babur. He had minted a large gold coin, as he was fond of doing, after he established his kingdom in India. This heavy gold coin was sent to Kabul, with special instructions to play a practical joke on the court jester Asas, who had stayed behind in Kabul. Asas was to be blindfolded and the coin was to be hung around his neck. Asas was intrigued and worried about the heavy weight around his neck, not knowing what it was. However, when he realized that it was a gold coin, Asas jumped with joy and pranced around the room, repeatedly saying that no one shall ever take it from him.

Gulbadan Begum describes her father's death when her brother had fallen ill at the age of twenty-two. She tells that Babur was depressed to see his son seriously ill and dying. For four days he circumambulated the bed of his son repeatedly, praying to Allah, begging to be taken to the eternal world in his son's place. As if by miracle, his prayers were answered. The son recovered and the forty-seven year old father died soon after.

Soon after his exile, Humayun had seen and fallen in love with a thirteen year old girl named Hamida Banu in the harem of Shah Husain Mirza. At first she refused to come to see the Emperor, who was much older than her. Finally she was advised by the other women of the harem to reconsider, and she consented to marry the Emperor. Two years later, in 1542, she bore Humayun a son named Akbar, the greatest of the Mughal rulers. Gulbadan Begum described the details of this incident and the marriage of Humayun and Hamida Banu with glee, and a hint of mischievousness in her manuscript.

Gulbadan also recorded the nomadic life style of Mughal women. Her younger days were spent in the typical style of the peripatetic Mughal family, wandering between Kabul and Delhi. During Humayun's exile the problem was further exaggerated. She had to live in Kabul with one of her step brothers, who later tried to recruit her husband to join him against Humayun. Gulbadan Begum persuaded her husband not to do so.

Pilgrimage to Mecca

Gulbadan Begum described in her memory a pilgrimage she took to Mecca, a distance of three thousand miles, crossing treacherous mountains and hostile deserts. Though they were of royal birth, the women of the harem were hardy and prepared to face hardships, especially since their lives were so intimately intertwined with the men and their fortunes. Gulbadan Begum stayed in Mecca for nearly four years and during her return a shipwreck in Aden kept her from returning to Agra for several months. She finally returned in 1582, seven years after she had set forth on her journey.

Akbar had provided for safe passage of his aunt on her Hajj and sent a noble as escort with several ladies in attendance. Lavish gifts were packed with her entourage that could be used as alms. Her arrival in Mecca caused quite a stir and people from as far as Syria and Asia Minor swarmed to Mecca to get a share of the bounty.

If Gulbadan Begum had written about the death of Humayun, when he tumbled down the steps in Purana Qila in Delhi, it has been lost. The manuscript seems to end abruptly in the year 1552, four years before the death of Humayun. It ends in mid-sentence, describing the blinding of Prince Kamran. As we know that Gulbadan Begum had received the directive to write the story of Humayun's rule by Akbar, long after the death of Humayun, it is reasonable to believe that the only available manuscript is an incomplete version of her writing. It is also believed that Akbar asked his aunt to write down from her memory so that Abul Fazal could use the information in his own writings about the emperor Akbar.

Maham Anga

Maham Anga (d.1562) was the wet nurse of the Mughal Emperor Akbar, and often referred as his foster mother as she took care of young Akbar, as his own mother, Hamida Banu Begum was mostly away, with his father, Humayun was i exile, thorough Akbar's growing years. She was the de facto regent of the Mughal state after the exclusion of Bairam Khan in 1560 to Akbar's assumption of full power in 1562, shortly before her death. The period is referred to by some historians as the "The Petticoat Government", suggesting that the 'foster mother cohort' attempted to keep Akbar as a puppet ruler after Bairam Khan's death. An alternative perspective is that this regency was considerably less oppressive than that of Bairam Khan, and ended in considerably less destruction than the Uzbeg Revolt of 1564-7.

Maham Anga was the mother of Adham Khan, Akbar's foster brother, and his violent execution for the murder of Ataga Khan, Akbar's favourite general Shams-ud-Din, at the hands of the young Emperor himself no less in November, 1561, profoundly affected her. She famously commented 'You have done well' to Akbar when he broke the news to her; she died shortly afterwards.

Her tomb and that of her son, known as Adham Khan's Tomb, was built by Akbar, and popularly named *Bhul-bulaiyan*, owing to the labyrinth in its structure, lies north of the Qutub Minar in Mehrauli.

Khairul Manazil

She also built a mosque, 'Khairul Manazil' ca 1561 CE. It later served as a *madarsa*, and now stands opposite, Purana Qila, Delhi on Mathura Road, south eats to Sher Shah Gate.

It was here that A slave tried to kill Akbar, after his return from hunting and moving towards Nizamuddin Dargah, but the arrow hit a soldier in his entourage instead, who was hurt, albeit not gravely.

Hamida Banu

Hamida Banu Begam, 'Maryam Makani' (1527-1604) was a wife of the second Mughal Emperor, Humayun, and the mother of Mughal Emperor, Akbar. Her important architectural legacy is the Humayun's Tomb, Delhi, which she commissioned in 1562 CE, and saw through its construction over the next eight years.

Biography

Hamida Banu Begum was born in 1527, to Shaikh Ali Akbar Jami, a Persian Shia, and a friend and preceptor to Mirza Hindal, the youngest son of first Mughal Emperor and Humayun's father, Babur. Ali Akbar Jami was also known as Mir Baba Dost, who belonged to the lineage of Ahmad Jami Zinda-fil. Hamida Banu's mother was Mah Afraz Begum, who married Ali Akbar Jami in Paat, Sindh.

She met Humayun, as a thirteen year old girl and frequenting Mirza Hindal's household, at a banquet given by Dildar Begum, Babar's wife and Humayun's stepmother in Alwar. Mughal Emperor, Humayun was in exile after his exodus from Delhi, due to the armies of Sher Shah Suri, who had ambitions of restoring Afghan rule in Delhi. Though initially she refused to meet him, eventually after forty days of perusing and eventually at the insistence of Dildar Begum, she agreed to marry the Emperor. The marriage took place on a day chosen by the Emperor, an avid astrologer, himself employing his astrolabe, at mid-day on a Monday in September, 1541 (Jumada al-awwal 948 AH) at Patr. Thus she became his junior wife, after Bega Begum (later known as Haji Begum, after *Hajji*), who was the elder wife.

Two years later, after a perilous journey through the desert, on 22 August 1542, she and Emperor Humayun reached at the Sindhi Fortress of Umarkot in central Sindh ruled by the Amir Hussein of Umarkot allied to the Mughals, at a small desert town, two months later she gave birth future Emperor, Akbar on the early morning of 15 October 1542 (fourth day of Rajab, 949 AH), he was given the name Humayun had heard in his dream at Lahore-the Emperor Jalalu-d-din Muhammad Akbar

In coming years, she took on numerous tough journeys to follow her husband, who was still in flight. First the beginning of the following December she and her new born went into camp at Jun, after travelling for ten or twelve days. Then in 1543, she made the perilous journey from Sindh, which had Qandahar for its goal, but in course of which Humayun had to take hasty flight from Shal-mastan, 'through a desert and waterless waste.' Leaving her little son behind, she accompanied her husband to Persia, here they visited the shrines of her ancestor, Ahmad-e Jami and Shiites shrine, of Ardabil in Iran, the place of origin of Safavid dynasty which helped them immensely in the following years.

In 1544, at a camp at Sabzawar, 93 miles south of Herat, she gave birth to a daughter, thereafter she returned from Persia with the army given to Humayun by Shah of Iran, Tahmasp I, and at Qandahar met Dildar Begum, and her son, Mirza Hindal. Thus, it was not until 15 November 1545 (Ramdan 10th, 952 AH) that she saw her son Akbar again, the scene of young Akbar recognizing his mother amongst a group of women has been keenly illustrated in Akbar's biography, *Akbarnama*. In 1548, she and Akbar accompanied Humayun to Kabul.

Meanwhile, Sher Shah Suri died in May 1545, and after that his son and successor, Islam Shah died too in 1554, disintegrating the Suri dynasty rule. In November 1554, when Humayun set out for India, she stayed back in Kabul. Though he took control of Delhi in 1555, he died within a year of his return, from a fall down the steps of his library at Purana Qila, Delhi, in 1556 at the age of 47, leaving behind a thirteen year old heir, Akbar, who was to become one of greatest emperors of the empire. Hamida Banu joined Akbar from Kabul, only during his second year of reign, 1557 CE, and stayed with him thereafter, she even intervened into politics on various occasions, most notable during the ouster of Mughal minister, Bairam Khan, when Akbar came of age in 1560.

Hamida now an Empress mother, commissioned the construction of Humayun's Tomb, Delhi, in around 1562 CE, six years after his death, and designed by Mirak Mirza Ghiyath, a Persian architect. Over the next eight years she personally supervised the construction of the tomb, where she too was buried after her death on 29 August, 1604 (19th Shahriyar, 1013 AH) in Agra, just a year before the death of her son Akbar and almost half a century after death of her husband, Humayun.

Throughout her years, she was held in high regard by her son Akbar, as English traveller Thomas Coryat recorded, Akbar carrying her palanquin himself across the river, during one of her journeys from Lahore to Agra. Later when Prince Salim, future king Jahangir, revolted against his father Akbar, she took upon the case of her grandson, and a reconciliation ensued thereafter, even though has plotted and got Akbar's favourite minister Abul-Fazal killed. Akbar shaved his head and chin only on two occasions, one at the death of foster-mother Jiji Anga and another at the death of his mother.

She was given the title, *Maryam-makani,* dwelling with Mary, posthumously, as she was considered, 'epitome of innocence' by Akbar.

Mumtaz Mahal

Mumtaz Mahal was the third wife of the Mughal Emperor Shah Jahan. It was in her memory that he built the magnificent monument of love and romance, known as the "Taj Mahal". Mumtaz Mahal, a Muslim Persian Princess, was originally known as Arjumand Banu Begum. So enthralling was her beauty that Shah Jahan (then Prince Khurram) fell in love with her at the first sight. Their marriage was solemnized five years later and from then on, started one of the most popular love stories of the world. Although she was the third wife of Shah Jahan, but at the same time, she was also his favourite. He even bestowed her with the name Mumtaz Mahal and the highest honor of the land-the royal seal, Mehr Uzaz.

Mumtaz Mahal became an inseparable companion of her husband till her death. She even accompanied him on his military endeavors and provided him with her counsel. Infact, she was a pillar of support, love and comfort to the emperor. Mumtaz Mahal gave birth to fourteen children of Shah Jahan. It was during the birth of their 14th child only that she left for the holy abode. It is said that she obtained a promise from Shah Jahan that he will build world's most beautiful monument in her memory. Whether this was true or not, but, Shah Jahan did build a magnificent monument as a tribute to her life. Today, it counts amongst the Seven Wonders of the World and is known as "The Taj Mahal".

6

Agrarian Relations: Mughal India

Introduction

A large pan of the agricultural surplus was alienated in the form of land revenue. Theoretically, the Emperor was the sole claimant as discussed in Unit 16. However, in actual practice, apart from the state and its agents, a number of intermediaries also took away huge amounts through various channels. In this Unit we will discuss the rights of various classes to land and its produce. We will also discuss the interrelationship between these classes.

Revenue Assignees and Grantees

The state adopted two ways to realise the land revenue from the peasants. First, the jagirdam were assigned certain areas with rights to collect revenue and utilise the same for their salary and to meet their military obligations. Secondly, it collected revenue through imperial revenue offers from the khaliso. The jamar had no permanent rights over the areas so assigned due to frequent transfers. His claims were confined to the authoristd land revenue and other taxes. Grantees Agrarian Relati-: Mqhal indls While the Jagirdars were given revenue assignments in lieu of cash salary, there was another category of people which was given revenue grants for their subsistence. This was the class of religious men who were patronised by t k state.

These grants were known as suyurghal or madad-i maash (aid for subsistence). A separate department under the charge of the sadr us sudur looked after these grants. If the aid was given in cash, it was known as wazifa. There were certain categories of people who were qualified to receive madad-i maaah. These grants did not invest the grantee with any right over land but were entitled to the prescribed revenue from its produce. Akbar put the ceiling of such grants of land to 100 bighas per person. The policy of Akbar was to grant half cultivable and half waste land to improve agriculture.

The Zamindars

The zamindan were present in practically every part of the Mughal Empire and held the most significant position in the agrarian structure of Mughal India. The word zamladar is derived from two Persian words-zamln (land) and dm (holder). During the pre-Mughal period, the word zamidar has been used in the sense of the chief of acoumeter. The fact that a chief had acknowledged the supremacy of a superior sovereign power made no difference to his position within his own domain, so long as he was allowed to retain it.

From Akbar's time onwards, this term was officially used for any person with any hereditary claim to a direct share in the peasant's produce. The early local terms such as khot and muqnddam in the Doab, mtarabi and blurt in Awadh, bloom in Rajasthan and bantb or vantb in Gujarat were replaced by the term zamidar. However, many of these terms continued to be used interchangeably with zamiadam in contemporary ackounts. The areas without zamiadan were termed niyati (peasant held).

Nurul Haran divides the zamindars into three categories:

a) Primary zomindors who had some proprietary rights over the land;

b) Secondary zrunindars who held the intermediary rights and helped the state incollecting land revenue; and

c) Autonomous chiefs-had autonomous rights in their temtories and paid a fixed amount to the Mughal State.

Zarnindari Rights

Zamindari did not signify a proprietary right in land. It was a claim on the produce of the soil, co-existing in a subordinate capacity, with the land revenue demand of the state. Yet, like any article of private property, it could, and was, freely bought and sold. It was also inheritable and divisible, that is, the heirs of a zamindar could divide the fiscal claims and perquisites of their inherited zamiadar, in accordance with the law of the land.

The zamindar acquired his rights by virtue of the historical tradition of control he and his kinsmen exercised over the inhabitants of particular villages. At some time, the zamindar had settled villages and distributed its land among the peasantry. In eastern Rajasthan, wasidar (a category of peasants) were settled by the bhomia (zamiadar as known there) in the village to undertake sometimes the cultivation of his personal lands. The zamindar rights, therefore, were not created by the ruling classes, but preceded them. The king, however, could create zrtollndari in villages where none existed. He could also dislodge a zamidar, but this was a right he exercised only in case of sedition or non-payment of revenue.

The medieval rulers recognised the rights of the zamindar, but were equally insistent on treating them as agents of the government for revenue collection. When the zamldul took this form, that is, it came to assist the government in the collection of revenue, for the service so rendered, the zamidar was entitled to a percentage of the total revenue collected. This percentage in officially ocuments is stated to be 10% and is described as nnnkar ("allowance"). When the administration decided to collect the revenue through its own agents, by-passing the zPmlnQr, the latter was entitled to a share in the collection of revenues called Multan. (proprietary right), and like nnnlrnr, was fixed at 10% of the total revenue collected.

In Gujarat, this claim of the zamindar was described as banth or vanth, but unlike malikana in Northern Iıdia, it was considerably higher. Like malikana, it was paid in the form of cash. In the Deccan, it was called chauth (lit. "one fourth"), and as the name suggests, stood at one-fourth of the revenues connected. Sardeshmukhi, another fiscal claim of the zamindar in the Deccan, was equivalent to 10% of the revenues.

Under the Marathas, the cesses of chauth and sardeshmukhi came to be realised not through a legal claim based on actual zamindari right, but by the sheer use of force. Under Shivaji, while the claim of the cumprised one-fourth of the chauth and the whole of surdeshmukhi, the other three-fourths of the chauth was to be retained by the Maratha feudatory barons.

Military Strength of Zamindars

The zamindars employed their footmen and cavalry. These troops helped them in the realisation of land revenue and subjugation of peasantry. Almost all zamindars had their own small or big qilachadgarhi or forts. According to the Ain-i Akbari, the troops of the zamindars in the whole Mughal Empire exceeded forty four lakhs. In Bengal they possessed thousands of boats.

Chaudhuris

As mentioned earlier, the zamindar played a prominent role in the collection of land revenue. Some of these zamindars were designated as chaudhuri for the purpose of collection of revenue. One of the. prominent zamindars of a pargana was appointed chaudhuri, generally one in each pargana.

The chaudhuri was suppose to collect the revenue from other zamindars of the pargana. Apart from thier customary nankar, these chaudhuris were entitled to another share in the land revenue collected by them. This was termed chaudhrai which amounted to two and a half per cent of the revenue collected. Unlike the zamindar, the chaudhuri was appointed by the state and could be removed for improper functioning.

Other Intermediaries

Each village had a number of hereditary officials. The most important of them was the village headman (muqaddam in Northern India and patel in the Deccan). He was the person responsible for the collection of land revenue and maintenance of law and order in the villages. For the services so rendered, he was granted a part of the village land revenue-free, though, in some cases, he was also remunerated in cash at a percentage of total land revenue realised. In addition, he was also entitled tc receive some amount of produce from peasants. In the task of the collection of land revenue the muqaddam was assisted by the village accountant (patwari in Northern India and kulkarni in the Deccan). The patwari's task was to maintain a record (bahi) of the revenue collected from the individual peasants and its payment to the state authorities. His records, therefore, were of immense help to the administration in assessing the revenue-paying capacity of the peasants and in fixing the total land revenue claim on the village. Like the muqaddam he was also remunerated by the grant of revenue.-free land or by a fixed commission in the total revenue collected.

However, being an employee of the village organisation, his allowance was much smaller than that of the village headman. The office and the accompanying privileges of both the muqaddam and patwari were hereditary.

Peasantry

In the earlier sections, we studied about the classes who enjoyed superior rights over the produce of the land. In this section we will discuss the main producing classes he main agrarian class, directly involved with the agricultural production, was the peasantry. Though the class had a number of strata within it, for the convenience of study we are including all of them under one nomenclature. The peasants constituted the primary class in rural society and the revenue collected from them sustained the whole state apparatus. We have noticed in Unit 16 that the peasant had to pay a large part of their produce as 'rand revenue. It appears that the bulk of the peasantry lived on the subsistence level of existence.

Land Rights of Peasantry

There has been a long debate among historians regarding the rights of the peasantry over land, Peasant's claim to land was not disregarded by the state, yet he was never allowed the right to free alienation. It appears that peasants had all the rights over land as long as he cultivated it. The zamindan or state had no right to evict the pessant as long as he cultivated the land and paid the revenue. It seems tha prietary rights in land were not quite developed during the Mughal period.

However, the most important aspect of the period is the varying claims over the produce of the land.

In contemporary accounts we come across a number of references to the fight of the peasantry from villages because of oppression or other problems. A number of instances are available about peasants settling individually or in groups in various regions. The mobility of the peasant was an established practice in Mughal India.

This mobility was more pronounced in cases of their oppression in one region or natural calamities like floods and famines.

Stratification of Peasantry

The peasantry was not a homogenous class. The stratification was due to inequalities in wealth and social status. Peasants with large resources cultivated bigger plots of land, and even employed labourers on his fields. They could acquire head-ship of a village jmuqddam or patel) and enjoy a superior share in the produce of other peasants. The divisions were so well-estwhed that they are dxerently desigpated even in official accounts anancor&. Richweasants a n referred to as LbudLorbt (self-cultivated) in Northern India, ghamhalas in Rajasthan and mirasdars in Maharashtra. The poor peasants are refer to as reza riaya (small peasant) in Northern India, paltis in kajasthan and kunbmn Maharashtra..

One major reason for this can be found in the wide prevalence of cash-nexus. Since land revenue in the larger part of India had to be paid in cash, peasants and cultivators were forced to carry their produce to the markets or sell it to merchants or moneylenders on the eve of harvest. In such a situation, those peasants who could cultivate cash crops would be placed in a better position, because of the higher prices they fetched in the market than those who, owing to their scarce resources, could only cutlivate food crops for which the prices were comparatively low.

Not all peasants could shift to cash crop cultivation since it involved much expenses (good seeds, better fertilisen, irrigation or facilities, and also more productive soil). The requirement of the payment of land revenue in cash would thus cause a widening gulf between the relatively better-off peasants whose resources allowed them to shift to cash crop cultivation and the poor peasants who found even the cultivation of food crops an arduous and expensive business.

The regressive nature of land revenue demand was another major factor that caused and intensified divisions within the peasantry. The incidence of land revenue demand being uniform for both the rich and the poor peasants, in actual fact it fell more heavily on the latter than on the former. The village organisation, or what has often loosely been described as the "village community", further perpetuated these divisions by levying lower revenue rates on the peasants, and calling upon the rent riaya to meet the deficit thus arising in the total revenue claim.

Economic inequalities were not the only basis of divisions within the peasantry. They were also divided between the permanent residents of the village and the temporary residents. Caste associations and kinship ties, even as they served as linkages that afforded supra-local affmitik were also at the same time sources of divisiveness kiow the class of peasants existed in rural India a large population of menial workers. Their number or their proportion to caste peasantry is almost impossible to estimate, yet, in all probability, they did constitute a significant portion of the rural population of India. They are described in the contemporary literature as chamam, balahars, theorise and dbanuks, etc. They were a cheap source of labour for the peasants and zamindars to work on their fields during the sowing and harvest seasons.

It was, therefore, in the interest of both of them (i.e., the peasants and zamhdars) to suppress and exploit them. The creation of a huge reserve of labour force for agricultural production reduced the cost of production, which enhanced the "surplus" produce of the peasant, and thus allowed a greater exploitation of land revenue by the ruling power. In the suppression of the menial workers, the state, the zamindars and the peasants were equal collaborators.

Village Community

Generally the peasants of a village had a majority of the same caste. Such villages were established historically by one clan or family. Apart from the peasants of the dominant caste of a village, there were menial workers who came from lower castes.

From the contemporary accounts it appears that in many activities these villages functioned as a community. It should not be taken to mean that there were any communal land holdings. The fields were definitely held by individual peasants. The revenue officials found it convenient to treat village as a unit for revenue assessment and collection. The description of the patwari as a village official supports this.

It is reported that the patwari was supposed to keep the account of individual peasants production and revenue liability. The payment to state was made by the village as a unit. The revenue from the individual peasants was put in a pool whose incharge was the patwari. From this pool, land revenue, fees and perquisites of certain officials and sundry common expenses of the village were paid. Even the loan taken from the moneylenders was paid back out of the village pool. The dominant group of people in a village constituted the village panchayat. The latter used to decide village affairs regarding dispute over land rights, disposal of waste land, etc. It was also responsible to the state for arresting criminals, compensating for the value of goods stolen or tracing them.

Relations Between Agrarian Classes

In the earlier sections of this Unit, we studied about various agrarian classes. We noticed that a number of groups appropriated a share in the surplus of the produce, i.e., jagirdars, religious grantees, zamlndars and various intermediaries at the village level. We have also studied about the producing class or peasantry. Here, in this section, we will study the relations between these classes.

Both the zamindar and the jagirdars fed upon the surplus produce of the peasant, and therefore, insofar as the exploitation of the peasantry was concerned, both acted as each other's collaborators. Yet, the zamindar, being permanently based would not allow exploitation that went beyond the alienation of surplus produce, for that would lead to exodus of the peasantry and desertion of agricultural operations which would in turn affect his own fiscal claims during the following year. The jagirdars, attitude is best reflected in Bernier's account who visited India in the mid-17th century. He writes that, because of the frequent transfers of jagirs the jagirdar governors and revenue contractors were not bothered about the deplorable state of peasantry. They therefore were interested in exploiting the peasantry to the maximum even at the cost of their desertion and fields lying unattended..

Jawahar Mal Bekas, an 18th century writer observes that the bldm (Jagirdar) of a day can in a moment remove a zomindar of five hundred years, and put in his stead a man who has been without a place for a life-time. Irfan Habib further elaborates his powers and writes that "as for peasants, the jagirdars claimed powers to detain them on the land, like serfs, and bring them back, if they ran away." In the second half of the 17th century due to the uncertainty of holding a jagir for a stipulated perio, the jagirdar oppressed peasants.-They had no regard for their welfare.

According to Irfan Habib, "While undoubtedly the Mughal administration sought to take meabres to regulate and moderate the jagirdar' exactions, it is not certain that these could reduce the pressure for short-term maximization of revenue by individual jagirdars. Such pressure not only inhibited extension of cultivation, but also involved the Mughal ruling class in a deepening conflict with the two major agrarian classes, the zamindars and the peasantry".

The divisions within the peasantry, as also the deep contractions that existed between the peasants and agricultural workers, acted as severe constraints and weakened the capabilities of this class. Disjointed and truncated, this class was quite incapable of confronting the medieval despotic states. It did, however, revolt for two reasons: one, when the revenue demand appropriated more than the surplus produce of the peasants, thereby threatening their very subsistence. Peasant revolts in these circumstances never went beyond asking for a reduction in revenue demand.

Peasants also revolted as followers of a zamindar who was leading a revolt against the state or jagirdar (mostly on the question of his claim to the produce of the soil), either in the hope that the end of revolt would lead to better conditions of living for them or simply as rendering a service to their overlord. Peasant revolts of this nature were actually zamindari revolts: the zamindars led them and the peasants served the purposes of the zamindars alone. We shall be discussing these zamindar-led peasant revolt in a separate Unit.

1669 Jat Uprising

Paradoxical though it might appear and strange though it might seem, the Jat uprising of 1669 in India under the leader Gokula occurred at a time when the Mughal government was by no means weak or imbecile. In fact this period of Aurangzeb's reign witnessed the climax of the Mughal Empire., during the early medieval period frequent breakdown of law and order often induced the Jats to adopt a refractory course. But, with the establishment of the Mughal rule, law and order was effectively established and we do not come across any major Jat revolt during the century and a half proceeding the reign of Aurangzeb. Though in 1638 Murshid Quli Khan, the Mughal faujdar of Mathura was killed during an operation against Jats. During the reign of Aurangzeb, the faujdar of Mathura in 1669 was none other than Abdun Nabi who incurred the wrath of people.

Causes of the Revolt

The underlying causes of the Jat revolt of 1669 have not been properly analysed so far. Historians have generally ascribed the said rebellion to Aurangzeb's religious discrimination and the oppression of local officers.,. These, however seem to have been the contributory causes but neither the sole nor the dominant factors which precipitated the revolt. The real cause of the Jat rebellion of 1669 lay deeper than have been assigned to it so far.

One of the main causes may be sought in the changed nature and scope of the Mughal government under Aurangzeb which was detrimental to the democratic and tribal way of life of the Jat fraternity. Akbar assiduously tried to build a comprehensive state based on religious and social freedom, respect for village autonomy and willing acquiescence of the people at large. The Nature of the Mugal despotism generally retained its previous character under Jahangir. In Spite of Shahjahan's intolerant attitude in the beginning, the government in his times also displayed a "sense of Justice "and kept the interests of the people in its view.

But, with the accession of Aurangzeb, the comprehensive nature of the state gradually yielded to a narrow and over centralized despotic regime., A despotic system rests upon the personality of the ruler, which motivates the entire administrative machinery.

The over-centralized set-up accompanied by the narrow outlook of the ruler, was naturally antagonistic to the tribal and democratic outlook of the Jats. An instinctive attachment to democratic ways and a "sturdy independence "have throughout been their chief characteristics. They have a pronounced aversion to external interference and have been accustomed to self governance of their internal affairs.

Giving due regard to their tradition customs and laws, Akbar issued two firmans, dated 8th Ramaza, 987 A.H. and 11th Ramzan, 989 A.H. granting internal freedom to the clan councils of the Jats of the upper Doab region in religious matters and "to carry out their functions according to their ancient customs and laws" Akbar's sagacious policy seems to have been followed until the time of Shah Jahan. Jahangir sometimes showed the top Jat leaders the unique favour of calling them to his audience and giving Khilats.

But Aurangzeb reversed this policy. He "restricted the activities" of their customary institutions. This along with his religious fanaticism, created concern among the Jats. They discussed this issue in a meeting at Chhaprauli in 1661 (1718 V.S) and decided to protest against the new laws and pleaded for the reversion of the policy of the Delhi court.,

The courageous Jats who had reminiscences of their republican past and who still retained that spirit could hardly afford to remain quiet before in immensely centralized system based on a narrow outlook which threatened to devour their traditional tribal and democratic ways.

Probably, not less significant was the role of the economic factors in leading the Jat peasantry to rebellion. Emperor assigned a certain piece of land to the officials in lieu of their pay and also to enable them to defray the expenses over their troops on condition of their paying a sum to the Emperor out of the surplus revenue. Such grants were called Jagirs Since they were mainly grants of revenue out of which the holders (Who were usually Mansabdars) maintained their quota of troops for the Empire, the tendency was to fix revenue at the highest possible rate almost equal to the surplus produce. Even this high rate went on increasing with the passage of time under the circumstances the peasants were financially hit very hard. They were usually left with the barest minimum needed for supporting their lives.,

What added further to the hardships of the cultivators was the frequent transfer of the jagirs to different assignees. The jagirdars held their jagirs at the pleasure of the Emperor. Bhimsen remarks "There is no hope of a jagir being left with the same officer next year.", This constant insecurity of the tenure of office proved unfortunate in two ways. Firstly it offered little incentive to the holders to exert for alleviating the distress of their tenantry. Instead it led them to employ all possible tactics to extort money from the Peasantry. Secondly, quite often at the time of the transfer the hard hit peasants of the same Jagir were pressurized to pay the same sum twice, first to the collectors of the outgoing jagirdar and then to those of the incoming one. Thus this system ended in a mad looting of the peasants by the rival collectors.,

If the peasants refused to pay the revenue, very severe punishment was meted out to them. At times they were left with no other option than to sell their women, children and cattle, or to run away form their home to avoid extermination through-ill-treatment.

In its actual operation Mughal assignment system became extremely "ruinous to the peasants and ultimately harmful to the interests of the Empire" The exploitation by the collectors increased as time went on. At last a stage was reached when " excessive acts of oppression" by the officers could lead some of the peasants to shifting their hand from plough to the sword, as happened in the case of the Jats following the atrocities of Abdun Nabi. We know it on the testimony of Shah Waliullah that "the cultivators of the villages between Delhi and Akbarabad were of the Jat caste.

Against this background, it was quite natural for the Jats to ventilate their resentment over the prevailing assignment system as agriculture occupied the uppermost place in the there life.

It is obvious that an oppressive system goes hard with the agriculturists. Its sharp reaction among the Jats, culminating into a rebellion, appears to have been because of their adventurous disposition and martial character.

The Jats had been a race of warrior agriculturists.

Highly disapproved of the enhanced revenue, the levying of the "harmful taxes" and "looting by government tax collectors "they were prone to opposing such thing and other oppressions even by force, if the occasion demanded this may explain better why in face of similar provocations other weak agricultural communities remained more or less inactive while the Jat peasants unsheathed their swords.

Apart form it, the Jats more than any other people, are reputed to be deeply attached to personal freedom and to resenting external control.,,

Aurangzeb pursued a fourfold course with regard to his religious policy, namely, promotion of Islamic practices, regulations against the Hindus, conversion to Islam and destruction of temples.

His supreme object was to make both Muslim and non-Muslim conform to the orthodox holy law. Hence he issued regulations aiming at suppressing the un-Islamic ceremonies and encouraging Muslim ways among the people at large.

In 1665 restrictions were imposed on the public celebration of the Hindu festivals of Holi and Diwali., In 1668, the Hindu fairs were prohibited in the Empire. In 1665 discriminative duties were imposed upon the Hindus. They were ordered to pay 5% while the Muslim merely 2.5% duty on their goods. In 1667, the Muslims were totally freed form this burden.,

These steps apart from being a source of revenue were intended to pressurise the Hindu into accepting Islam. In addition, Aurangzeb adopted seductive methods to attract the non Muslims to Islam, he offered posts money grants, public honour and even amnesty as rewards for embracing Islam.

Above all Aurangzeb embarked upon the policy of temple demolition; here he displayed his characteristic subtlety of approach. Early in 1659 he declared that his Canon Law prohibited the construction of new temples but did no ordain the demolition of the old ones. Gradually he opened out.

The temples of Somnath were razed to the ground early in his reign. In 1665, he ordered to redemolish the repaired temples of Gujarat which had once been destroyed by him during his viceroyalty of the province. He next ordered the pulling down of all the newly constructed temples in Orissa. In 1669, he fully unmasked himself. In that year he issued a general order for the destruction of the Hindu Schools and temples and the suppression of their teaching and religious practices throughout the Empire several temples pulled down in the wake of this order included those of Malarna and Vishwanath. Thus, within a short span of 11 years, Aurangzeb reversed the liberal and tolerant approach of Akbar, While Akbar's liberalism had secured him the willing co-operation of his people Aurangzeb's bigotry created mounting discontent among the suffering non Muslims.,

Mathura, the birth centre of the Jat rising, suffered heavily in Aurangzeb's reign. This venerated place of Hindu worship was naturally an object of annoyance to Aurangzeb. He appointed Abdun Nabi, "a religious man", as faujdar of the place to "suppress the Hindus". This officer amassed through questionable means, cash worth 93000 mohars and thirteen lakhs of Rupees and valuables worth four and a half Lakhs., Abdun Nabi demolished a temple in the city and upon its ruins erected a Jama Masjid in 1661-1662. Next, in pursuance of Aurangzeb's order, he removed the stone railing of the famous temple of Keshava Rai in 1666.

All these acts must have provoked the Jats further. We know that during the Sultanate danger to or suppression of their religion generated disaffection among them. There is no reason to believe that a more systematic religious persecutions by zealot Aurangazeb did not offend the religious feelings of the Jats.

Generally speaking the Jats have never been orthodox in their religious belief.,, They do not bother about the philosophical or the ethical nuances of religion, but the outward ritualistic aspects do commonly touch them. Hence, measures like the closing of fairs and festivals and desecration of religious places could not but have caused concern among them.,

The religious bigotry of Aurangzeb and the consequent suffering of the non Muslims however had not assumed full proportion by 1668 – 1669. Jiziya, orders for the exclusion of the Hindus from public officers and even the destruction of the temple of Keshava Rai at Mathura followed later. And yet the Jats under Gokula unfurled the banner of revolt.

The 'floating literature' or the" Sakhas "as they are called among the Jats and other local people refers to the visit of Samarth Guru Ram Das, who exhorted the Jats for insurrection.

He urged them to meet excess with excess. He also impressed upon them that tyranny is a sin but to tolerate tyranny is greater sin. Having been urged and inspired by the Guru, Gokula took a vow to save the Hindus from destruction and rose in rebellion.

The Jats being restive, fuel was ready. Only fire was needed and it was according to the "Sakhas" provided by Ram Das.

K.R.Qanuago observes that in the revolt of 1669 "one flare of the might conflagration kindled throughout India by the missionary zeal of the Emperor" and revived the Hindu Nationalism. Thus religious factors played and appreciable part in the Jat Insurrection.

The economic causes although important, may not be over-emphasized. The vices in the operation of the assignment system did not multiply overnight in the reign of Aurangzeb. Their increasing tendency was discernible even before him. But when the tightening grip of Aurangeb threatened the age old democratic and tribal traditions of the Jats, the economic factors made their weight felt heavily.

From the foregoing discussion it may be concluded that the Jat rebellion of 1669 was essentially the result of the political provocation aggravated by the economic discontent and set ablaze by the religious persecution.

The Outbreak of the Rebellion

The year 1669 witnessed, the bursting forth of the pent up fury of the Jats into a very powerful revolt under the inspiring leadership of Gokula, the zamindar of Tilpat. A remarkable feature of this rebellion was its composite character. Though the Jats counted for its majority and provided leadership to it, it consisted of other local people as well such as, Mev, Meena, Ahir, Gujar, Naruka, Panwar and others. The rebels gathered at the village of Sahora (about 6 miles from Mathura). Abdun Nabi, the faujdar of Mathura, attacked them. At first he appeared to be gaining ground, but in the middle of the fighting he was killed on 12 may, 1669 (21st Zil-Hijja, 1079 A.H.).

Overjoyed at this success, Gokula ravaged the paragana and town of Sadabad (24 miles from Mathura) in the Daob. The turbulance spread to Agra District also whereto Radandaz Khan was sent (13 May 1669 – 22nd Zil-Hijja, 1079 A.H.) with a force to put down the rebels. Aurangazeb appointed Saf Shikan Khan as the new faujdar of Mathura. As arms failed to prevail, diplomacy was resorted to. The Mughal government offered to forgive Gokula provided he surrendered his spoils. But Gukula spurned the offer.

On the other side, as the situation was assuming serious proportions, the Emperor had to proceed (28 November- 14th Rajab, 1080 A.H.) in person to the Disturbed area. On his way on 4 December 1669 (20th Rajab, 1080 A.H.) Aurangazeb learnt of the circumstance of rebellion in the villages of Rewara, Chandarakanta and Sarkhud (Sarkharu ?). He dispatched Hasan Ali khan to attack these places.

Till noon the insurgent fought with bows and muskets. Getting desperate thereafter, many of them having performed the jauhar of their women fell upon the Khan, A fierce fight raged till the evening in which many imperialists and 300 rebels were killed. Hasan Ali Khan returned to the Emperor, taking 250 male and female prisoners. Aurangazeb was pleased with his performance. He made him the faujdar of Mathura in place of Saf Shikan Khan who had obviously failed in suppressing the rebels.

Under Hasan Ali Khan, were placed 2,000 barqandaztroops 1000 archers 1000 musketeers 1,000 rocketmen, and 25 pieces of cannons. Amanulla, the faujdar of the environs of Agra, was also ordered to help Hasan Ali. The latter immediately got engaged in quelling the rebellion. In January 1670, Gokula with 20,000 Jat and other followers, rushed forward to face the imperialists at a place 20 miles from Tilpat.

Both the sides suffered many casualties in the battle in which the Jats, despite showing utmost bravery, could not cope with the trained Mughals and their artillery. They retreated to Tilpat. Hasan Ali followed them and besieged the fortalice. Fighting continued for three days in which muskets and bows were used by the contestants. On the fourth day, the royalists charged the besieged from all sides and having made a breach in the walls entered Tilpat. Then ensued a sanguinary conflict.

The Jats displayed their reckless courage and undaunted valour. The experienced Mughals gained the day but not before losing 4,000 men. Of the vanquished 5000 lay dead, while 7000 were arrested. Gokula, with his two associates including " Sonki" (Udai Singh Singhi), was captured alive through the efforts of Shaikh Razi-ud-Din, the peshkar of Hassan Ali. They and other prisoners were presented to the Emperor. Being furious, he ordered Gokula and Singh to be cut limb on the Chabutara of the Kotwali (Agra). Other captives either met fate of their leader or were put in chains.

Aftermath of the Rebellion

Never before in the history of the Mughal Empire had the standard of such a formidable rebellion been raised by the Jats as was done by those of Mathura under Gokula in 1669. Although the rebellion failed, it had considerable though indirect, repercussions upon the future course of the Jat History and in the long run upon the Mughal Empire itself. The crushing defeat of the Jats in 1669 was not without a lesson. It exposed to them certain strategic flaws in their ways of fighting.

They had seen their 20,000 gallant brethren being easily routed by the Mughal forces in a face to face combat. It must have been laid bare to them that, in the absence of proper military training and sufficient equipment their reckless courage and obstinate valour alone would not prove effective against the mighty Mughal army. Besides, the fall of Tilpat within the short duration of three days must have pointed out to them the hopeless vulnerability of their defence and its corresponding implications. The military tactics of Raja Ram and Churaman II clearly indicate that the Jats had benefited from the failure of 1669.

They gradually turned to making a change in their existing military methods. The subsequent Jat leaders grew alive to the efficacy of discipline and proper equipment in warfare. There developed an increasing tendency to build their forts in the fastness of dense Jungles capable of withholding the onslaught of powerful armies. Likewise they avoided the rashness of Gokula in inviting pitched battles with the mighty Mughals.

Gukula's rebellion also gave to the posterity an inspiration of political nature, namely, the usefulness of working under a united leadership.

We know that the Jats had the reputation of being impatient of any external control. Although success did not crown them in 1669, it was perhaps, heartening for them to perceive that their joint efforts could gather so powerful a momentum as to disturb even the Mughal Emperor, compelling him to rush to the disturbed region. On the other hand, it was disheartening to them that the effectiveness of their resistance withered away once their chief leader Gokula was no more.

This seems to have emphasized to the Jats the advantage to working united under a common leader. Although progress in this direction was necessarily slow in due course it proved to be of considerable political importance to them. Once their combined efforts proved fruitful under later leaders and bright future prospects appeared ahead. Their circumstantial union assumed a little fixed character.

Consideration of common benefit might also have been instrumental in leading the tribal and democratic Jats to prefer, accept and finally adopt the institution of kingship. To such circumstances may be traced the genesis of the Jat state of Bharatpur and the eventual emergence of the principalities of Patiala, Nabha and Jhind which were republican until recently.

In the light of the above considerations it seems that from the viewpoint of the long term interests of the Jats, Gokula's abortive exertions were no less significant than the more fruitful struggles of Raja Ram and Churaman II. The brighter careers of these two have dimmed the image of Gokula whose full importance has not been duly appreciated so for. The circumstances in which they worked were not altogether similar. Gokula had to face more formidable odds than the two later fortunate Jat leaders. It is doubtful whether, even with their better organizing capacity their success could have been assured in Gokua's circumstances. It is difficult to resist the conclusion that though Gokula failed, his failure paved the way for the subsequent success of Raja Ram and Churaman II.

Prior to the Jat uprising, other revolt had taken place in a different part of the Empire. But they were not so powerful and the place of their occurrence were comparatively too distant from the capital. The rebellion under Gokula was, however quite different. From the point of view of time, dimension and place it was the first fierce repudiation of the authority of Aurangzeb under his very seat. Though such evidence is not forthcoming, the possibility cannot be ruled out that his audaciousness provided a stimulus to the later rebels such as the Satnamis.

Aurangazeb pursued a course which seems to have estranged the Jats further. He wrecked terrible vengeance upon them. Apart from the treatment meted out to 7,000 captives, the family of their leader, Gokula was forcibly tried to convert to Islam. Even after the fall of Gokula the Mughal forces kept on imprisoning and plundering the Jats. Not content with it, as it were, Aurangzeb broke loose his fury upon the temple of Keshava Rai. It was levelled to the ground (during the month of Ramzan, 1080 A.H. 13 January to 11 February 1670) and mosque was built upon its site.

Its idols were desecrated and later buried under the footsteps of the Begum Sahiba mosque at Agra. The name of Mathura was changed to 'Islamabad' and that of Brindaban to 'Mominabad.' The temples and idols of the rest of the holy places in the Brij were gradually destroyed. This added insult to injury. The affront inflicted upon the families of their leader and kinsmen must have outraged the feelings of the entire tribe in whose social consciousness and tribal sentiments have always been uppermost.

Jat people are normally moderate light-hearted and not unmanageable unless of course when excited. It can hardly be called an act of political wisdom on his part to have tried to put down the warlike and stubborn Jats in ruthless manner.

So long as the Emperor had a firm grip over the north the Jats remained subdued but as soon as it loosened, their pent up fury was let loose and they resumed their lawless course with added vigour. Thus the policy of Aurangzeb towards them defeated its very object and in the long run proved harmful for the Empire. It has been rightly remarked that a little indiscretion and persistence in a wrong policy " converted " peaceful husbandmen (Jats) into flaming warriors as it did friends (Rajputs) into foes.

Unit 37 Potentialities of Capitalistic Development

This is the last U N ~ of your present course @HI-04). By now you must have become intimately familiar with the many facets of Medieval India during the 16th-18th centuries. Here we do not intend to give a resume of the subject-matter of the foregoing Blocks. Instead, we will raise an important question and try to respond to it. We have dispensed with the formal mode of structuring in this Unit so that you read the entire argument in a flow. The question we are going to address here relates to the economic structure of Medieval India.

It has often been asked why India failed to industrialise and evolve a capitalistic economy before the British conquest. In other words, was there any potentiality of emergence of capitalism in Mughal India along the lines of what happened in Europe?

This, query was casually probed by W.H. Moreland (India at the Death of Akbar, London, 1920; From Akbar to Aurangzeb, London, 1923) and Brij Narain (Indian Economic Lib, Past and Present, Lahore, 1929). However, since 19608, there has been a regular debate on this question beginning with Moms D. Morris (1963) and Toru Matsui and followed by Bipn Chandra and Tapan Raychaudhuri (1968). But their views largely dwell on the 19th century India. It will, however, be more fruitful to us if we focus attention on the status of the Mughal economy. A pioneering enquiry on these lines was conducted by Irfan Habib in 'Potentialities of Capitalistic development in the Economy of Mughal.

In fact what we are concered for this Unit is not why a capitalist structure did not emerge during the Mughal period; our query is whether we can see signals of capitalist development within the Mughal economy. Significantly Europe did not possess capitalist economy in the 17th century. Capitalism started emerging, for example in England, from the second half of the 18th century only. It was, by and large, merchant capitalism that prevailed in England at this time, not industrial capitular.

To begin with, we must be clear about what do we understand by the term capitalism. Thereafter we may begin to investigate the presence or absence of its features in Mughal economy. Let us list the most important features of early capitalism:

i) Control of capital over production-processes;
ii) Money or market relations;
iii) "Immense accumulation of commoditiesn (Karl Mark); and
iv) Breakthrough in production-technology.

That the merchants of Medieval India possessed considerable capital cannot be questioned. Estimates of their wealth come from European records. We are told that in 1663 some merchants of Sumit owned more than 5 or 6 million rupees. Mulls Abdul Ghafur of Surat had assets worth 8 million rupees. He also owned twenty ships (bepeen 300 and 800 tons each).

The English factors testify that the volume of his trading transactions was no less than that of their company. Another Surat merchant Viji Von is reproted to have held an "estate" of the value of 8 million rupees. Manrique (1630) was amazed by the immense wealth of the merchants of *Agn;* he saw money piled up in some merchants' houses that "looked like grain heapsn.

Besides, the merchants put their money into commercial circulation. The wealth of the non-mercantilrc groups too was invested in trading ventures. This included the Mughal Emperors, royal ladies, princes and nobles-many of whom had their own ships. True, their investment was less than that of the merchants; but the important point here is that their involvement increased the size of "money-market" in its own way.

The system of credit and banking in Mughal India was well developed. You have already read about the role and functions of the sarrat who acted as a banker remitting money and issuing bills of exchange called hundi (Bolock 6, Unit 24).

The sarraf also discounted the hundb of merchants thus enlarging the volume of money for commerce. Another well-developed financial practice related to the insurance of goods in transit (both inland and marine). Moreover, institutions of money lending (and interest), for commercial purposes including bottomry and respondentia, were also prevalent. Clearly then the basic financial and economic institutions were in operation in good measure during the 17th and 18th centuries.

This may have put the Medieval economy on to the road to capitalism. Again, commodity production was taking place on a vast scale, especially of textiles, saltpetre, indigo, etc. Procurement of these commodities was made easier both for the Indian and foreign merchants by the institution of brokery. Means of transport, too were fairly well-established keeping in view the constraints of Medieval times.

Ture capitalist relations may develop only when capital would dominate and control large areas of production process. This is the principal difference between industrial and merchant capital. The latter is not directly involved with manufacture. In other words, production was not controlled by merchants: it was camed out by independent artisans who owned the tools, invested their money in buying raw material, worked at their respective homes (Domestic Craft System), owned the finished goods and sold the latter at the market. Capitalism destroys all these features, turning the independent artisans into wage-workers. As an upshot, industrial capital takes over gradually the means of production and controls the entire system.

But the changeover from merchant to industrial capitalism was not abrupt or sudden. There was a transitory stage that arose within merchant capitalism itself. It is called putting-out system (you have already read about it in Block 6, Unit 22). 'Therefore, it is pertinent to examine the nature and extent of this tramitory phase in Medieval India, that is, the progressive control of labour and production by capital.

The penetration of merchant capital into the existing artisan-level mode of production could occur through the putting-out system (dadni) which seek to have been quite an established practice, though on a small scale, even prior to the 17th century. The brokers come into the picture because the advances to the primary producers by the merchants were made through them: Let us first set out the economic structure of the putting-out system, That Indian economy during the 17th century was a, sellers' (i.e., producers') market.

There was tremendous demand and the large number of competitive buyers flooding the market. Thus, from the merchants' point of view, especially of those engaged in foreign trade, the putting-out system excluded his rivals and secured him timely delivery of stipulated quantity of commodity in accordance with his specifications at previously agreed rates. On the other hand, the primary producer accepted advance since he had to cope with extensive orders for which he may not have adequate money to buy raw materials.

Thus, the putting-out system rendered economic services to both the merchant and the artisan. In this context, the degree of penetration of merchant capital into the production-process through the putting-out system could be assessed by examining whether the merchant advanced cabs or n w materials (or both) and the tools of production to the artisan. Taking the textile industry, we have adequate evidence for advance being given in cash to infer that it was an established practice. Bult evidence for raw material is quite insufficient o show its wide use, while that for instruments of production is almost negligible.

Here it must be pointed out that the need for giving raw material (yam) to the weavers arose from the cowidention that the yam obtained by weavers themselves was often of inferior quality, even when granted cabs advance. It appears that some profit accrued to the weaver when he himself purchased yarn or raw silk of a quality questionable from the merchants' point of view. Thus it may be reasonably assumed that the weaver did not always welcome the supply of raw material from the merchant as this possibly wiped off the little "cut" they could otherwise get.

This partly explains the scarcity of data on this particular practice, that is, the advance being made in raw material. The same could be said about Gujarat with the difference that probably this practice was adopted on a comparatively large scale than in Bengal. But there is no evidence to convince us that it ever acquired a very dominant form of the putting-out system there.

Even Chicherov, despite his strong advocacy of that development of capitalistic relations, is struck by the scarcity of data on the advancing of raw material, that is, yam, to the weavers. He himself explains that "the supply of raw material's never posed a problem" in the rural areas because "cotton-growing, which was extraordinarily extensive and in some areas almost universal, was a typical economic-geographical feature of India; cotton could be grown on every farm or bought on the nearest market".

He adds, "spinning, widespread not only in the so weavers' home but also in ordinary peasant families, created a constant and vast source of raw materials for the weaving trade". Thus, it may safely be concluded that the most distinguishing feature of the putting-out system during the 17th century was the practice of cash-advance.

From this point we can pass on to the part played by the practice of cash-advance in transforming the relationa of production. Considering the prime motive of giving cash-advances to the artisan, we do not notice any distinct tendency on the part of the merchantry to intervene deliberately in the production process in such a manner as to bring about a radical change in the relations of production.

True, the producer was "tied" to the merchant in the sense that now he was under an obligation to fulfil his commitment, that is, to provide the merchant with the commodity produced by him in accordance with the merchant's specifications within a limited time and at an agreed price. But the artisan a till retained the ownership of the tools of production and in this case raw metals, too. What really happened was that he had merely sold off his produce in return for advance payment out of his free will.

There does not appear to exist any extraordinary economic compulsion (except poverty) for him to accept such orders from the merchant; nor does the latter appears to have employed non-economic coercion to compel him to enter into such a deal. Instead, the merchant had to induce the producer to accept the advance payment in his own interest. For example, in 1665 the English factors wrote from Surat:

> *"Calicoes are soe bought up by the Dutch etc. that we are forced to pray and pay for what we have and take it as a* courtesy *(italics ours) that the weavers will vouchsafe to receive out money 8 and 10 months beforehand, which is the only thing that tyes them to us."*

Here, the merchants felt obliged to the weavers for their acceptance of the advance money. But even this "tie-up" was very slender. In 1647 the English factors at Thatta wrote to Surat:

> *"Besides, those wesvers are a company of base rougues, for, notwithstanding wee give them money aforehand part of the yeare, and that in the time of there greatest want, yet if any*

> *pedling cloth inerchant comes to buy, they leave us and worked for him, though he gives one money aforehand; being the ordinary base make is more facill and easy to weave then ours, with which they must take some paines."*

Again, in 1622, they wrote from Broach: "wee must give out our money beforehand, and receive the proceeds of it at the weavers and brokers pleasure". Thus, it is indeed incongruous and Chicherov talks of "economic bondage",

"economic dependence", "physical coercion" and "merchant monopoly" with regard to the relations between the merchant and the producer during the 17th century. The artisan had merely turned into a "contract-producer" from and "independent" one. True he was no longer the owner of his produce, but he was not yet alienated h m the ownership or raw material and tools of production, long as the artisan worked within the domestic system of craft-production, real capitalistic relations of production could not be generated.

That the putting-out system did not deprive the producer of his tools and often raw material clearly indicates that the control of labour by merchant capital was indeed very weak. Until this alienation took place, commodity-production manufactory or, in other words, aseemblage of large number of workers at one place at the same time for the production of the commodity under a superior capitalist direction could not emerge. But at this stage the putting-out system itself, along with the brokers, would ultimately disappear, yielding place to new relations of production. Nor do we find any evidence for the creation of surplus value, say, through

"depression of wages", during the 17th century so that a part of the labour time could remain unpaid for. Quite obviously in the absence of the exercise of non-economic coercion by the merchants, this was not possible so long as the tools of production were retained by the artisan, working within the domestic system. Since the tools were simple and cheap to be made or purchased and no technological breakthrough was achieved rendering them costlier, beyond the means of an average artisan, the latter was not alienated from them. Here we may recall the observation of Mark:

> *"The process, therefore, that clears the way for the capitalist system, can be none other than the process which takes away from the labourer the possession of his means of production;*

> *a process that transforms, on the one hand, the social means of subsistence and of production into capital; on the other, the immediate producers into wage-labourers."*

However, we do not propose to hold that merchant capital did not exercise any influence on the organization of production. The putting-out system through which it operated did encroach on the "independent" status of the primary producer, transforming him into a "contract-worker". It also cut him off from the market—a process which was inherent m the system itself. Again, the sporadic examples of karkbanas maintained and the dyeing and refining "houses" erected by the foreign merchants in Gujarat and Bengal do indicate the direction of change during the latter half of the 17th century.

Yet these changes were not fundamental nor so widespread as to compel us to discover in them elements which could promote real capitalistic relations. After all these were changes within the existing mode of production, wherein merchant capital had a very feeble hold over the production process. Therefore, it will be incorrect to say that merchant capital "broke through the traditional bonds of production" in 17th century India: it had only nibbled a small part of it, of not much consequence.

It is pertinent to ask why did merchant capital, operating through the putting-out system, fail to exercise any worthwhile control over labour? That the failure did not spring from a lack of its development has been examined by Irfan Habib. We have already suggested that the enlargement of demand and the flooding of the market with a largt: umber of competitive buyers had put the primary producer in a favourable situation; the absence of gny extraordinary economic compulsion or non-economic coercion left the artisan free to strike a deal with whomsoever he considered best.

Another important reason was the coexistence of the independent artisan-level production with the putting-out system (which turned the artisan into a contract labourer) probably on a scale larger than the latter or at least on equal footing. Besides, territorial and occupational mobility of the artisan was yet another factor which often may gave rescued him from falling into "economic bondage" or "dependence" as a result of his poverty, on which Chicherov lays so much stress.

Finally, as we have shown above, the interests of the broker and merchant did not always coincide. The former tried to seize upon and opportunity to get some irregular income through underhand mechanism: his victims were both the producer and the merchant. Thus he did not always act in a manner which could promote the interest of merchant capital; rather he worked sometimes in collusion with the artisan.

All this actuallly strengthens the opinion of Man:

> *"The independent and predominant development of capital a's merchant's capital is tantamount to the non-subjection of production to capital, and hence to capital developing on the basis of an alien social mode of production which is also independent of it. The independent development of merchant's capital, therefore, stands in inverse' proportion, to the general economic development of society."*

Perhaps it would not have been difficult for some merchants, especially for "broker-contractors" (middlemen merchants) who were in close proximity with the production-process, to evolve into manufacturing entrepreneurs: the examples of karkhanas maintained by the Mughal emperors, nobles and occasionally by the foreign companies should have served as models. But a mere change in the organization of production unaccompanied by basic changes in technology could not cut much ice.

7

India-The Roaring Trade Partner of Europe

Right from ancient times till the establishment of the British Empire, India was famed for her fabulous wealth. Even during the medieval period, i.e. roughly from the 12th to the 16th centuries, the country was prosperous despite the frequent political upheavals. A notable feature of this period was the growth of towns in various parts of the country. This development was the result of the political and economic policies followed by the Muslim rulers. These towns grew into trade and industrial centres which in turn led to the general prosperity.

During the Sultanate period, which lasted from the early 13th to the early 16th centuries, the economy of the towns flourished. This was due to the establishment of a sound currency system based on the silver tanks and the copper dirham. Ibn Batuta the 14th century Moorish traveller had visited India during the Sultanate period. He had described the teeming markets of the big cities in the Gangetic plains, Malwa, Gujarat and Southern India. The important centres of trade and industry were Delhi, Lahore, Bombay, Ahmedabad, Sonargaon and Jaunpur. Coastal towns also developed into booming industrial centres with large populations.

During the two hundred years of Mughal rule i.e. from the 16th to the 18th centuries the urbanisation of India received a further impetus. The Mughal era witnessed the establishment of a stable centre and a uniform provincial government. During this age of relative peace and security, trade and commerce flourished. The burgeoning foreign trade led to the development of market places not only in the towns but also in the villages. The production of handicrafts increased in order to keep up with the demand for them in foreign countries.

The prime urban centres during the Mughal era were Agra, Delhi, Lahore, Multan, Thatta and Srinagar in the north. The important cities in the west included Ahmedabad, Bombay (then known as Khambat), Surat, Ujjain and Patan (in Gujarat). The flourishing trade centres in the eastern part of the country were Dacca, Hoogli, Patna, Chitgaon and Murshidabad. Most of these cities boasted of sizeable populations.

Products and Manufactures

The accounts of foreign travellers contain descriptions of the wide variety of exquisite goods sold in the markets of those days. India was famous for its textiles, which formed one of the chief items of export. Duarte Barbosa a Portuguese official in Cochin in the early 16th century described Gujarat, in the western region as a leading cotton trade centre. Textiles from Gujarat were exported to the Arab countries and to South-east Asia. Patola, which is a kind of silk dyed in natural colours, was highly popular in South-east Asia. It was very much in demand among the wealthy classes in Malaysia, Indonesia, and the Phillipines.

In the east Bengal was another important region for a wide variety of textiles. Ibn Batuta the 14th century Moorish traveller saw many cotton trade centres during his sojourn in Bengal. Silks were also manufactured there. The textile products included quilts of embroidered tussar, or munga on a cotton or jute, silk and brocade edged handkerchiefs. Dhaka muslin was renowned for its fineness. Kasimbazaar in Bengal was an important trade centre for cotton and silk goods. Sirbund, a type of cloth used for tying turbans was manufactured in Bengal. It was highly popular in Europe.

Similarly, Malabar in Kerala was also famous for its coloured and printed cloth material. The other important textiles producing centres in the south were Golconda, Shaliat and Pulicat. The last two were major trading centres for a wide variety of cottons. Golconda was famous for its Kalamkaaris. These were finely painted cotton fabrics with motifs from Hindu mythology. They were exported through the port city of Masulipatnam. Palampores, which were another variety of painted fabrics, were popular in the Mughal and Deccan courts. These were bedspreads made of Calico cloth. The borders of these pieces were block printed while the centre depicted deoicted the 'Tree of Life' motif made by hand. Indian textiles whether from Bengal, Gujarat or the South were highly appreciated abroad for their fine texture, elaborate design and brilliant colours.

Hardwood furniture, embellished with inlay work was a very popular item. The furniture was modelled on the European design but the expensive carvings and inlays were inspired by the ornate Mughal style. The production centres were in Sindh, Gujarat and the Deccan. Mother-of pearl inlay against a black lac background was a traditional design in Gujarat.

Carpets were used both in ancient and medieval India but it was in the 16th century during the Mughal era that the skill of carpet weaving touched new heights. It had become an important profession by then and all the major courts of the country encouraged it. The carpets produced during the Mughal era depicted either animals in combat or flowers. The flowers were woven so meticulously that they could be easily identified. The affinity of the Great Mughals with nature is evident from the designs of the carpets made during their times.

Many varieties of ornamental work in cut stones, ivory, pearl and tortoise shells were produced in South India. Pearl fishing was a major industry here. Diamonds were procured from the Deccan while sapphires and rubies were imported from Pegu and Ceylon. Major centres were established at Pulicat, Calicut and Vijaynagar for cutting and polishing these stones.

Indian arts and crafts were patronised by Indian rulers. They were unmatched for their beauty and skill and were popular in the European countries. During the Mughal era the European traders used to employ local artisans at the manufacturing centres set up by them at various places in India.

Domestic Trade

Foreign travellers gave extensive accounts about domestic trade in medieval India. Ibn Batuta had described Delhi as a major trade centre. The most superior quality rice and sugar from Kannauj, wheat from Punjab and betel leaves from Dhar in Madhya Pradesh found their way to the markets of Delhi. Well-maintained roads linking various parts of the country facilitated domestic trade. The threat from bandits did not in any way affect the flow of goods as merchants travelled in well-armed groups to ensure their security. According to Barbosa's account, trade between Gujarat and Malwa was possible owing to the routes established in this area. The roads facilitated the exchange of goods between the different parts of the country. Limbodar in Gujarat and Dabhol in Maharashtra were major trade centres, which linked the northern and southern halves of the country. Accounts of foreign travellers give instances of the trade between Vijaynagar and Bhatkal in Goa with 5000-6000 bulls carrying goods between the two places. Vijaynagar traded in diamonds with other southern cities.

River routes also facilitated trade between different parts of the country. Boats carrying goods used to ply on the Indus and the Ganges. Some of the merchants had their own large boats.

Different communities dominated trade in various parts of the country. Multani and Punjabi merchants handled the business in the north, while in Gujarat and Rajasthan it was in the hands of the Bhats. Foreign traders from Central Asia, known as Khorasanis engaged in this profession all over India. Members of the nobility and the royalty took an interest in trading activities. They set up their own manufacturing centres wherein local artisans were employed.

Internal trade flourished due to the organised system set up by the government. The 14th century Sultan Alauddin Khilji for instance, used to strictly supervise the market places. Shopkeepers, who were caught violating the rules, were severely punished. However, the trading community used to face unfair treatment from the government officials. Sometimes they were forced by these officials to sell their products at reduced rates or on credit, thus incurring heavy losses in the process. The price list fixed by the government brought in low returns for the traders.

During the period of the later Mughals in the 18th century, the royalty and the nobility either purchased luxury goods at very low prices or did not pay at all. Such circumstances forced the trader to hoard his wealth and lead a frugal existence.

Foreign Trade

India's exports far exceeded her imports both in the number of items as well as in volume. The chief articles of import were horses, from Kabul and Arabia, dry fruits and precious stones. India also imported glassware from Europe, high grade textiles like satin from West Asia, while China supplied raw silk and porcelain. Foreign luxury goods were highly popular among the royalty and the nobility. These included wines, dry fruits, precious stones, corals, scented oils, perfumes and velvets.

During the Sultanate period articles of everyday use as well as luxury articles were exported to Syria, Arabia and Persia from Bengal and Cambay. These included silks, gold-embroidered cloth caps, exquisitely designed clay pots and pans, guns, knives and scissors. The other prime articles of export were sugar, indigo, oils, ivory sandalwood, spices, diamonds and other precious gems and coconuts.

Arab traders shipped Indian goods to European countries through the Red Sea and the Mediterranean ports. Indian products were also sent to East Africa, Malaya, China and the Far East. In China, Indian textiles were valued more than silk. Trade was also conducted through overland routes with Afghanistan, Central Asia and Persia. The route lay through Kashmir, Quetta and the Khyber Pass. Iraq and Bukhara were the other countries with which India conducted trade via the land route.

Foreign trade was in the hands of both local and foreign merchants. Many European travellers had settled in the coastal regions. Limbodar in Gujarat was a major exporting centre. Horses imported from Arabia were sent from the port of Bhatkal in Goa to the southern kingdoms. Imports like bronze, iron, wax, gold and wool were brought in through Goa, Calicut, Cochin and Quilon. The traders of Malabar, Gujarat and foreign settlers controlled business in the port cities of Calicut, Khambat, and Mangalore. Chinese ships docked at Quilon and Calicut while in Khambat the volume of trade was such that 3000 ships visited this port annually. This fact gives an idea of the magnitude of India's foreign trade during the medieval period.

Trade with China and Southeast Asia was mainly carried on through the port of Sonargaon now known as Dacca. Vijaynagar, which was the richest and most extensive state in the 15th and 16th centuries, enjoyed the most voluminous maritime trade with diverse countries such as Persia, Arabia, Africa, the Malayan Archipelago, Burma, China and the numerous islands in the Indian

Ocean. The magnitude of trade can be surmised from the fact that there were 300 ports to facilitate the movement of goods. The shipbuilding industry flourished in the coastal towns.

The city of Vijaynagar was a teeming marketplace for both exports and imports. The fabulous wealth of the Empire left the foreigners dumbfounded. The people, irrespective of which strata of society they belonged to, possessed vast quantities of gold, diamonds and material wealth. Domingo Paes described the citizens as being heavily bejewelled. Abdur Razzak, the Khurasani ambassador to the court of Vijaynagar, refers to the treasury which had chambers filled with molten gold.

The merchant community in the other parts of the country was a prosperous lot. The Gujarati and Marwari businessmen who controlled the trade between the coastal towns and North India were extremely wealthy and spent large sums for the construction of temples. The Multanis who were Hindus and the Khurasanis who were Muslim foreigners controlled the trade with Central and West Asia. Many of these Multanis and Khurasanis settled in Delhi where they lived luxurious lives. Cambay was also home to an affluent mercantile community.

Thus India had always enjoyed a favourable balance in her trade relations with other countries. Her earnings from the export of textiles, sugar, spices and indigo alone went up to crores of rupees. The state coffers were amply stocked with gold and silver.

The Decline in Prosperity

However the political conditions in India in the 18th century brought about a sea change in the situation. This period was marked by decline of the Mughal government and the rise of the Maratha power. After Aurangzeb, who was the last of the great Mughal Emperors, the state crumbled and it could not protect the mercantile community as before. Though the regional powers did extend patronage to the artisans and manufacturers, they did not have the economic and military means to sustain it. Consequently trade dwindled. The Maratha invasions in northern India also adversely affected trade and commerce.

The rise of the British East India Company in the mid 18th century dealt a fatal blow to the prosperity of the country. The victory of the English over the Nawab of Bengal at the Battle of

Plassey in 1757 marked a turning point in the fortunes of the country. In order to disrupt the trade relations between the Indian mercantile community and the foreigners, the Company imposed heavy duties on both imports and exports. After the Company had established its supremacy in Bengal, it prevented merchants from Asian countries from coming to the eastern provinces for trading purposes. The export of Indian textiles to England was totally banned.

The Company increasingly monopolised the foreign trade in India thereby reducing the mercantile community to bankruptcy. Not only did it cripple the indigenous manufactures, but also it started importing various items such as cloth, utensils, horses, etc. from England. This so adversely affected the Indian traders that they turned to other professions for their livelihood. The great trading community, which had flourished during the Mughal rule, had dwindled to non-existence by the end of the eighteenth century. Thus the once glorious arts and crafts of India died a natural death.

Trade between Western Europe and the Mughal Empire in the 17th Century

Contact between Western Europe and the Mughal empire was put into practice in the very beginning of the 17th century. The Portuguese, English, and later on, the Dutch were the ones to communicate with the Mughal empire. As the first Islamic power on the Indian subcontinent, the Mughal empire was more interested in assimilating the land, studying the history, customs and religion of the people occupying this area, and communicating with the other two Islamic empires – the Saffavid and the Ottoman Empires.

The Mughal empire was blessed with very strong leaders, however, very different in approach and strategy. Akbar the Great was known for his tolerance towards unorthodox Muslims and Hindus. The Akbarnama, a book written by Abul Fazal on the life and rule of Akbar, gives a lot of evidence on how Hinduism was viewed and explained by the Muslims. Along with being tolerant towards his Hindu and Muslim subjects, Akbar welcomed Portuguese Jesuits, which allowed Portugal to enter the trade with Indian goods. At the very end of his rule, the British, Dutch, and Portuguese started trade with the Mughal empire as well. Even though the trade started during the reign of Akbar the Great, his son Jahangir was the one to strengthen this economic activity in the Indian subcontinent.

Premises of Western Europe for the trade

The English and Dutch were granted 21-year permission of monopoly in the "East Indies", which followed by the retorted answer from the Indian landlords – they encouraged the establishment of coastal posts for trade. Half a century afterwards, the competition for trade in the Indian Ocean was enhanced by the setting up of the French East India Company in 1664. It followed Jean-Baptiste Colbert's theory of Mercantilism that claimed to keep the national exports greater than the imports. In his Memorandum on English Alliances and Memorandum to the King on Finances written in 1669 and 1670 respectively, Jean-Baptiste Colbert defended his theory and tried to figure out a way of how to undercut the Dutch trade.

This document gave evidence on the strength of the Netherlands' trade in the 17th century not only in India but also in the Caribbean. Moreover, it gave the precise numbers of the Dutch superiority over both the British and the French – 15,000 to 16,000 vessels per year versus 3,000 to 4,000 for the British and 500 to 600 for the French. The British managed to increase the trade with textile with 22.7 million square meters over a period of just twenty years. Ironically, they did that in the very same year that France intervened in the Indian trade..

The need for Alcohol Established the First Trading Contacts

One of the items traded was alcohol drinks. During Babur's and Jahangir's reign the trade was especially directed towards alcohol exchange. It probably was the same during the rest of the Great Mughals' reigns but the autobiographies and court chronicles had very little information about this issue. Moreover, these sources cannot be very reliable because the emperors reviewed them. However, there are records and journals written by individuals that were either travelling or were members of the Mughal court, which strongly suggest the overuse of alcohol and its social connection within the people and castes.

The Great Mughals were not only connoisseurs of alcohol, they were often overusing it, too. Jahangir died of alcohol abuse. Alcohol was also considered a gift of goodwill, especially between sailors and merchants. Evidence of that were the records and journals of the British East India company. Its employees often requested for wine supply for themselves and for gifts for the monarch. It was used not only for special occasions but also as a regular act of just revering the emperor. Jahangir was the emperor who was the most associated to alcohol but all the rest of the Great Mughals appreciated it too, with the exception of Jahangir's father Akbar. Wine and alcohol in general was as well used for negotiations and, was therefore a very important part of the trading process.

The Implementation of Trade on the Local Level in India and the Various Trading Posts

The trade in India was implemented mainly on the coast. During the 17th century there were two big Islamic empires between Western Europe and the Mughal empire – the Saffavid and the Ottoman Empires – their trade was implemented only by ships. Therefore, the main ports were on the coast of both the Arabian Sea and the Bay of Bengal with the small exception of Calcutta, located on the bank of river Hooghly, yet still accessible by water.

Bombay and Surat on the Arabian sea coast and Madras (today's Chennai) or - as the British named it - Fort St. George, were the four main locations of Indo-European trade during the 17th century. Trade as a tool for the Early World Globalization was very prosperous and profitable for both the European and the Indian merchants. Consequently, the local Indian landlords gained a lot of power and money.

Since the emperor's power was not as centralized and certainly was not recognized by all of the people of different origin living within the borders of the Mughal empire, the local potentates stood against the emperor and formed autonomous or semiautonomous states. This separation made it easy afterwards for the already penetrated British powers to put the end of the Mughal empire in the mid 19th century.

The Detrimental Outcomes of the Trade on the Mughal Empire

Two and a half centuries of trade between India and Western Europe led to the downfall of an initially agriculturally-orientated empire with strong military forces and tolerance towards its subjects and their different religious beliefs (with the exception of Aurangzeb). All three Islamic empires found either their collapse or a significant weakening by the 19th century. European countries, however, were growing, expanding, developing, coming up with new movements, intentions, technology.

Even though they were essentially separated by the Ottoman and Safavid empire, the common interest, the trade, helped Europe to permanently settle into the Indian lands. The most comprehensive and clear sources about the Mughal empire were the factory records of the British East India company, which suggests that trade was the only way of communication between Western Europe and the Mughal empire. The trade was carried out by the same countries, only there were variations of the proportion of import for those countries, depending on what was going on at that time in Europe and on the alliances the countries tight themselves into.

The pattern of Globalization and World's entanglement was traced in 17th century through trade. This way the European countries found their place in the Mughal empire, gradually gaining more power over the trade and, consequently, over the empire until the British colonized the Indian subcontinent in the 19th century. The European language was primarily spread amongst coastal regions, in particular large trading centres and sometimes throughout big commercial towns which were based inland.

Thomas Roe

Sir Thomas Roe (or Row) (c. 1581 – 6 November 1644) was an English diplomat of the Elizabethan and Jacobean periods. Roe was an accomplished scholar and a patron of learning.

Life

The son of Robert Rowe, and of Elinor, daughter of Robert Jermy of Worstead in Norfolk, he was born at Low Leyton near Wanstead in Essex, and at the age of twelve (1593), matriculated at Magdalen College, Oxford. Shortly afterwards, he joined one of the Inns of Court, and became esquire of the body to Queen Elizabeth I of England. He was knighted by James I in 1605, and became intimate with Henry, Prince of Wales, and also with his sister Elizabeth, afterwards briefly Queen of Bohemia, with whom he maintained a correspondence and whose cause he championed. In 1610 he was sent by Prince Henry on a mission to the West Indies, during which he visited Guiana and the Amazon River. However, he failed then, and in two subsequent expeditions, to discover the gold he was seeking.

In 1614, he was elected Member of Parliament for Tamworth.His reputation resulted mainly from the success of his embassy in 1615-18 to the court at Agra, India of the Great Mogul, Jahangir, the principal object of the mission being to obtain protection for an English factory at Surat. At the Mughal court, Roe became a favourite of Jahangir; indeed, he was his drinking partner. This greatly enhanced Roe's status with the Mughals.

Roe was appointed ambassador to the Ottoman Empire in 1621. He obtained an extension of the privileges of the English merchants, concluded a treaty with Algiers in 1624, by which he secured the liberation of several hundred English captives, and gained the support, by an English subsidy, of the Transylvanian Prince Bethlen Gabor for the European Protestant alliance and the cause of the Palatinate.

Through his friendship with the Ecumenical Patriarch of Constantinople, Cyril Lucaris, the famous *Codex Alexandrinus* was presented to James I, and Roe himself collected several valuable manuscripts which he subsequently presented to the Bodleian Library. 29 Greek and other manuscripts, including an original copy of the synodal epistles of the council of Basle, he presented in 1628 to the Bodleian Library. A collection of 242 coins was given by his widow, at his desire, to the Bodleian Library after his death. He also searched for Greek marbles in behalf of the Duke of Buckingham and the second Earl of Arundel.

In 1629, he was successful in another mission undertaken to arrange a peace between Sweden and Poland. In so doing, he was able to help free Gustavus Adolphus of Sweden to intervene decisively in the Thirty Years War on the side of the Protestant German princes. Roe also negotiated treaties with Danzig and Denmark, returning home in 1630, when a gold medal was struck in his honour. In 1631, he sponsored the Arctic exploration of Luke Fox; Roes Welcome Sound was named in his honor.

In January 1637, he was appointed chancellor of the Order of the Garter, with a pension of £1200 a year.

Subsequently, he took part in the peace conferences at Hamburg, Regensburg and Vienna, and used his influence to obtain the restoration of the Palatinate, the emperor declaring that he had "scarce ever met with an ambassador till now." In June 1640, he was made a privy councillor, and in October was returned to parliament as member for the University of Oxford, where his unrivaled knowledge of foreign affairs, commerce and finance, together with his learning and eloquence, gained for him in another sphere considerable reputation.

He married Eleanor, daughter of Sir Thomas Carr of Stamford

Peter Mundy

Life

He came from Penryn in Cornwall. In 1609 he accompanied his father to Rouen, and was then sent to Gascony to learn French. In May 1611 he went as a cabin-boy in a merchant ship, and gradually rose in life until he became of independent circumstances.

Mundy's drawing of the Ascension Flightless Crake, now extinct.

He visited Constantinople, returning to London overland, and afterwards made a journey to Spain. On 6 March 1628 he left Blackwall for Surat, where he arrived on 30 September 1628. In November 1630 he was sent to Agra, and remained there until 17 December 1631, when he proceeded to Puttana on the borders of Bengal. He returned to Agra and Surat, and leaving the latter in February 1634, arrived off Dover on 9 September 1634. This portion of his travels is contained in the Harleian MS. 2286, and in the Addit. MSS. 19278-80.

He went on further voyages to India, China, and Japan, when he started from the Downs on 14 April 1636. The fleet of four ships and two pinnaces were sent out by Sir William Courten, and Mundy seems to have been employed as a factor.

His journals end somewhat abruptly, but a manuscript in the Rawlinson collection at the Bodleian Library continues the narrative of his life, including journeys to Denmark, Prussia, and Russia, which lasted from 1639 to 1648. Mundy himself made the drawings for the volume and traced his routes in red on the maps of Hondius.

Francois Bernier

Francois Bernier (1625–1688) was a French physician and traveller, born at Joue-Etiau/Anjou. For 12 years he was the personal physician of the Mughal emperor Aurangzeb.

His 1684 publication *Nouvelle division de la terre par Les differences especes ou races qui rehabilitant* is considered the first published post-Classical classification of humans into distinct races. He also wrote *Travels in the Mughal Empire*, which is mainly about the reigns of Dara Shikoh and Aurangzeb. It is based on his own extensive journeys and observations, and on information from eminent Mughal courtiers who had witnessed the events at first hand.

Life

A son of farmers, Francois Bernier, was orphaned very young and was cared for by his uncle, the cure de Chanzeaux. At age 15, he moved to Paris to study at the College de Clermont (the future Lycee Louis-le-Grand) where he was invited to stay at the home of his younger friend Chapelle, the natural son of Luillier who was a counsellor at the parliament in Metz. There Bernier most probably met Cyrano de Bergerac and Moliere, and certainly the philosopher Pierre Gassendi (1592-1655), whose aide and secretary he became.

In 1652 during a prolonged stay with Gassendi in the south of France, he managed to become a medical doctor on the strength of a speed-course at the famous Faculte de Montpellier: an intensive three-month course gave the medical degree providing one did not practice on French national territory.

Liberated from his ties to France by the death of Gassend in 1655, he set out on his twelve-year journey to the East, at 36 years of age: Palestine, Egypt, one year in Cairo, Arabia, and an attempt to enter Ethiopia which was frustrated by civil war in the interior. In 1658 he debarked at Surat in India, in Gujarat state. Attached at first and for a short while to the retinue of Dara Shikoh – the history of whose downfall he was to record – he was installed as a medical doctor at the court of Aurangzeb, the last of the great Mughal emperors.

A tour of inspection by Aurangzeb (1664-1665) gave Bernier the opportunity to describe Kashmir, the first and for a long time the only European to do so. In: "Voyages de F. Bernier (angevin) contenant la description des Etats du Grand Mogol, de l'Indoustan, du royaume de Kachemire" (David-Paul Maret ed., Amsterdam, 1699). He subsequently visited the other extreme of the empire in Bengal. European medical training was highly esteemed amongst the Mughal and gave him access to all ranks of the court, even on medically required occasions to the Emperor's harem.

After his return from Kashmir, he travelled around on his own, meeting with Jean-Baptiste Tavernier in Bengal and — while preparing for a journey to Persia at Surat — with Jean Chardin, that other great traveller in the Orient (1666).

He returned once more to Surat (1668) to write a memory on Indian commerce for the use of Jean-Baptiste Colbert. In 1669 Bernier left India for Paris, to stay. In 1671 he almost was jailed for writing in defense of the ideas of Rene Descartes, against whom a judicial arrest had been issued — an exploit he followed with an "Abrege de la Philosophie de Gassendi", also not a subject to arouse official approval (1674). Meanwhile he was a favoured guest at some of the great literary salons, for example that of Marguerite de la Sabliere, who introduced him to Jean de La Fontaine; or at that of Ninon de Lenclos. (His much-debated text on "races" — "A New Division of the Earth", of which the second half is dedicated to feminine beauty — may be read against this background.) In 1685 Bernier visited London where he met with some famous exiles from France: Hortense Mancini, Duchesse de Mazarin, niece of the redoubtable Cardinal; Saint-Evremond; others. He returned to Paris via the Netherlands, where he probably visited his philosophical correspondent Pierre Bayle.

Bernier died in 1688, the year that saw the publication of his "Lettre sur le quietism des Indes".

Foremost among his correspondents while he was in India had been Jean Chapelain, who shipped him crates of books, Melchisedech The venot, and Francois de La Mothe-Le-Vayer. From Chapelain's correspondence we know of a link with the elder Petis de la Croix, whose son Francois Petis de la Croix was sent on a language course to Persia two years after Bernier's return from India.

Note: this description of the life of Francois Bernier is abstracted from a French introduction by France Bhattacharya to an edition of "Voyage dans Les Etats du Grand Mogol" (Paris: Fayard, 1981).

Danishmand Khan

In India, Bernier came under the protection of Daneshmand Khan, an important official at the court of Aurangzeb. Mullah Shafiai was secretary of state for foreign affairs, grand master of the horse, later treasurer (Mir Bakshi) and governor of Delhi (died 1670). Bernier and Daneshmand seem to have been on terms of mutual esteem, and Bernier always refers to him as "my Agha".

Two excerpts from "Travels in the Mughal Empire" illustrate the interchange that followed. The importance of the detail could only fully be appreciated in the last decades of the 20th century, following the contributions by Henry Corbin and Seyyed Hossein Nasr to the history of Islamic philosophy.

A candidate for becoming Bernier's "pandit" probably would have come from the circle around Hindu scholars such as Jagannatha Panditaraja, who still was at work under Shah Jahan, or Kavindracharya, who taught Dara Sikhoh Sanskrit. His intellectual partner could be someone like Zulfaqar Ardistani (died 1670), author of the *Dabistan-i Mazahib*, an overview of religious diversity (Jewish, Christian Buddhist, Hindu, Muslim...). He was educated perhaps by Mir Abul-Qasim Astrabadi Findiriski a link between the religious tolerance aspect of the great project of Persian translations, initiated by Akbar and continued by his great-grandson Dara Shikoh, and the School of Isfahan near the end of the Safavid reign; or perhaps he was educated by Hakim Kamran Shirazi, to whom Mir Findiriski referred as "elder brother", who studied Christian theology and the Gospel under Portuguese priests, travelled to India to study Sanskrit Shastra, lived with the yogi Chatrupa at Benares, and died, chanting the liberation of the philosophers, at the age of 100. Those were scholars who had a knowledge of Greek peripatetic philosophers (mashshaun, falasifa— in the Arabic translations), as well as respect for Ibn Sina and Shihabuddin Yahya Suhrawardi Maqtul (Hikmat al Ishraq).

France Battacharya notes that she removed, in her critical edition based on the 1724 edition, the chapter "Lettre a Chapelle sur less atomes" — as being not so relevant to the context.

Francois Bernier developed a racial classification system in his *New division of Earth by the different species or races which inhabit it.* He declared in this paper that Native Americans, North Africans and South Asians have little physical dissimilarities from Europeans other than their dark skin. He is counted as one of the first anthropologists to specify race using physical characteristics.

Jean-Baptiste Tavernier

Jean-Baptiste Tavernier (1605 – July 1689) was a French traveller and pioneer of trade with India, born in Paris, where his father Gabriel and uncle Melchior, Protestants from Antwerp, pursued the profession of cartographers and engravers.

The conversations he heard in his father's house inspired Tavernier with an early desire to travel, and in his sixteenth year he had already visited England, the Low Countries and Germany, and seen something of war with the imperialist Colonel Hans Brenner, whom he met at Nuremberg. Four and a half years in the household of Brenner's uncle, the Viceroy of Hungary (1624-29), and a briefer connection in 1629 with the Duke of Rethel and his father the duke of Nevers, prince of Mantua, gave him the habit of courts, which was invaluable to him in later years; and at the defense of Mantua in 1629, and in Germany in the following year with Colonel Walter Butler (afterwards notorious through the death of Wallenstein), he gained some military experience.

In The Six Voyages Tavernier states that he departed from Butler's company (1630) with the intention to travel to Ratisbon (Regensburg) to attend Ferdinand III investiture as King of Romans. However, the actual investiture did not take place until 1636. It is probable, therefore, that he actually attended the ceremony between his first and second voyages. By his own account he had seen Italy, Switzerland, Germany, Poland and Hungary, as well as France, England and the Low Countries, and spoke the principal languages of these countries.

He was now eager to visit the East; and at Ratisbon he, with the help of Pere Joseph, Cardinal Richelieu's agent and *Eminence gris* he was able to join the retinue of a pair of French travelers, M. de Chapes and M. de St Liebau, who had received a mission to the Levant. In their company he reached Constantinople early in 1631, where he spent eleven months, and then proceeded by Tokat, Erzerum and Erivan to Persia. His farthest point in this first journey was Isfahan; he returned by Baghdad, Aleppo, Alexandretta, Malta and Italy, and was again in Paris in 1633. Of the next five years of his life nothing is known with certainty, but it was possibly during this period that he became controller of the household of the duke of Orleans. He certainly claimed the Duke's patronage twice in his *Le Six Voyages*. In September 1638 he began a second journey (1638-43) by Aleppo to Persia, and thence to India as far as Agra and Golkonda.

His visit to the court of the Great Mogul-Emperor Shah Jahan at the time-and to the diamond mines was connected with the plans realized more fully in his later voyages, in which Tavernier travelled as a merchant of the highest rank, trading in costly jewels and other precious wares, and finding his chief customers among the greatest princes of the East. The second journey was followed by four others. In his third (1643-49) he went as far as Java, and returned by the Cape; but his relations with the Dutch proved not wholly satisfactory, and a long lawsuit on his return yielded but imperfect redress.

During his last two voyages, 1657-1662, 1664-1668) he did not proceed beyond India. The details of these voyages are often obscure; but they completed an extraordinary knowledge of the routes of overland Eastern trade, and brought the now famous merchant into close and friendly communication with the greatest Oriental potentates. They also secured for him a large fortune and great reputation at home. He was presented to Louis XIV, in whose service he had travelled sixty thousand leagues by land, received letters of nobility (on 16 February 1669), and in the following year purchased the barony of Aubonne, near Geneva. In 1662 he had married Madeleine Goisse, daughter of a Parisian jeweller.

Thus settled in ease and affluence, Tavernier occupied himself, as it would seem at the desire of the king, in publishing the account of his journeys. He had neither the equipment nor the tastes of a scientific traveller, but in all that referred to commerce his knowledge was vast and could not fail to be of much public service. He set to work therefore with the aid of Samuel Chappuzeau, a French Protestant *litterateur*, and produced a *Nouvelle Relation de l'Interieur du Serail du Grand Seigneur* (4 to, Paris, 1675), based on two visits to Constantinople in his first and sixth journeys.

This was followed by *Le Six Voyages de J. B. Tavernier* (2 vols. 4 to, Paris, 1676) and by a supplementary *Recueil de Plusieurs Relations* (4 to, Paris, 1679), in which he was assisted by a certain La Chapelle. This last contains an account of Japan, gathered from merchants and others, and one of Tongking, derived from the observations of his brother Daniel, who had shared his second voyage and settled at Batavia; it contained also a violent attack on the agents of the Dutch East India Company, at whose hands Tavernier had suffered more than one wrong. This attack was elaborately answered in Dutch by Havan Quellenburgh (*Vindicfie Batavicae,* Amst., 2684), but made more noise because Arnauld drew from it some material unfavourable to Protestantism for his *Apologie pour less Catholiques* (1681), and so brought on the traveller a ferocious onslaught in Jurieu's *Esprit de M. Arnauld* (2684). Tavernier made no reply to Jurieu.

The closing years of Tavernier's life are obscure; the time was not favourable for a Protestant. In 1684 Tavernier travelled to Brandenburg at the request of the Elector Fredrick William to discuss the Elector's scheme to charter his own East India Company. The scheme, unfortunately, came to nothing.

In 1679 Louis XIV began to seriously undermine his Protestant subjects. He established the Bureau of Conversion to reward Catholic converts. In January 1685, Tavernier managed to sell his Chateau Aubonne to Marquis Henri du Quesne for 138,000 livres plus 3,000 livres for horses and carriages. His timing was good, In October of the same year, Louis XIV repealed the Edict of Nantes. Louis then instituted the Verification of Nobility which deprived non-Catholics of noble titles.

In 1687, despite an edict prohibiting Protestants from leaving France, he left Paris ant travelled to Switzerland, in 1689 he passed through Berlin and Copenhagen and entered Russia on a passport from the King of Sweden, perhaps with the intent of travelling overland to India. It is not known if he met with Czar Peter who was just 17 years old at that time. Tavernier died in Moscow in July 1689 at the age of 84. It appears that he had still business relations in the East; but the true reason for the final journey of this indefatigable old man remains a mystery.

Tavernier's travells, though often reprinted and translated, have a defect: the narrative is much confused by his plan of often deserting the chronological order and giving instead notes from various journeys about certain routes. It is true that this defect, while it makes the biographer's task more difficult, is hardly a blemish in view of the object of the writer, who sought mainly to furnish a guide to other merchants. A careful attempt to disentangle the thread of a life still in many parts obscure has been made by Charles Joret, *Jean-Baptiste Tavernier dapres des Documents Nouveaux*, 8vo, Paris, 1886, where the literature of the subject is fully given.

For the 400th anniversary of Tavernier's birth in 2005, the Swiss filmmaker Philippe Nicolet made a full-length film about him called *Les voyages en Orient du Baron d'Aubonne*. Another Swiss, the sculptor Jacques Basler, has made a life-sized bronze effigy of the great 17th-century traveller which looks out over Lake Geneva at Chexbres.

Niccolo Manucci

Ne a Venise et fils de broyeur depices, Manucci decide a quinzeans, en 1653, dembarquer pour Smyrne. Pris sous son aile par Henry Bard, ambassador anglais de Charles II aupres du Chah de Perse et de l'Empereur des Indes, il poursuit sa route au-dela de Smyrne pendant plus de deux ans, par la Turquie et la Perse, jusqua Bandar Abbas puis Surat. Il parcourt l'Inde, offrant ses services comme mercenaire dans larmee de Dara Shikoh de 1656 a 1659, puis aupres de Jai Singh et de son fils Kirat Singh. Vers 1670, ilabandonne cette carriere militaire et pratique la medicine, apres en avoid appris Les rudiments lors d'un sejour chez Les Jesuites de Delhi. Apres setre dabord etabli a son compte a Lahore, il entre au service de Shah Alam, ne parvenant des lors pas a lui echapper malgre plusieurs tentatives. Il exerce cependant aussi des activites de negociant et d'agent diplomatique.

Tansen

Miyan Tansen or Ramtanu Pandey (1493 or 1506 – 1586 or 1589) is considered among the greatest composer-musicians in Hindustani classical music. He was an extraordinarily gifted vocalist, known for a large number of compositions, and also an instrumentalist who popularized and improved the rabab (of Central Asian origin).

He was among the Navaratnas (nine jewels) at the court of the Mughal Emperor Akbar. Akbar gave him the title *Miyan* (an honorific, meaning learned man).

Early Life and Background

Tansen as a historical personality is difficult to extract from the extensive legend that surrounds him. It is reasonably certain that he was born into a Hindu Brahmin family, possibly in 1506, though some legends give it as 1493; possibly in the village Behat near Gwalior. His father Mukund Mishra was a poet and accomplished musician, who for some time was a temple priest in Varanasi. Tansen's name as a child was Ramtanu (he may have had other nicknames/names like Tanna and Mukul).

He was born at a time when a number of Persian and Central Asian motifs were fusing with Indian classical music, his influence was central to creating the Hindustani classical ethos as we know today. A number of descendants and disciples have also considerably enriched the tradition. Almost all gharanas of Hindustani classical music claim some connection with the Tansen lineage.

According to legend, he was noted for his imitations of animal calls and birdsong.

Career

At some point, he was discipled for some time to Swami Haridas, the legendary composer from Vrindavan and part of the stellar Gwalior court of Raja Mansingh Tomar (1486-1516 AD), specializing in the dhrupad style of singing. One legend has that Haridas was passing through the forests when the five-year old Ramtanu's imitation of a tiger impressed the musician saint. Another version is that his father sent him to Haridas. From Haridas, Tansen acquired not only his love for dhrupad but also his interest in compositions in the local language. This was the time when the Bhakti tradition was fomenting a shift from Sanskrit to the local idiom (Brajbhasa and Hindi), and Tansen's compositions also highlight this trend. At some point during his apprenticeship, Tansen's father died, and he returned home, where it is said he used to sing at a local Shiva temple. In any event, Tansen went to Muhammad Ghaus who eventually became his spiritual mentor. He also married Husseini (lit. *beautiful one*),

> *"However, beyond a reference of Tansen's name in a list of his disciples Miyan Tansen's name is not found among the names of the Mureeds (Fans) of the Shuttari Tariqat-a Sufi spiritual lineage founded by Shaykh Muhammad Ghaus of Gwalior."*

The burial of Tansen in his shaykh's mausoleum is thought to indicate proof of his conversion to the faith of his spiritual guide. Usually, the most prominent disciples of a saint are buried near the master's mausoleum, not much historical detail is known about their actual encounter.

The interaction with Ghaus in the Sufi tradition and the earlier training with Swami Haridas in the Bhakti tradition led to a fusion of these streams in the work of Tansen. As it is, the mystic streams of Sufism and Bhakti had considerable philosophical and stylistic overlap; Ghaus in his text *Bahr-ul-Hayat* (Ocean of Life) devotes several chapters to Yoga practices. In Tansen's music, we find he continues to compose in Brajbhasha invoking traditional motifs such as Krishna or Shiva.

Tansen was also influenced by other singers in the Gwalior court and also the musically proficient queen, Mriganayani (lit *doe-eyed*), whose romance with the king had been forged on her singing; she remained a friend even after the death of the king. Other musicians at Gwalior may have included Baiju Bawra.

Eventually, he joined the court of King Ramachandra Baghela of Rewa, India, where he remained from 1555-1562. It appears that the Mughal emperor Akbar heard of his prowess and sent his emissary Jalaluddin Qurchi to Ramachandra, who had little choice but to acquiesce, and Tansen went to Akbar's court in 1562.

Another legend is that Akbar's daughter Meherunnissa was enamoured by Tansen and had a role in his coming to Akbar's court. Tansen later converted to Islam from Hinduism, apparently on the eve of his marriage with Akbar's daughter.

Tansen joined Akbar's court eventually becoming one of the treasured Navaratnas (lit *nava*=nine, *ratna*=jewel) of his court. It was Akbar who gave him the honorific title *Miyan*, and he is usually referred to today as Miyan Tansen. Legend has it that in his first performance, he was gifted one lakh (100,000) gold coins.

The presence of musicians like Tansen in Akbar's court has been related by historians to the theoretical position of making the empire's audible presence felt among the population, a mechanism related to *Naubat* or ritual performance.

The fort at Fatehpur Sikri is strongly associated with Tansen's tenure at Akbar's court. Near the emperor's chambers, a pond was built with a small island in the middle, where musical performances were given. Today, this tank, called *Anup Talao*, can be seen near the public audience hall *Diwan-i-Aam*-a central platform reachable via four footbridges. It is said that Tansen would perform different ragas at different times of day, and the emperor and his select audience would honour him with coins.

Family

Tanras Khan, Bilas Khan, Hamirsen, Suratsen and Saraswati Devi, all musicians. Bilas Khan is said to have created raga Bilaskhani Todi after Tansen's death; an interesting legend of this improvisation, has it that Bilas composed it while grief-stricken at the wake itself, and that Tansen's corpse moved one hand in approval of the new melody.

Tansen's blood descendants – the Senia gharana-held considerable prestige in musical circles for several centuries. The royal courts of Rewa, India, Rampur and Jaipur among others, retained many noted members of Tansen lineage, including Nayak Wazir Khan (guru of Allauddin Khan) and Mohammed Ali Khan. Wazir Khan, who is of Saraswati Devi lineage, was also a musicologist who wrote the *Risala Mousibi*. One of the last of the line, Dr. Dabir Khan, (1905-1972, Saraswati Devi lineage) was a dhrupadiya and a beenkar, at Radio Calcutta.

Musical Legacy

The legendary musical prowess of Tansen surpasses all other legends in Indian and Pakistani music. In terms of influence, he can be compared only to the prolific sufi composer Amir Khusro (1253-1325), or to bhakti tradition composers such as Kabir or Haridas. The sitar is said to have been invented by Amir Khusro (1253-1325), a devotee of the Chistiyya order, after the Persian 'Setar', from the saz group of musical instruments

Several of his raga compositions have become mainstays of the Hindustani/Ancient Pakistani tradition, and these are often prefaced with *Miyan ki* ("of the Miyan"), e.g. Miyan ki Todi, Miyan ki Malhar, Miyan ki Mand, Miyan ka Sarang; in addition he is the creator of major ragas like Darbari Kanada, Darbari Todi, and Rageshwari.

Tansen also authored *Sangeeta Sara* and *Rajmala* which constitute important documents on music.

Almost every gharana (school) tries to trace its origin to him, though some try to go further back to Amir Khusro. As for the Dhrupad style of singing, this was formalized essentially through the practice by composers like Tansen and Haridas, as well as others like Baiju Bawra who may have been a contemporary.

After Tansen, some of the ideas from the rabab were fused with the traditional Indian stringed instrument, veena; one of the results of this fusion is the instrument sarod, which does not have frets and is popular today because of its perceived closeness to the vocal style.

The famous qawwals, the Sabri Brothers of Pakistan claim lineage from Miyan Tansen

Legends

The bulk of Tansen's biography as it is handed down in the musical literature consists of legends.

Among the legends about Tansen are stories of his bringing down the rains with Raga Megh Malhar and starting fires with the legendary raga Deepak. Other legends tell of his ability to bring wild animals to listen with attention (or to talk their language). Once, a wild white elephant was captured, but it was fierce and could not be tamed. Finally, Tansen sang to the elephant who calmed down and the emperor was able to ride him.

Many aficionados are convinced that his death was caused by a conflagration while he was singing the raga Deepak.

Tansen is considered to be one of the greatest musicians that ever lived. He was the court musician of the famous Mogul Emperor Akbar (16th century). He was so highly valued in the court that he was called one of the "Nine Jewels" in his court *(navarathna).*

He was born in a Hindu community and had his musical training under the great Swami Haridas. He then went to the court of the Raja Ram Baghela, a great patron of the arts. From there he migrated to the court of Akbar.

It is said that Tansen could work miracles with his singing. This is called *nada siddha* in Sanskrit. He is supposed to have acquired such supernatural abilities through the association with the saintly Swami Haridas. It is said that on occasion he could create rain by singing the monsoon *rag Megh Malhar*. It is also said that he could create fire by singing *rag Dipak*.

Baiju Bawra

Baiju Bawra or Baijnath Prasad or Baijnath Mishra (1542-1613) was an Indian dhrupad singer. He was the court musician of Raja

Mansingh of Gwalher, now Gwalior, along with Nayak Charju, Bakshu, and others. Much of the information on Baiju Bawra is legendary and not historically verifiable.

Early Life

Bawra was born in either Chanderi (in Gwalior) or in Champaner (in Gujarat) on Sharad Purnima in the month of Ashwini in 1599 according to Vikram Samvat calendar (1542 CE). He was called Bawra (crazy) because he was insanely in love with a dancer in Chanderi. Baiju learnt Dhrupad music in Dagurvaani in Vrindavan.

Career

Bawra was a musician at the court of the Raja of Chanderi (now in the Guna District of Madhya Pradesh). Later, he became a musician at the court of Raja Mansingh of Gwalher (modern Gwalior in Madhya Pradesh). Sultan Bahadur Shah of Gujarat had also patronized Baiju.

Like Tansen, the musician at the court of Mughal Emperor Akbar, Bawra was a disciple of Swami Haridas (1512-1607). According to another legend, he was a contemporary of Amir Khusro.

According to historical books preserved in Jai Vilas Mahal in Gwalior, he would light oil lamps by singing Raga Deepak, make it rain by singing the ragas Megh, Megh Malhar, or Gaud Malhar, and bloom flowers by singing raga Bahar.

Contemporary Singers

Besides Tansen, renowned singers, Baba Ram Das, who composed raga Ramdasi Malhar, and Nayak Charju, who composed raga Charju ki Malhar, were Baiju's contemporaries.

Historian Abul Fazal at Emperor Akbar's court and historian Faqirullah at Emperor Aurangzeb's court have written that Baiju defeated Tansen in a singing competition at the court of Akbar. Tansen then touched Baiju's feet and asked for his own life. In response, kind-hearted Baiju went back to Gwalior.

Gopal Nayak, a court musician in the state of Kashmir, India, was a student of Baiju. The king of Kashmir challenged Baiju against Gopal Nayak. Baiju sang raga Bhimpalasi. Instead of singing in response, feeling overwhelmed, Gopal Nayak cried in the court.

After this defeat, Gopal died and his body was cremated on the bank of river Satluj. When the bones in Gopal's body were thrown in the river following the cremation, they sank. According to a legend, Gopal's widow then asked Baiju to retrieve her husband's bones. Responding, Baiju taught a new version of Malhar to her daughter, Meera, and after a week's training, Meera sang that raga on the bank of Satluj in front of a crowd. As soon as she finished the Dhrupad, her father's bones emerged on the bank out of the river. From that time on, that raga is known as Meera ki Malhar.

Swami Haridas

Swami Haridas was a spiritual poet and classical musician. Credited with a large body of devotional compositions, especially in the Dhrupad style, he is also the founder of the Haridasi school of mysticism, still found today in North India. His work influenced both the classical music and the Bhakti movements of North India, especially those devoted to Krishna's consort Radha. He is accounted a follower of the Nimbarka Sampradaya, the major Vaisnava tradition of exclusive devotion to Radha-Krishna. He was the disciple of Purandara Dasa and the teacher of Tansen.

Biography

The details of Haridas's life are not well known. According to one school of thought he was born in 1480 in Rajpur, near Brindavan. His father's name was Gangadhar and his mother's name was Chitra Devi. In this version of his life story Haridas is said to have died in 1575. A second school holds that Haridas's father was a Saraswat Brahmin from Multan and that his mother's name was Ganga Devi. The family migrated to a village called Khairwali Sarak, near Aligarh in Uttar Pradesh. Haridas was born there in 1512 and the village is now called Haridaspur in his honor. This school holds that he died in 1607.

Swami Haridas spent some time at the Gwalior court of Raja Mansingh Tomar, whose patronage of Hindustani classical music, and particularly the dhrupad style, left an indelible mark in the period c. 1485-1510. In Tomar's court were a galaxy of musicians such as Bhanu and Baiju Bawra and he was eulogised by Tansen. Haridas was in his element at the court, and composed a large number of songs in Brij Bhasha and Hindi.

He was deeply learned and widely acquainted with the music

of his time. Mention is found in his works of stringed instruments such as the kinnari and aghouti, and of drums such as the mridanga and daff. He mentions the *ragas* of Kedar, Gauri (raga), Malhar and Basant. Swami Haridas is said to have been the teacher of Tansen, one of the 'nine gems' of Akbar's court, and the renowned dhrupad singer and composer Baiju.

He later shifted his residence to Vrindavan, the playground of the immortal cowherd Krishna and his lover Radha. There he built his *ashram* (hermitage) in Nidhivan and sang his songs of the love of Radha-Krishna. Following the example of Swami Shribhatta, Haridas continued to praise the Lord until the Lord manifested himself. Swami Haridas' spiritual disciples included Vitthal and Krishna Das who fostered his tradition of devotional music. Groups (*samaj*, like the *sankeertan* of Bengal and the *bhajana goshti* of South India) of devotees came together and sang of the Lord of Vrindavan.

His samadhi (tomb) is still in Nidhivan, Vrindavan. He is sometimes said to have been the incarnation of Lalita Sakhi, the legendary friend who consoled Radha in her lovelorn state.

Songs of Swami Haridas

Haridas's compositions may be classed as Vishnupadas. Even his *prabandhas* that do not refer to Krishna have come to be known as Vishnupadas, perhaps because of the mystic source of his music but also because they are musically constructed in a manner similar to dhrupads. He is also said to have written *tirvats*, *ragamalas* and other forms. There are around 128 compositions attributed to him, of which eighteen are philosophical (*siddhanta pada*) and a hundred and ten devotional (*keli mala*).

He describes Radha and Krishna's sporting beautifully:

Swami Haridas belonged to the tradition of *madhura bhakti*-Adoration expressed in conjugal imagery. Haridas's theology embraces not merely the Love of Krishna and Radha but also the witnessing of the Love, a state of mind called rasa. In an ecstatic condition of trance he sings of the play of Krishna among the bowers of Vrindavan. More than Krishna, Radha was the central personality of all his poems.

8

Mughal Music

During the Mughal rule in India, Indian Classical music emerged as two separate traditions-north Indian Hindustani and the south Indian Carnatic, mainly because of the Islamic influence.

The Hindustani system may be thought as a mixture of traditional Indian musical concepts and Persian performance practice. Many new musical forms like Khayal and Ghazal, and new instruments like Sitar, Sarod and Tabla emerged under the Mughal Rule.

Dhrupad, the earliest form of Hindustani music, which emerged around 13th century, reached its pinnacle during the reign of Akbar. The Khayal form of music can be thought of as the ultimate blending of Indian musical theory and Persian musical expression. The concept of a 'Raag' was made popular during the Mughal rule.

Music in Mughal India

Tansen the famous singer at Akbar's court is credited with having enriched the Hindustani school by composing many new melodies or ragas. One of the most popular of these was the raga Darbari. Jahangir and ShahJahan continued patronizing music in the royal court. New styles of singing such as the khayal and thumri became popular. However music in all forms continued to be patronized by Aurangzeb's queens and by the nobles. That is the reason for largest number of books on classical Indian music in Persian were written during Aurangzeb's reign. But some of the most important developments in the field of music took place only in the 18th century during the reign of Muhammad Shah.

Tansen

Considered as the greatest musician in India, Tansen (1506-1589) is instrumental in the creation of the classical music that dominates the north of India. He was considered as one of the Navaratnas (Nine Gems) in the court of Emperor Akbar. Tansen was born in a Hindu family in a place called Gwalior located in Madhya Pradesh. His father was a famous poet by the name of Mukund Mishra. Tansen was named Tannu Mishra when he was born. To know more about the fascinating life history of this great musician, go through this biography of Mian Tansen.

He received the prefix "Mian" from Emperor Akbar. As a young boy, Tansen learnt music from his Guru, Shri Haridas Swamy. He was considered to be a legendary teacher of that time. It is said that Tansen has no equal apart from his teacher. Such was his passion for music that he is said to have performed astonishing miracles merely by singing. He could bring rain by singing in a particular Raag known as Megh Malhar. Similarly he could start a fire by singing in Raag Deepak. He has also composed several Ragas that have been the foundation of classical music like Bhairav, Darbari Todi, Darbari Kanada, Malhar, Sarang and Rageshwari.

There is no particular evidence of the origin of each and every school of music. Since he is the greatest musician, every school of music tries to trace its origin from him. The Dhrupad style of music is likely to have been started by him and his Guru. Some of his important works on music are the Rajmala and Sangeet Sara. Such was the power of his music that when he used to sing in the court of Akbar, candles used to light up automatically. Even today, Tansen is considered to be the greatest of all and there is no comparison when it comes to his style of singing. His contribution to the world of music is priceless and is still worshipped by leading singers and composers of the world.

Persian Influence on Mughal Music

The advent of Islamic rule under the Delhi Sultanate and later the Mughal Empire over northern India caused considerable cultural interchange. Increasingly, musicians received patronage in the courts of the new rulers, who in their turn, started taking increasing interest in local music forms. While the initial generations may have been rooted in cultural traditions outside India, they gradually adopted many aspects from their kingdoms which retained the traditional Hindu culture. This helped spur the fusion of Hindu and Muslim ideas to bring forth new forms of musical synthesis like qawwali and khayal.

The most influential musician from the Delhi Sultanate period was Amir Khusrau (1253-1325), sometimes called the father of modern Hindustani classical music. A prolific composer in Persian, Turkish, Arabic, as well as Braj Bhasha, he is credited with systematizing many aspects of Hindustani music, and also introducing several ragas such as Yaman Kalyan, Zeelaf and Sarpada. He created the qawwali genre, which fuses Persian melody and beat on a dhrupad like structure. A number of instruments (such as the sitar and tabla) were also introduced in his time.

Amir Khusrau is sometimes credited with the origins of the khayal form, but the record of his compositions do not appear to support this. The compositions by the court musician Niyamat Khan (*Sadarang*) in the court of Muhammad Shah 'Rangiley' bear a closer affinity to the modern khyal, and suggests that while khyal already existed in some form, 'Sadarang' may have been the father of modern day khyal.

Much of the musical forms innovated by these pioneers merged with the Hindu tradition, composed in the popular language of the people (as opposed to Sanskrit) in the work of composers like Kabir or Nanak. This can be seen as part of a larger Bhakti tradition, (strongly related to the Vaishnavite movement) which remained influential across several centuries; notable figures include Jayadeva (11th century), Vidyapati (1375 AD), Chandidas (14th-15th century), and Meerabai (1555-1603 AD).

As the Mughal Empire came into closer contact with Hindus, especially under Jalal ud-Din Akbar, music and dance also flourished. Particularly, the legendary musician Tansen is recognized as having introduced a number of innovations, ragas as well as particular compositions. Legend has it that upon his rendition of a night-time raga in the morning, the entire city fell under a hush and clouds gathered in the sky, or that he could light fires by singing raga Deepak, which is supposed to be composed of notes in high octaves.

At the royal house of Gwalior, Raja Mansingh Tomar (1486-1516 AD) also participated in the shift from Sanskrit to the local idiom (Hindi) as the language for classical songs. He himself penned several volumes of compositions on religious and secular themes, and was also responsible for the major compilation, the *Mankutuhal* (book of curiosity), which outlined the major forms of music prevalent at the time. In particular, the musical form known as dhrupad saw considerable development in his court and remained a strong point of the Gwalior gharana for many centuries.

After the dissolution of the Mughal empire, the patronage of music continued in smaller princely kingdoms like Lucknow, Patiala, and Banaras, giving rise to the diversity of styles that is today known as gharanas. Many musician families obtained large grants of land which made them self sufficient, at least for a few generations (e.g. the Sham Chaurasia gharana). Meanwhile the Bhakti and Sufi traditions continued to develop, and interact with the different gharanas and groups.

Zeb-un-nisa, Jani, Lal Kunwar and Muhammad Shah Rangeela

Two of them were Mughal princesses who deserve to be remembered. One was Jani Begum, the daughter of Dara Shikoh, later married to Aurangzeb's son Azam. The second was Zeb-un-nisa, Aurangzeb's daughter. The third was Lal Kanwar, a dancing girl destined to be a queen.

Zeb-un-nisa, like her uncle Dara Shikoh, was devoted to studies from her childhood. Being the daughter of the reigning Emperor, she was given Tees Hazari, the imposing garden house that had once belonged to Jahan Ara, as her jagir (property). Here she built an excellent library. It was better than any other private collections of the time. She employed many scholars to write literary work.

Others were employed to copy manuscripts. She paid the scholars handsomely. She loved poetry and was a special patron of the poets. In fact she was a poet herself and wrote in Persian under the pen name of Makhvi (the concealed one). After her death Zeb-un-nisa was buried in Tees Hazari. But when the British took over, they ruined the garden completely. Later with the advent of the railways Zeb-un-nisa's tomb was pulled down and the railway tracks laid over it.

Jani, the darling of grandfather Shah Jahan and adored by father Dara Shikoh, was brought up by Jahan Ara when Aurangzeb demolished the rest of her family. She stands out as an incredible character in the gory history of the Red Fort. Jani was totally void of bitterness and hatred despite her tragic life. She did not believe in the doctrine of 'eye for an eye'.

She constantly upheld Babar's example, who had laid down his own life for his son Humayun, rather than remember those who had butchered and tortured their own brothers and kinsmen. She was so sweet, and so free from hatred and any resentment, that even Aurangzeb eventually came under her spell and could not help loving her. He went to Jahan Ara himself and formally asked for her hand in marriage to Azam, his second and most favourite son. The wedding was celebrated with great pomp and show.

Azam was a brave soldier. Jani Begum always accompanied him to the battlefield. Once when fighting in Deccan Azam's life was in real danger and Aurangzeb himself ordered him to come back. But Azam sent word, Saying, "Moharnrnad Azam, his two sons and Begum will not retreat from this post of danger so long as he is alive. After my death His Majesty may have my corpse removed for burial. My followers may stay or go as they please."

On hearing this, Aurangzeb sent a relief force. But it was Jani who saved his life by following him on elephant with Anirudh Singh, whom she called her son. The battle was won as a result of their combined effort. The entire city rejoiced when Azam returned to the Red Fort with Jani.

After Aurangzeb's death Azam became the next Emperor, succeeding the throne on March 14, 1707. But his reign lasted a bare three months. He was succeeded by Bahadur Shah I who hardly set his foot inside the Red Fort because he had to be on the move all the time, pacifying his troubled kingdom to the best of his ability. Many historians have called him an able king and administrator. Percival writes: "The gallery of the great Mughals is completed by Aurangzeb's son Bahadur Shah, commonly neglected because his reign lasted barely five years.

He waged the usual war of succession with resolution, skill and unusual humanity. He made a settlement with the implacable Marathas, tranquilized the Rajputs, decisively defeated the Sikhs in Punjab and took their last Guru into his service. He travelled throughout his reign and only came to rest at Lahore during the last few months of his life." His son Jahandar Shah succeeded him on March 29, 1712. Jahandar was fond of dance and music and beautiful women. He was no good as a king or as an administrator. Delhi was plunged into utter chaos and misrule during his reign. A lot of it was due to Lal Kunwar, a dancing-girl whom he married later, giving her the supreme position of Empress. She had him under her thumb and soon became the real power behind the throne. Her hold over the Emperor is aptly brought out in the Son-et-Lumiere.

We hear Jahandar Shah addressing her as "the form of an angel and the voice of a nightingale." when Lal Kunwar protests, saying that she is only a slave, he announces that henceforth she would be known as Begum Imtiaz Mahal. Lal Kunwar says, "But I shall have to live in the palace then...How will I see Zohra ?" The king enquires who Zohra is. Lal Kunwar replies, "Zohra ? She is my best friend. She sells water-melons... the sweetest water-melons in Delhi." The king appoints Zohra as her chief lady-in-waiting, so that she might live in the palace with her. Then Lal Kunwar asks, "But what about Niyamat? He is my brother and plays the Sarangi." The king appoints Niyamat the Governor of Multan!

There is an interesting story according to which Zulfikar Khan, the Emperor's wazir, is said to have demanded 1,000 sarangis as bribe from the brother of Lal Kunwar. When the Emperor asked him what he was going to do with so many sarangis, the wazir told him that since sarangi players were being made Governors, he wanted to present a sarangi to each of the nobles in the Empire, so that they too might qualify themselves for the service of the Emperor!

In the words of another historian: "Lal Kunwar's brothers and relations swaggered through the streets, committing every kind of outrage while the Emperor gave himself to drinking and other vices." Jahandar Shah came to be known as the "Lord of Misrule". The once glorious Diwan-i-Khas was reduced to a farcical emblem from where one foolish decree followed another.

Incredible as it might seem, Lal Kunwar belonged to the family of Tansen, the famous singer at Akbar's court, revered to this day. Lal Kunwar, though beautiful and skilled in singing, was prone to crazy whims, many of them brutal and heartless. And Jahandar Shah gave in to all of them. When she remarked one day that she had never seen a boat sink with people drowning Jahandar Shah immediately ordered a boat to be taken to the Yamuna and made to sink. So that Lal Kunwar might watch the agony of the drowning people! When she said that she was curious to know what the Faiz canal would look like without the trees on both sides, the Emperor ordered the trees to be felled down immediately.

Of course it is not quite fair to blame just Lal Kunwar for these follies. The besotted Emperor who gave these crazy orders should be blamed even more. The only thing that may be said in Lal Kanwar's favor was that she was truly devoted to Jahandar all her life and had once saved his life in the battlefield when he was badly wounded. She rushed to the field on her own elephant and carried him to safety, looking after him until he was able to resume fighting once again.

Jahandar Shah's reign was short-lived. His nephew Farrukhsiyar who entered Delhi in a procession on February 12, 1713 strangled him to death. He ordered that the head of Jahandar Shah should be carried on the point of a long bamboo pole and paraded all over the city. The severed body was laid across another elephant. The new king, an otherwise cowardly, contemptible and good-for-nothing man, reveled in gruesome deeds.

It was during his reign that the Sikh Guru Banda Bahadur was executed. The captive Guru and his 740 followers were brought to Delhi and paraded through the city in a most humiliating manner before they were killed. But they maintained their dignity and showed no signs of dejection. Nor did any of them offer to change their religion in order to save their heads!

Farrukhsiyar, in his turn, was assassinated in the Nakkar Khana of the Red Fort in 1718 by the Sayyid Brothers. After a quick succession of two rulers, whose reigns lasted for just a few months, Mohammad Shah, the grandson of Bahadur Shah I, took over as the new king. He was the last Mughal Emperor to sit on the Peacock Throne. People called him Mohammed Shah Rangeela (the Merry Monarch) because the only thing he cared for was merry-making! He loved wine, music and dancing-girls-three things that dominated his life.

His favourite pastimes were watching animal and bird fights, mimics, jokers, play actors, puppeteers, acrobats, and conjurers. As a result all these crafts were developed and patronized during his reign. The Bhagat Baz or play-actors performed plays based on epics like the Ramayana and Mahabharata. Bahuropees (actors who dressed up as different characters) were patronized too, and so were the dancers, known as nats and natnis.

But Muhammad Shah Rangeela's reign is considered important for a special reason. It is because some important cultural developments took place during the time. It was during his reign that Wali Deccani, said to be the first Urdu poet, came to Delhi with his collection of Urdu poetry. The new language was developed and recognized as never before and provided a new meeting ground for the Hindus and the Muslims. Rangeela was the Emperor who made Urdu a court language.

From a mere dialect it was given the status of a full-fledged language. Khayal, a new style of classical singing, was also developed to perfection during this period. In fact it grew so popular that the old style of Dhrupad was virtually pushed aside. Both Qawwali and the dance form of kathak made great strides during this period. Nawab Salar Jung in his Muraqqa-i-Delhi mentions many famous musicians in the court of Rangeela Shah, such as Naimat Khan, a great veena player, and Feroz Khan. The Emperor gave them the titles of Sadarang and Adarang.

But every single thing Rangeela did was accompanied by bouts of drinking. During one such carousal, the Persians, led by Emperor Nadir Shah, invaded India. But the merry monarch was too busy to take the messenger's warning seriously. *"Hanooz Dilli Door Ast"* (it's a long way to Delhi) said he, pouring more and yet more wine from the goblet. By the time he really woke up to the seriousness of the situation it was too late. Nadir Shah and his men were already at the threshold of the seventh city of Delhi.

Mughal Contribution to Indian Literature

The Mughals established a mighty empire that dominated India for more than two centuries. Their passion for literature and knowledge commissioned excellent literary works. They add luster and wealth to the literatures of India.

Printing in India

Most of the Indian literatures were in palm leaves till the arrival of the printing technology in the sixteenth century. Printing was a turning point in the Indian history. It came with the missionary movement of the Portuguese and others. Fifty-nine years after the landing of Vasco da Gama in India, the printing press opened its account at Goa, a few decades after the beginning of the 16th century. Within a hundred years of the printing of Gutenberg's Bible in Germany, India initiated its groping towards fashioning of types for the many Indian languages.

Mughal Empire which was established in the north in the sixteenth century and the Vijayanagara Empire in the south witnessed the changes that were brought by the printing technology in India.

Mughal Contribution To Literature

There was tremendous literary activity during the Mughal period, because with the return of a stable and prosperous empire. There was once again patronage for the literary works. Languages like Persian, Sanskrit, Hindi and Urdu saw tremendous creative activity as did many vernacular languages. The Mughal Emperors, themselves interested in literature, encouraged literary contributions. Vast number of works were written during the period of the Mughals.

The Three Categories of Contributions

We can easily divide the contributions of the Mughals into three categories: historical works, translations, poetry and novels. Our understanding of the Mughal period was greatly enhanced by these books, and most of the historical works of this period provide us with a fairly reliable source of information. The important historical works written in this time were Ain-I-Akbari, and Akbarnama by Abul Fazal, the Tarikh-I-Alfi by Mulla Daud. Akbar, though was not educated in any formal educational institution, could contribute much to literature.

Jehangir possessed a keen interest in literature, and his autobiography is one of the finest amongst the Mughal emperors. During his reign important historical works like Maasir-I-Jahangir, the Igbalnamah-I-Jahangiri and the Zubud-ut-Tawaikh were written.

Great Translations

Many important works in translation were also written during this period, with the translation of the epics, the Mahabharata and the Ramayana taking place. Many of the Vedas were also translated and several previous historical books were also translated. All this translation added to the wealth of Indian literature and spread ancient knowledge to a greater audience. This renewed interest in Indian literature would be an important tool used by the social reformers of the eighteenth century to educate the people about what the ancient texts really said as opposed to the distorted interpretations that were being followed.

New Contributions

The Mughal empire encouraged a large number of poets and writers and hence there were a lot of new contributions published in this era. During the reign of Akbar, Jehangir and Shah Jahan the literary people had tremendous patronage and many remarkable works were composed. Since the Mughal emperors had integrated themselves into Indian society, they patronized many Indian languages leading to some good quality literature being developed for these languages. The main themes of the period were essentially religious, covering most of the major religions of the period.

One of the fine Hindu works composed during this time was Ramcharitmanasa (the life of Rama) by Tulsidasa, which was a simplified version of the Ramayana. In Bengal there was a lot of work being created in Vaishnava literature. Writers like Krishnada and Kaviraj were popular authors of the time. Many biographies were also written during this period.

Valuable Contributions

The Mughals established a mighty empire that dominated India for more than two centuries. Their passion for nature and literature contributed much for the Indian literature. Books were very precious to the Mughal kings. Expensive and laborious contributions were as marked the symbols of royal wealth, power and intelligence.

At the height of the Mughal power, the imperial studios hummed with the activity of hundreds papermakers, printers and business people of books. Today we can see and enjoy the books and manuscripts illustrated with exquisite miniature paintings of the Mughal Emperors treasured by museums around the world. The Mughal contribution to the Indian literatures is really great.

9

Aurangzeb's Religious Policy: Its Emergence and Impact on Mughal Polity

Aurangzeb was the third son of the Mughal emperor Shah Jahan; his mother was Mumtaz Mahal, who is buried in the Taj Mahal. Aurangzeb showed his ability in administrative and military matters in various appointments, which gradually caused him to envy his eldest brother Dara Shikoh, the designated successor to the throne.

In 1657 Shah Jahan became seriously ill, and the rivalry between Dara Shikoh and Aurangzeb turned into open confrontation. Shah Jahan recovered unexpectedly, but the struggle for succession continued. Aurangzeb placed his father under house arrest, drove one brother into death, had two other brothers executed and in 1658 declared himself emperor of the Mughal empire, assuming the name 'Alangir ("the World Seizer").

Aurangzeb did not share the interest of his ancestors and relatives in the arts, drink and the good life generally but was serious-minded and religious. He inherited an empire that had flourished for nearly a century under the wise administrative and economic procedures introduced by his great-grandfather Akbar the Great. The economic boom had led to the development of artisanal activity in all villages, and the municipalities had become economically much less dependent on the central power.

Aurangzeb tried to stem the growing independence of the different parts of his empire by returning to autocratic rule. He abandoned the policy of separation of religion and state and turned away from the policy of religious tolerance that during the previous three generations had kept Muslims, Hindus, Sikhs, Christians and others together in peace and common destiny. In 1675 he executed the Sikh guru Tegh Bahadur because of his refusal to convert to Islam. The Sikh rebellion that followed continued throughout Aurangzeb's reign; relations between Sikhs and Muslims have been strained ever since.

In 1679 Aurangzeb reintroduced the jizya, a poll tax for non-Muslims that had been abolished by Akbar the Great a century earlier. The result was a revolt of the Hindu Rajputs, supported by Aurangzeb's third son Akbar, in 1680-1681. In the south of the empire the Maratha kingdom was conquered and broken up and its ruler Sambhaji executed in 1689, which started a long and exhausting guerilla campaign by the Maratha Hindu population.

The ongoing struggles placed severe strain on the empire's finances, and increased taxation led to several peasant revolts, often but not always under the guise of religious movements.

At Aurangzeb's death the empire was larger than before but severely weakened. It survived for another 150 years but was in constant religious strife. What Akbar the Great had so splendidly begun collapsed 300 years later under the colonial onslaught, because the empire's economic progress did not lead to the political reform that would have allowed further development.

Jizyah According to Satish Chandra

Aurangzeb introduced the Jizyah, but, cautions Satish Chandra, "it was not meant to be an economic pressure for forcing Hindus to convert to Islam, for its incidence was to be light." For this assertion Satish Chandra gives two bits of proof, so to say. First, "women, children, the disabled, the indigent, that is, those whose income was less than the means of subsistence, were exempted as were those in government service." How could even Aurangzeb have exacted a tax from those "whose income was less than the means of subsistence?" And why would he exact a discriminatory and humiliating tax from those who were in government service, that is, from those who were already serving his interests and those of the Islamic State? The second proof that Satish Chandra gives is that "in fact, only an insignificant section of Hindus changed their religion due to this tax" — but could that not have been because of the firm attachment of Hindus to their faith, because of their tenacity rather than because of the liberality of Aurangzeb?

The Jizyah was not meant either to meet "a difficult financial situation". Its reimposition was in fact, says Satish Chandra, "both political and ideological in nature." Political in the sense that "it was meant to rally the Muslims for the defence of the State against the Marathas and the Rajputs who were up in arms, and possibly against the Muslim States of Deccan, especially Golconda, which was in alliance with the infidels." A parity twice-over — one, that Aurangzeb was only trying to rally the Muslims just as those opposing him had rallied the Marathas and Rajputs. And, in any case, the ones who were opposing him were "infidels"

> *"Jizyah was to be collected by honest; God-fearing Muslims who were specially appointed for the purpose and its proceeds were reserved for the Ulema." As the proceeds went to Ulama, there was a secular reason for exacting the tax — it was to be "a type of bribe for the theologians among whom there was a lot of unemployment,"*

Aurangzeb's Administration

Aurangzeb ruled for almost 50 years. During his long reign, the Mughal Empire reached territorial climax. Aurangzeb proved to be a hardworking ruler and never spared himself or his subordinates in the task of government. He was a stirct disciplinarism who did not spare his own sons, during his reign he introduced few administrative changes. According to histories, Aurangzeb brought changes in administration. Those were that the senior Hindu officers in the finance ministry were retained and even promoted, although in Banaras and some other places and Brahmans were harassed, and Hindu temples were also demolished by orthodox mobs. Aurangzeb stopped this desecration, but, in accordance with Islamic Sharia rules no new temples would be elected. A high proved mansabdar was appointed as censor of morals (muhtasib) to prevent drinking and to make Muslim changes to Quranic Laws.

There were many changes regarding festival's celebration also. Like celebration of Iranian Naw festival, which falls on the day the sun enters Aries was banned The "Kalima", or the confession of faith, was no longer stamped on coins, to prevent the holy words from being defiled by unbelievers or heretics. These reforms in no way undermined Hindu political and economic interests. Aurangzeb also used to send gift to holy men of Mecca-Madina & those were suppose to be distributed among poor or needy but to Aurangzeb's disappointment the funds were misused. In other words some historiams used different way of describing Aurangzeb's reign. They divided his reign into two phases. First phase was from 1658-1679 and second was from 1679 to his death 1707. And these were divided again into severed sub-phases. Other Historians defines economy measures, tax, Hindu temples etc. in the reign of Aurangzeb. There were many ceremonies, which were used to perform, were also stopped like the practices of the Emperor putting a Tika or saffrom paste on the forehead of a new raja was stopped. Practices, which were considered against Islamic spirit, were banned. Public displays of Holi and Muharram procession were also stopped. The courtiers were also asked not to wear silk gowns or gowns of mixed silk and cottons.

Taxs

There were taxs. Basically there were many taxs and we are told that Khalisa areas alone, rahdari had yielded 25 lakhs of rupees a year. Another tax was pandari or ground rent for stalls in the bazar in the capital and others towns. Another vexation tax, which was abolished in 1666, was the octroi duty on Tobacco.

Economy Measures

According to the history of Aurangzeb, in thirteenth years, it was reported that expenses had exceeded income during the preceding twelve years. Some of the measures of economy adopted by Aurangzeb were the retrenchment of many items in the expenditure of the Emperor, the princes and Begums. It seems that Aurangzeb was keen to promote trade among Muslim who depended almost exclusively on the state support. In 1665, he reduced the duty on import of goods by Muslim traders from 5% to 2 ½% and two years later abolished it altogether. But he had to reimpose it when he found Muslim traders were abusing it by presenting goods of Hindu traders as theirs. So ultimately it was kept 2½% for the Muslims. Many temples were being destructed by him also.

Aurangzeb's Religious Policy

According to historians Aurangzeb reversed Akbar's Policy of religious toleration. He basically used those policies which were already introduced by his predecessor but those were not that strong so again Aurangzeb during his reign again used those policies and one of them in Religious policy.

Aurangzeb's religious policy was largely based on his analysis of the first half of Aurangzeb's reign, which in his opinion was climaxed by the reinposition of Jizyah (poll tax). The other orthodox measures of Aurangzeb were insidious attempts on his part to establish an Islamic state in India which in effect implied conversion of the entire population to Islam and the extinction of every form a dissent. The religion policy of Mughal was largely the reflection of the personal religious views etc. It was a very narrow and orthodoxy kind of policy taken by Aurangzeb. He put ban on the practice, which were considered as against Islamic spirit. And many ceremonies and festivals were banned that time. Many temples were also destroyed that time. It was earlier found that long standing temple should not be demolished but no new temples allowed to be built. But later on it was found that many temples were demolished. And this was so because Aurangzeb started fearing for his political existence because there were some temple where both Hindu & Muslim used to go and learn teachings and Aurangzeb thinking that these kind of practice may hamper therefore, there should be stopped so demolishment took place. There was also tax, which was imposed on non-Muslims like Jizyah.

Jizyah

It was that tax which was reimposed by Aurangzeb on the non-muslims. Aurangzeb considered reimpostion of Jizyah, but postponed the matter due to "certain political exigencies". That it was reimpossed twenty-two years after Aurangzeb's accession to the throne is clear indication that its institution was on account of political considerations. Jizyah was used to be collected by honest God-fearing Muslims, who were especially appointed for this purpose. Because of this tax many got converted and enjoyed benefits but many did not left their religion and were being harassed. There were exception in this tax was that the women, children and the person who can not earn even for his own livelihood will be taken into consideration. So basically Jizyah was not an Income Tax but was a kind of property tax, which is imposed only in non-Muslim. These many let Islam grow.

Policy's Impact

There been several bad impacts of Aurangzeb's policies. Some historians had said that Aurangzeb's policies made Mughal very weak. Earlier there was no respect left for Islam and its adherents; mosques were without splendour, while idol-temples flourished; the requisites of canonical practice remained closed under bolts, while the gates of irreligious practices were flung open. That time Aurangzeb was the defender of the truth faith, converts to Islam were made much of. Many temples were given order of destruction and instead mosques built. But now because of this religious policy Mughal State had failed to yield the expected dividends. Now Aurangzeb faced difficult task of bringing under Imperial control the extensive country extending up to Jinji, populated by Hindu population and simultaneoudy he had to deal with Marathas. And situation became so worst that there seem like Aurangzeb need to make some modification in his policy. His attitude towards Hindu temples also varied from time to time according to circumstance that is political exigencies. And his attitude towards Marathas also varied. But policy was not changed. During that time many festivals & ceremonies banned and all practice, which is found against Islamic spirit, were also banned. Jizyah's impact was also very bad. Altogether, Jizyah came into picture because of religious policy. This tax was for non-Muslims. And basic impact of this Jizyah was that people got converted into Islamic religion so as to escape from Jizyah and enjoy profits of being Islamic.

But many people who were not Islamic were treated badly. Many people used to close their shops and observe hartals against the measure. But even though Jizyah had not led to any large conversion. And in this Jizyah there started lot of corruption. Aurangzeb's religious policy led to series of contractions, which he found hard to resolve.

Conclusion

After reading or researching it can said that Aurangzeb was very orthodox regarding his religious policy but indeed was a hardworking personality and he was of such kind that he did not even allow his officers to be spare. But even Aurangzeb got only disappointment. Reason can be that he was very orthodox regarding religious policies and also Jizyah. Religious policy was basically concern with Islamic spirits. And Jizyah was there because of this Religious policy, People who do not belonged to Islamic religion or who were non-Muslim were charged with this Jizyah tax. To conclude Aurangzeb;s religious policy we will have to went through a numbers of phases. Through Aurangzeb's policy he brought system under tremendous pressure especially by his religious policy and also political policies. Aurangzeb's religious policy should be seen in a wider context. Aurangzeb was orthodox in his outlook and tried to remain within the framework of Islamic law. But this law was development outside India in a vastly dissimilar situation, and could hardly be applied rigidly to India. His failure to respect the susceptibilities of his non-Muslim subjects can be seen on many occasions. And his re-imposition of Jizyah did not help him to rally the Muslims to his side or generate a greater sense of loyalty towards a state based on Islamic Law. So overall his policies had weakened his administration. And religious policy played very important role in his reign. Aurangzeb died in 1707 and after his death's Mughal became weaker then before. And it stood nearly for some 100 years and then lost, as there were many problems regarding religion also but alone religion was not the reason but there were many reasons behind.

Rise of British Power

Meanwhile, far-reaching developments had taken place outside the capital. Alivardi Khan, the able governor of Bengal, died on April 10, 1756, and was succeeded by his grandson, Mirza Mohammad, better known as Siraj-ud-daula. The disruptive forces which had been kept under check by Alivardi got out of hand and overwhelmed the government. Alivardi's commander-in-chief, Mir Jafar, to whom his half-sister was married, started plotting against Siraj-ud-daula, and for a short time was removed from the command. Another reason for weakness was the existence of the East India Company, which had established at Calcutta not only a commercial, but a political center. A third was the attitude of the Hindu zamindars, bankers, and officials who, always influential in Bengal, had grown very powerful since the days of Murshid Quli Khan.

Alivardi Khan made no distinction between the Hindus and the Muslims. He had gained his position with the support of the Hindu notables, and they shared the government with him. This had not reconciled them to a Muslim ruler; or perhaps they recognized that a new power might soon overthrow his rule, and they wanted to be on the winning side. In any case, as an official of the East India Company had written two years before Alivardi's death: "[Hindu] rajas and inhabitants were disaffected to the Moor government and secretly wished for a change and opportunity of throwing off their tyrannical yoke." These three forces sealed the fate of Siraj-ud-daula. The familiar story of British activities need not be told here, but the role of the treacherous Mir Jafar, generally held responsible for the fate of Siraj, was comparatively a minor one. More significant was the alliance of the Hindu merchants with the East India Company. This new alignment, as much as any single factor, must be taken into account in explaining the end of Muslim rule in Bengal.

The battle fought at Plassey, a few miles outside Murshidabad, has been called by a modern British writer "the most miserable skirmish ever to be called a decisive battle." An army of which the commander-in-chief had been won over and took no part in the battle, can hardly offer spirited contests. Siraj-ud-daula's Hindu paymaster, Mir Madan, however, was loyal to the nawab, and fell in action. Clive's spirited leadership and British organization, coupled with the help they received from the powerful local elements, resulted in the rout and flight of Siraj-ud-daula. On June 28, 1757, Clive installed Mir Jafar on the masnad of Murshidabad and four days later Siraj-ud-daula was executed.

The legal position in Bengal had not changed with the British victory at Plassey, for the nawab was still in charge of the administration. But the officials of the East India Company expected him to do their bidding, and a clash was inevitable if a nawab sought to impose policies counter to British interests. The clash came when Nawab Mir Qasim, who had succeeded the incompetent Mir Jafar, tried to collect internal revenue from the English traders. According to an agreement, only the East India Company itself was to be free from the tax; in practice, every company servant traded on his own account and refused to pay any duty. In desperation, since his revenues were disappearing, Mir Qasim abolished all internal duties, thus removing the English advantage over the Indian traders. The British refused to accept this, and Mir Qasim left Bengal to organize an attack on the British. Support of a half-hearted kind came from Emperor Shah Alam and Shuja-ud-daula, the Wazir of Oudh, who had followed the general pattern of the time by establishing himself as a semi-independent ruler. The Mughal and the British forces met at Buxar in October, 1764, and while the British suffered fairly heavy losses, they won a clear victory. The results of the battle of Buxar were more far-reaching than those of Plassey. Even before the battle the British had attempted to facilitate the military task by diplomatic means, and the newly crowned Shah Alam was only a fugitive from Delhi, but the East India Company had gained a victory against what appeared to be the combined army of the emperor and the rulers of Bengal and Oudh. It gave greater prestige to British arms than had the earlier victory over a provincial government. It also altered Shuja-ud-daula's course of action. Henceforth dependence on the British became a cardinal point of his policy, and Oudh was, for all practical purposes, drawn into the orbit of the British influence. Most important of all, Emperor Shah Alam was forced to give the East India Company the diwani, or civil government, of Bengal, Bihar, and Orissa in return for the districts of Allahabad and Kora and an annual payment of two and a half million rupees. This provided the legal basis for British rule in Bengal.

Emperor Shah Alam remained in Allahabad for some years after the battle of Buxar, but he returned to Delhi in 1772, after the death of his wazir, Najib-ud-daula, who had been the actual ruler of the city for a decade. Motivated either by his own greed for money, or under the influence of the Marathas, who were supporting him for their own ends, Shah Alam attacked Zabita Khan, the powerful son of Najib-ud-daula, who was the leader of the Rohilla Afghans who had established themselves to the east of Delhi. In one punitive expedition against the family stronghold of Ghausgarh, Zabita Khan's relatives were treated with great cruelty. According to tradition, his son, Ghulam Qadir, was castrated and made to serve as page in the palace at Delhi, but a few years later, Ghulam Qadir was able to exact a terrible revenge.

Affairs in the capital were following a tortuous course, with the nobles intriguing against each other for the spoils of the decaying empire. One able administrator, Najaf Khan, succeeded for a time in organizing a small effective army to maintain order, but he eventually succumbed to the debilitating atmosphere.

Without any able or loyal followers, the emperor took a momentous step. In 1785 he invited the great Maratha chieftain

Mahadaji Sindhia of Gwalior to take charge of the Delhi administration. Appointed commander-in-chief and supreme regent (wakil-i-mutliq) of the empire, Sindhia tried to get the cooperation of Ghulam Qadir dealing with the Sikhs, but Ghulam Qadir, waiting for a chance to repay the humiliation he and his family had suffered at the hands of Shah Alam, had no desire to strengthen the emperor's rule.

His opportunity came in 1787, when Sindhia was defeated by the Rajputs. Ghulam Qadir entered Delhi in September, 1787, and forced the emperor to appoint him Mir Bakhshi or paymaster, and regent. He was driven out of Delhi by the emperor's supporters, but entered the city again the following year, deposed Shah Alam, and blinded him.

A drunken ruffian, Ghulam Qadir behaved with gross brutality to the emperor and his family. Three servants and two water-carriers who tried to help the bleeding emperor were killed. According to one account, Ghulam would pull the beard of the old monarch, and say: "Serves you right. This is the return for your action at Ghausgarh." Servants were tortured and made to reveal the hidden treasures, and the entire palace was ransacked to find the buried wealth.

After ten horrible weeks during which the honor of the royal family and prestige of the Mughal empire reached its lowest ebb, Ghulam Qadir left with the booty for his stronghold. Sindhia's officers hunted him down and captured him in December, 1788. He was put to death with tortures which equalled his own fiendish cruelties.

When Delhi was retaken by the Marathas, the blind Shah Alam was enthroned again. While his action reconciled the people to Sindhia's rule, it meant that Delhi was being drawn into the great struggle then taking place between the Marathas and the British.

An account of that struggle and of British expansion is outside the scope of this chapter, for the British did not defeat Mughal India, but its successor states, both Muslim and Hindu. Conquest was cautiously achieved. Periods of rapid expansion alternated with long periods of consolidation. Military action was effectively aided by diplomatic activity. Local differences and jealousies were most skilfully exploited. The Company's forces were normally able to depend on the direct or indirect cooperation of the commander, or at least some of the major leaders, of the troops confronting them. At Plassey it was Mir Jafar; at Buxar, the differences between Shuja-ud-daula and Mir Qasim were fully exploited. In fact, British success owed as much to diplomatic skill and the demoralized state of Indian society as to valor and military organization.

The great period of expansion initiated during the governor-generalship (1798–1805) of Lord Wellesley saw Delhi and the Mughal emperor pass under British sway. But even as late as 1798 this absorption did not seem inevitable, for an attempt was made to create a confederacy of the Afghan king, the wazir of Oudh, and a number of Maratha chiefs, to strengthen the position of the emperor. Wellesley took the plan seriously enough to stir up trouble between the Persian and the Afghan courts, so that the Afghan ruler would not be able to give any attention to India.

More important for the fate of the Mughals was Wellesley's war with the Marathas in 1803. In a two-pronged attack, they were defeated in the Deccan and North India. Sindhia's defeat meant the capture of Delhi, and with this the Mughal empire, long a dependent of the Marathas, passed into British control. Yet after a century of decline, the Mughal emperor still remained a symbol of greatness that was not easily defaced. To many British, his continuance seemed absurd, at best an empty pageant. Yet as events were to show in 1857, even the last flickering shadow of Mughal greatness still appeared to be a possible center of power.

Causes of the Mughal Decline

Before turning to these last years of the Mughal empire, it may be useful to summarize what appear to have been certain general causes of Mughal decline, leaving aside such specific causes as external invasions and internal rebellions. One feature of Islamic power in India, as elsewhere, was the failure to make progress in certain vital fields. For example, even Akbar failed to see the possibilities in the introduction of printing. The scarcity of books resulted in comparative ignorance, low standards of education, and limitation of the subjects of study. Because of this, the governing classes were ignorant of the affairs of the outside world. The position becomes clear if we compare the books on India printed in Europe during the eighteenth century with the knowledge of the West current in India. The interest on the part of Europeans that led travellers like Bernier to make reports on their travels finds no parallel in Mughal India. So far from being concerned with Europe, the Mughals, after *Ain-i-Akbari*, made no real addition to their knowledge even of their own dominions.

The stagnation visible in the intellectual field was visible also in the military sphere. Babur had introduced gunpowder in India, but after him there was no advance in military equipment, although the organization and discipline of forces had been completely revolutionized in the West. The Portuguese had brought ships on which cannons were mounted, and had thus introduced a new element which made them masters of the Indian Ocean. What was a fortified wall round the country became a highway, and opened up the empire to those countries which had not remained stagnant. Mughal helplessness on the sea was obvious from the days of Akbar. Their ships could not sail to Mecca without a safe-conduct permit from the Portuguese. Sir Thomas Roe had warned Jahangir that if Prince Shah Jahan as governor of Gujarat turned the English out, "then he must expect we would do our justice upon the seas." The failure of the Mughals to develop a powerful navy and control the seas surrounding their dominions was a direct cause of their replacement by an European power having these advantages.

On land no real progress or large-scale training of local personnel in the use of artillery was made in Mughal India, and the best they could do was to hire foreigners for manning the artillery. The military weakness resulting from this was obvious, and was clearly visible to foreign observers. Bernier wrote in the early years of Aurangzeb's reign:" I could never see these soldiers, destitute of order, and marching with the irregularity of a herd of animals, without reflecting upon the ease with which five-and-twenty thousand of our veterans from the army in Flanders, commanded by Prince Conde or Marshal Turenne would overcome these armies, however numerous." With this condition of the Mughal army, the downfall of the empire was only a question of time.

Another factor which contributed to the fall of the Mughal empire was the moral decay of the ruling classes. This was partly due to the affluent standard of living maintained by monarchs like Shah Jahan and queens like Nur Jahan. Ostentatious luxury became the ambition of everyone who could afford it, and the puritanical

Aurangzeb's attempts to arrest the tide were without success. The evil had gone too far and was only driven underground, to reappear within ten years of the emperor's death, in the uncontrolled orgies of his grandson Jahandar Shah. Perhaps Aurangzeb's extreme asceticism and self-denial only intensified the reaction of the nobility. Many a Maratha hill fortress captured after long and dreary siege was lost because the Mughal commander, unwilling to spend the monsoon months in his lonely perch, came down to the plains, while the hardy Marathas, awaiting the opportunity, moved in.

The moral decline of the nobility, showed itself in lack of discipline, laziness, evasion of duties, and even treacherous conduct. It also made them rapacious and heartless in dealing with the public. The extravagant standards that the Mughal bureaucrats tried to maintain were not possible without corruption, extortion, and the enrichment of the officers at the expense of the state and the people. These evils increased as Mughal authority weakened, but their seeds had been sown in earlier days and were a natural result of the efforts of the officers to maintain standards beyond their means.

These were the basic factors responsible for the downfall of the Mughal empire, but others were contributory. The fact that after the death of Aurangzeb no ruler of real vigor and resourcefulness came to the throne made recovery of the lost position almost impossible. Even Aurangzeb's long life was an asset of doubtful value in its last stages. He drove himself hard and resolutely, conscientiously performing his duties, but at the age of ninety he was subject to the laws governing all human machines. When he died, his son and successor Bahadur Shah was already an old man of sixty. He began well but was on the throne for barely six years, and with his death a disastrous chapter opened in Mughal annals.

Directly related to the troubles of this period was the absence of a well-defined law of succession to ensure the continuity of government. The result was that each son of a deceased king felt that he had an equal claim to the crown, and succession to the throne was invariably accompanied by bloody warfare. The disaster was compounded when the imperial princes, who were often viceroys governing vast territories, started making secret pacts with soldiers to ensure their support for the time when the fateful struggle would begin. Soon not only the imperial army but forces external to the empire—the East India Company, the Marathas, the Sikhs—were being used by claimants to the throne of Delhi, as well as to control of the provincial kingdoms. The results were fatal.

Influence on the Indian Subcontinent

A major Mughal contribution to the Indian Subcontinent was their unique architecture. Many monuments were built by the Muslim emperors, especially Shahjahan, during the Mughal era including the UNESCO World Heritage Site Taj Mahal, which is known to be one of the finer examples of Mughal architecture. Other World Heritage Sites includes the Humayun's Tomb, Fatehpur Sikri, Red Fort, Agra Fort and Lahore Fort.

The palaces, tombs and forts built by the dynasty stands today in Delhi, Aurangabad, Fatehpur Sikri, Agra, Jaipur, Lahore, Kabul, Sheikhupura and many other cities of India, Pakistan, Afghanistan and Bangladesh. With few memories of Central Asia, Babur's descendents absorbed traits and customs of the Indian Subcontinent, and became more or less naturalised. The Mughal period would be the first to witness the blending of Indian, Iranian and Central Asian customs and traditions.

Contributions such as:

- Centralised, imperialistic government which brought together many smaller kingdoms.
- Persian art and culture amalgamated with Indian art and culture.
- New trade routes to Arab and Turkic lands.
- The development of Mughlai cuisine.
- The Urdu language developed from the Hindi language by borrowing heavily from Persian as well as Arabic and Chaghatai Turkic. Urdu developed as a result of the fusion of the Indian and Islamic cultures during the Mughal period. Modern Hindi which uses Sanskrit-based vocabulary along with loan words from Persian and Arabic, is mutually intelligible with Urdu.
- Mughal Architecture found its way into local Indian architecture, most conspicuously in the palaces built by Rajputs and Sikh rulers.
- Landscape gardening.

Although the land the Mughals once ruled has separated into what is now India, Pakistan, Bangladesh and Afghanistan their influence can still be seen widely today. Tombs of the emperors are spread throughout India, Afghanistan and Pakistan. There are 16 million descendants spread throughout the Subcontinent and possibly the world.

Mughal Society

The Indian economy remained as prosporous under the Mughals as it was, because of the creation of a road system and a uniform currency, together with the unification of the country. Manufactured goods and peasant-grown cash crops were sold throughout the world.

Key industries included shipbuilding (the Indian shipbuilding industry was as advanced as the European, and Indians sold ships to European firms), textiles, and steel.

The Mughals maintained a small fleet, which merely carried pilgrims to Mecca, imported a few Arab horses, transported soldiers over rivers, and fought pirates; however, the Siddis of Janjira and the Marathas sent ships to China, and the eastern limits of Africa, together with some Mughal subjects carrying out private-sector trade.

Cities and towns boomed under the Mughals; however, for the most part, they were military and political centres, not manufacturing or commerce centres. Only those guilds which produced goods for the bureaucracy made goods in the towns; most industry was based in rural areas. The nobility was a heterogeneous body; while it primarily consisted of Rajput aristocrats and foreigners from Muslim countries, people of all castes and nationalities could gain a title from the emperor.

The middle class of openly affluent traders consisted of a few wealthy merchants living in the coastal towns; the bulk of the merchants pretended to be poor to avoid taxation.

The bulk of the people were poor. The standard of living of the poor was as low as, or somewhat higher than, the standard of living of the Indian poor under the British Raj; whatever benefits the British brought with canals and modern industry were neutralized by rising population growth, high taxes, and the collapse of traditional industry in the nineteenth century.

Science and Technology

Astronomy

In the Mughal Empire, the 16th and 17th centuries saw a synthesis between Islamic astronomy and Indian astronomy, where Islamic observational techniques and instruments were combined with Hindu computational techniques. While there appears to have been little concern for theoretical astronomy, Muslim and Hindu astronomers in India continued to make advances in observational astronomy and produced nearly a hundred Zij treatises. Humayun built a personal observatory near Delhi, while Jahangir and Shah Jahan were also intending to build observatories but were unable to do so. The instruments and observational techniques used at the Mughal observatories were mainly derived from the Islamic tradition, and the computational techniqes from the Hindu tradition. In particular, one of the most remarkable astronomical instruments invented in Mughal India is the seamless celestial globe.

Technology

Fathullah Shirazi (c. 1582), a Persian-Indian polymath and mechanical engineer who worked for Akbar the Great in the Mughal Empire, invented the autocannon, the earliest multi-shot gun. As opposed to the polybolos and repeating crossbows used earlier in ancient Greece and China, respectively, Shirazi's rapid-firing gun had multiple gun barrels that fired hand cannons loaded with gunpowder.

The first prefabricated homes and movable structures were invented in 16th century Mughal India by Akbar the Great. These structures were reported by Arif Qandahari in 1579.

Considered one of the most remarkable feats in metallurgy, the seamless globe and celestial globe were invented in Kashmir by Ali Kashmiri ibn Luqman in 998 AH (1589-90 CE), and twenty other such globes were later produced in Lahore and Kashmir during the Mughal Empire.

Before they were rediscovered in the 1980s, it was believed by modern metallurgists to be technically impossible to produce metal globes without any seams, even with modern technology. These Mughal metallurgists pioneered the method of lost-wax casting while producing these seamless globes.

Fathullah Shirazi

Fathullah Shirazi (c. 1582), sometimes referred to as Amir Fathullah Shirazi, was a Persian-Indian polymath—a scholar, Islamic jurist, finance minister, mechanical engineer, inventor, mathematician, astronomer, physician, philosopher and artist—who worked for Akbar the Great, ruler of the Mughal Empire. Shirazi was given the title of 'Azuddudaulah, translated as "the arm of the empire."

Biography

Mir Fathullah Shirazi was a polymath who worked as an imperial finance minister for Akbar the Great. According to Abul-Fazl ibn Mubarak's *Akbarnama,* when Shirazi died, Akbar mourned his death:

[Akbar] grieved at the departure of this memorial of former sages. He often said that the Mir was his *vakil,* Indian philosophy, physician, and astronomer, and that no one could understand the amount of his grief for him. "Had he fallen into the hands of the Franks, and they had demanded all my treasures in exchange for him, I should gladly have entered into such a profitable traffic, and have bought that precious jewel cheap."

Inventions

Among the inventions credited to him was a military weapon, fashioned for killing infantry: the first known autocannon. As opposed to the polybolos and repeating crossbows used earlier in Ancient Greece and China, respectively, Shirazi's rapid-firing machine had multiple gun barrels that fired hand cannon.

Another cannon-related machine he created could clean sixteen gun barrels simultaneously, and was operated by a cow. He also developed a seventeen-barrelled cannon, fired with a matchlock.

Not all of his creations were intended for warfare, however, including a carriage, which was called comfortable by Abul-Fazl ibn Mubarak. It could also be used to grind corn, when not transporting passengers.

Economic and Social Developments under the Mughals

It was the normal policy of the Timurid rulers, both in their original Central Asian homelands and in India, to encourage trade. As in much else, Sher Shah Suri during his brief reign (1538–1545) set a pattern that was followed by the later Mughals, especially Akbar, when he encouraged trade by linking together various parts of the country through an efficient system of roads and abolishing many inland tolls and duties. The Mughals maintained this general policy, but their rule was distinguished by the importance which foreign trade attained by the end of the sixteenth century. This was partly the result of the discovery of the new sea-route to India; but even so, progress would have been limited if conditions within the country had not been favourable.

Trade and Industry

Both Akbar and Jahangir interested themselves in the foreign seaborne trade, and Akbar himself took part in commercial activities for a time. The Mughals welcomed the foreign trader, provided ample protection and security for his transactions, and levied a very low custom duty (usually no more than 2½ percent ad valorem). Furthermore, the expansion of local handicrafts and industry resulted in a reservoir of exportable goods. Indian exports consisted mainly of manufactured articles, with cotton cloth in great demand in Europe and elsewhere. Indigo, saltpeter, spices, opium, sugar, woolen and silk cloth of various kinds, yarn, asafoetida, salt, beads, borax, turmeric, lac, sealing wax, and drugs of various kinds, were also exported. The principal imports were bullion, horses, and a certain quantity of luxury goods for the upper classes, like raw silk, coral, amber, precious stones, superior textiles (silk, velvet, brocade, broadcloth), perfumes, drugs, china goods, and European wines. By and large, however, in return for their goods Indian merchants insisted on payment in gold or silver. Naturally this was not popular in England and the rest of Europe, and writers on economic affairs in the seventeenth century frequently complained, as did Sir Thomas Roe, that "Europe bleedeth to enrich Asia." The demand for articles supplied by India was so great, however, and her requirements of European goods so limited, that Europe was obliged to trade on India's own terms until the eighteenth century, when special measures were taken in England and elsewhere to discourage the demand for Indian goods.

The manufacture of cotton goods had assumed such extensive proportions that in addition to satisfying her own needs, India sent cloth to almost half the world: the east coast of Africa, Arabia,

Egypt, Southeast Asia, as well as Europe. The textile industry, well established in Akbar's day, continued to flourish under his successors, and soon the operations of Dutch and English traders brought India into direct touch with Western markets. This resulted in great demand for Indian cotton goods from Europe, which naturally increased production at home. Even the silk industry—especially in Bengal—was in flourishing condition. Bernier wrote: "There is in Bengal such a quantity of cotton and silk, that the kingdom may be called the common storehouse for these two kinds of merchandise, not of Hindoustan or the Empire of the Great Mogol only, but of all the neighbouring kingdoms, and even of Europe."

Apart from silk and cotton textiles, other industries were shawl and carpet weaving, woolen goods, pottery, leather goods, and articles made of wood. Owing to its proximity to sources of suitable timbers, Chittagong specialized in shipbuilding, and at one time supplied ships to distant Istanbul. The commercial side of the industry was in the hands of middlemen, but the Mughal government, like the earlier sultans, made its own contribution. The emperor controlled a large number of royal workshops, busily turning out articles for his own use, for his household, for the court, and for the imperial army.

Akbar took a special interest in the development of indigenous industry. He was directly responsible for the expansion of silk weaving at Lahore, Agra, Fathpur-Sikri, and in Gujarat. He opened a large number of factories at important centers, importing master weavers from Persia, Kashmir, and Turkistan.

Akbar frequently visited the workshops near the palace to watch the artisans at work, which encouraged the craftsmen and raised their status. It is said that he took such an interest in the industry that to foster demand he "ordered people of certain ranks to wear particular kinds of locally woven coverings ... an order which resulted in the establishment of a large number of shawl manufactories in Lahore; and inducements were offered to foreign carpet-weavers to settle in Agra, Fathepur Sikri, and Lahore, and manufacture carpets to compete with those imported from Persia." In the course of time, the foreign traders established close contracts with important markets in India, and new articles which were more in demand in Western Europe began to be produced in increasing quantities. Among the foreign inventions that excited

Akbar's interest was an organ, "one of the wonders of creation," that had been brought from Europe.

Urban Life

All foreign travellers speak of the wealth and prosperity of Mughal cities and large towns. Monserrate stated that Lahore in 1581 was "not second to any city in Europe or Asia." Finch, who travelled in the early days of Jahangir, found both Agra and Lahore to be much larger than London, and his testimony is supported by others. Other cities like Surat ("A city of good quantity, with many fair merchants and houses therein"), Ahmadabad, Allahabad, Benares, and Patna similarly excited the admiration of visitors. The new port towns of Bombay, Calcutta, Madras, and Karachi developed under British rule, but they had their predecessors in Satgaon, Surat, Cambay, Lari Bunder, and other ports.

The efficient system of city government under the Mughals encouraged trade. The pivot of urban administration was the kotwal, the city governor. In addition to his executive and judicial powers, it was his duty to prevent and detect crime, to perform many of the functions now assigned to the municipal boards, to regulate prices, and in general, to be responsible for the peace and prosperity of the city. The efficient discharge of these duties depended on the personality of the individual city governor, but the Mughals tried to ensure high standards by making the kotwal personally responsible for the property and the security of the citizens. Akbar had decreed (probably following Sher Shah Suri's example of fixing the responsibility on village chiefs for highway robberies in their territory) that the kotwal was to either recover stolen goods or be held responsible for their loss. That this was not only a pious hope is borne out by the testimony of several foreign travellers who state that the kotwal was personally liable to make good the value of any stolen property which he was unable to recover. The kotwals often found pretexts to evade the ultimate responsibility, but in general they took elabourate measures to prevent thefts.

Most of this flourishing commerce was in the hands of the traditional Hindu merchant classes, whose business acumen was proverbial. Their caste guilds added to the skills in trade and commerce that they had learned through the centuries. Not only were their disputes settled by their panchayats, but they would frequently impose pressure on the government by organized action. Foreign visitors record that the governors and kotwals were very sensitive to this, and in spite of hardships inseparable from a despotic system of administration, the business communities had their own means of obtaining redress. Bernier, writing during Aurangzeb's time, declared that the Hindus possessed "almost exclusively the trade and wealth of the country." If Muslims enjoyed advantages in higher administrative posts and in the army, Hindu merchants maintained the monopoly in trade and finance that they had during the sultanate. A Dutch traveler in the early seventeenth century was struck by the fact that few Muslims engaged in handicraft industries, and that even when a Muslim merchant did have a large business, he employed Hindu bookkeepers and agents. Banking was almost exclusively in Hindu hands. In the years of the decline of the Mughals, a rich Hindu banker would finance his favourite rival claimant for the throne. The role of Jagat Seth of Murshidabad in the history of Bengal is well known. Even the "war of succession" out of which Aurangzeb emerged victorious was financed by a loan of five and a half lakhs of rupees from the Jain bankers of Ahmadabad. Here one sees a contrast with British rule, when the British not only monopolized the higher civil service posts but also controlled most of the major industries as well as the great banks and trading agencies.

Rural Conditions

Conditions in the rural areas during the Mughal period were much the same as at present, with one important difference—the Muslim rulers had scarcely disturbed the old organization of the villages. The panchayats continued to settle most disputes, with the state impinging very little on village life, except for the collection of land revenue, and even this was very often done on a village basis rather than through individuals, with the age-old arrangements being preserved. The incidence of land revenue was substantially higher under the Mughals and in Hindu states like Vijayanagar than in British India, but the administration was more flexible, both in theory and in practice, in its assessment and collection. Apart from the remission of land revenue when crops failed, there was reduction in government demand even when bumper crops caused prices to fall. For example, between 1585 and 1590 very large sums had to be written off because a series of exceptionally good harvests had resulted in a surplus, and peasants could not sell their crops. The state also advanced loans to the cultivators, and occasionally provided seed as well as implements for digging wells. Loans advanced to the cultivators for seeds, implements, bullocks, or digging of wells were called *taqavi*—an expression which has continued in modern land revenue administration.

Health and Medical Facilities

A feature noticed by many foreign travellers was the good health of the local inhabitants. Fryer, writing of the mortality among the English at Bombay and the adjacent parts, says that "the country people lived to a good old age, supposed to be the reward of their temperance." Bernier also speaks of "general habits of sobriety among the people," though this did not apply to a few cases among the upper classes or the royal family. The European travellers found "less vigour among the people than in the colder climates, but greater enjoyment of health." From their accounts, even the climate would appear to have been healthy. "Gout, stone complaints in the kidneys, catarrh ... are nearly unknown; and persons who arrive in the country afflicted with any of these disorders soon experience a complete cure." The Mughal emphasis on physical fitness and encouragement of out-of-door manly games also raised the general standard of health. The ideal was that everyone was to be trained to be a soldier, a good rider, a keen shikari, and able to distinguish himself in games. Ovington found that the English at Surat were "much less vigorous and athletic in their bodies than Indians." It is possible that the drinking habits of the Europeans made them an easy prey to ill-health in the tropics.

Public hospitals had been provided in Muslim India, at least since the days of Firuz Tughluq (1351–1388), and though it would be ridiculous to compare them with the arrangements introduced by the British, the system seems to have been extended during the Mughal period. Jahangir states in his autobiography that on his accession to the throne he ordered the establishment, at government expense, of hospitals in large cities. That this order was actually made effective is shown by the records of salaries paid by the government and of grants for the distribution of medicine.

The supply of local physicians was not plentiful; and judged by the demand for European doctors, particularly surgeons, they were apparently not equal to all demands. The general health of the inhabitants suggests, however, that the medical services were not completely inadequate, and the local physicians were able to deal with normal problems. As early as 1616 they knew the important characteristics of the bubonic plague and suggested suitable preventive measures. According to an account in *Iqbal Nama,* which was written in Jahangir's reign: "When the disease was about to break out, a mouse would rush out of its hole, as if mad, and striking itself against the door and the walls of the house, would expire. If immediately after this signal the occupants left the house and went away to the jungle, their lives were safe. If otherwise, the inhabitants of the village would be spirited away by the hands of death." As modern scholars have pointed out, this observation includes two facts about the plague whose significance has been corroborated by modern science: the association of the death of rodents with the disease, and the necessity of evacuating the infected quarter.

A crude form of vaccination against smallpox seems to have been employed by Eastern doctors, for it was vaguely realized that the introduction of a mild form of cowpox prevented the virulent form of smallpox. An article in the Asiatic Register of London for 1804 contained a translation of a memorandum by Nawab Mirza Mehdi Ali Khan describing from personal observations the method adopted by a Hindu medical practitioner of Benares. A thread drenched in "the matter of a pustule on the cow" was placed on the arms of a child to cause an easy irruption, thus avoiding a virulent attack of smallpox.

In ancient times, the use of medicines had been well developed among the Hindus, but dissection was considered to be irreligious. The Muslims, who did not have this restriction, performed a number of operations. As Elphinstone pointed out: "Their surgery is as remarkableas their medicine especially when we recollect their ignorance of anatomy. They cut for the stone, couched for the cataract, and extracted the feotus from the womb, and in their early works enunciate no less than one hundred and twenty-seven surgical works." According to Manucci, Muslim surgeons could provide artificial limbs.

Social Customs

The marriage customs of Hindus and Muslims had many

similarities. Early marriages were much in vogue amongst the Hindus, with seven considered the proper age for a girl to be married. To leave a daughter unmarried beyond twelve years of age was to risk the displeasure of one's caste. The Muslims also betrothed their children between the ages of six and eight, but the marriage was generally not solemnized before they had attained the age of puberty.

Among the wealthier classes polygamy and divorce are said to have been very common. The custom of secluding women, known as purdah, was very strictly observed. Marriage negotiations were undertaken by the professional broker or the friends of either party. The marriage ceremonies were more or less the same as they are at present, and the character of the average Indian or Pakistani home and the socio-ethical ideas which influence it have not undergone any fundamental change. The son's duty to his parents and the wife's duty to her husband were viewed almost as religious obligations. "Superstitions played a prominent part in the daily life of the people. Charms were used not merely to ensnare a restive husband but also to secure such other ends as the birth of a son or cure of a disease. The fear of the evil eye was ever present ... and the young child was considered particularly susceptible. ... People believed in all sorts of omens."Astrologers were very much in demand, even at the Mughal court.

The Muslim aristocrats lived in great houses decorated with rich hangings and carpets. Their clothing was made of finest cotton or silk, decorated with gold; and they carried beautiful scimitars. There was a considerable element of ostentatious display involved in this, however, for their domestic arrangements did not match the outward splendour of their dress and equipment. Manucci, a keen observer, refers to Pathans who came to court "well-clad and well-armed, caracolling on fine horses richly caparisoned and followed by several servants," but when they reached home, divested themselves of "all this finery, and tying a scanty cloth around their loins and wrapping a rag around their head, they take their seat on a mat, and live on ... rice and lentils or badly cooked cow's flesh of low quality, which is very abundant in the Mogul country and very cheap."

The courtly manners and the elabourate etiquette of the Muslim upper classes impressed foreign visitors. In social gatherings they spoke "in a very low voice with much order, moderation, gravity, and sweetness. ... Betel and betelnut were presented to the visitors and they were escorted with much civility at the time of departure. Rigid forms were observed at meals. ... Dice was their favourite indoor game. Polo or chaugan—for which there was a special playground at Dacca—elephant-fights, hunting, excursions and picnics, were also very popular." The grandees rode in palkis, preceded by uniformed mounted servants. Many "drove in fine two-wheeled carts, carved with gilt and gold, covered in silk, and drawn by two little bulls which could race with the fastest horses."

The Position of the Hindus

The Hindu upper classes undoubtedly shared in the material culture of the Mughals, for, as already noted, they had a virtual monopoly of trade and finance. Furthermore, they had long held many high posts in the government. The contrast between the position of Hindus under the Mughals and of Indians in general under the British was often made by Indian historians during the period of the nationalist movement. Thus a Hindu historian writing in 1940 could argue that "under Shah Jahan Hindus occupied a higher status in the government than that occupied by the Indians today." The vitality of the Hindus was shown in more than their ability to maintain footholds within administrative and commercial life. Widespread religious movements, having, as we have seen, their roots partly in the vivifying contacts of Hinduism with Islam, had produced a religious enthusiasm among the masses that was transforming the older Brahmanical religion.

Although Muslim historians ignore this religious revival among the Hindus, there is enough evidence to indicate its importance during Mughal rule. The new regional literature of Bengal and Maharashtra, which owed much to the new movement, is a clear mirror of what was taking place in Hindu society. In Bengal, there was not only the rise of a new literature, but numerous temples were built during the late seventeenth century. The significance of this phenomenon becomes clear if it is remembered that practically throughout the second half of the seventeenth century, Aurangzeb was on the throne. His alleged ceaseless campaign of temple destruction obviously could have been neither thoroughgoing nor universal.

The developments in intellectual life were even more marked. The rise of Navadipa as a great center of Sanskritic learning, and the vogue of navyanyaya (new logic) belong to this period. In relation to Islam, Hinduism exhibited a new vigor, greater self-confidence, and even a spirit of defiance.

Hinduism is not generally thought of as a missionary religion, and it is often assumed that during Muslim rule conversions were only from Hinduism to Islam. This is, however, not true. Hinduism by now was very much on the offensive and was absorbing a number of Muslims. When Shah Jahan returned from Kashmir, in the sixth year of his reign, he discovered that Hindus of Bhadauri and Bhimbar were forcibly marrying Muslim girls and converting them to the Hindu faith. At death these women were cremated according to the Hindu rites. Jahangir had tried to stop this practice but with no success, and Shah Jahan also issued orders declaring such marriages unlawful. Four thousand such conversions are said to have been discovered. Many cases were also found in Gujarat and in parts of the Punjab. Partly to deal with such cases, and partly to conform to his early notions of an orthodox Muslim king, Shah Jahan established a special department to deal with conversions. After the tenth year of his reign, he seems to have ceased trying to prevent the proselytizing activities of the Hindus. There are several later cases of the conversion of Muslims, not recorded by the court historians. A number of Muslims—including at least two Muslim nobles, Mirza Salih and Mirza Haider—were converted to Hinduism by the vairagis, the wandering ascetics of the Chaitanya movement, which had become a powerful religious force in Bengal. There were also cases of conversions from Islam to Sikhism. When Guru Hargovind took up his residence at Kiratpur in the Punjab some time before 1645, he is said to have succeeded in converting a large number of Muslims. It was reported that not a Muslim was left between the hills near Kiratpur and the frontiers of Tibet and Khotan. His predecessor, Guru Arjan, had proselytized so actively that he incurred Jahangir's anger, and, as Jahangir mentions in his autobiography, the Hindu shrines of Kangra and Mathura attracted a number of Muslim pilgrims.

The Hindu position was so strong that in some places Aurangzeb's order for the collection of jizya was defied. On January 29, 1693, the officials in Malwa sent a soldier to collect jizya from a zamindar called Devi Singh. When he reached the place, Devi Singh's men fell upon him, pulled his beard and hair, and sent him back empty-handed. The emperor thereupon ordered a reduction in the jagir of Devi Singh. Earlier, another official had fared much worse. He himself proceeded to the jagir to collect the tax, but was killed by the Hindu mansabdar. Orders to destroy newly built temples met with similar opposition. A Muslim officer who was sent in 1671 to destroy temples at the ancient pilgrimage city of Ujjain was killed in a riot that broke out as he tried to carry out his orders.

Muslim historians, in order to show the extreme orthodoxy of Aurangzeb, have recorded many reports of temple destruction. On a closer scrutiny, however, there seem to be good grounds for believing that all the reports were not correct, and that quite often no action was taken on imperial orders. We read, for example, about the destruction of a certain temple at Somnath during the reign of Shah Jahan and again under Aurangzeb. It is likely that in this and in many similar cases, the temple was not destroyed on the first order. According to accounts by English merchants, Aurangzeb's officers would leave the temples standing on payment of large sums of money by the priests. However, new temples whose construction had not been authorized were often closed.

If the situation is closely examined, it appears that the complaint of Shaikh Ahmad that under Muslim rule as it existed in India, Islam was in need of greater protection than other religions does not appear to have been completely unfounded. Aurangzeb tried, of course, to reverse this trend, and some other rulers also had occasional spells of Islamic zeal, either from political or religious causes. But by and large, it is perhaps fair to say that during Muslim rule, Islam suffered from handicaps which almost outweighed the advantages it enjoyed as the religion of the ruling dynasty. This paradox becomes understandable if the basic Muslim political theory is kept in mind, under which the non-Muslim communities, so long as they paid certain taxes, were left to manage their own affairs. This local and communal autonomy severely circumscribed the sovereignty of the Muslim state, and in most matters the caste guilds and the village panchayats exercised real sovereignty, which they naturally utilized to safeguard their creed and way of life. It was this power which enabled them to evade, or even defy, unwelcome orders from the capital. A curious light on the situation is thrown by the penalties and economic losses which a Hindu had to suffer on the adoption of Islam. Practically until the end of Muslim rule, a Hindu who became a Muslim automatically lost all claim to ancestral property. This extraordinary position was a natural result of the application of Hindu law, which, according to the Muslim legal system, governed Hindu society even under Muslim government, and under which apostacy resulted in disinheritance. Shah Jahan, who began as an orthodox Muslim, tried to redress the balance by issuing orders that "family pressure should not prevent a Hindu from being admitted to Islam," and laid down that a convert should not be disinherited. Whether these orders could overcome the subtle but solid pressure of the joint family system and the power of the caste panchayats must remain a matter of speculation. The question, however, of handicaps or advantages of one community against another is not of fundamental significance. The important fact is that during normal times conditions of tolerance prevailed. This was of special interest to European visitors, almost all of whom commented on the concessions enjoyed by non-Muslims under Muslim rule. The Jesuits were critical of this policy of tolerance, declaring the destruction of Hindu temples by Muslims "a praiseworthy action," but noting their "carelessness" in allowing public performance of Hindu sacrifices and religious practices. When Akbar granted the followers of the Raushaniya sect the freedom to follow their religion, Monserrate sadly commented that "He cared little that in allowing everyone to follow his own religion he was in reality violating all religions."

Even in Aurangzeb's reign a cow could not be slaughtered in important places like Surat, and attempts made by some English merchants to obtain beef led to riots. According to one account: "In Surat the Hindus paid a fixed sum to the Mohammadans in return for sparing the cows. In 1608 a riot was caused at Surat by a drunken sailor Tom Tucker who killed a calf. Similar occurrences at Karwar and Honavar led to outbreaks, in one of which the whole factory was murdered." But nothing brings out the Mughal administration's respect for the susceptibilities of the Hindus as well as the experience of the Portuguese missionary traveler, Manrique. "In a village where he stopped for the night, one of his followers, a Musalman, killed two peacocks, birds sacred in the eyes of Hindus, and did his best to conceal the traces of his deed by burying their feathers. The sacrilege was, however, detected, the whole party arrested, and the offender sentenced to have a hand amputated, though this punishment was eventually commuted to a whipping by the local official, who explained that the emperor had taken an oath that he and his successors would let the Hindus live under their own laws and customs and tolerate no breach of them."

Although the Mughals interfered little with Hindu customs, there was one ancient practice which they sought to stop. This was sati, or the custom of widows, particularly those of the higher classes, burning themselves on their husbands' funeral pyres. Akbar had issued general orders prohibiting sati, and in one noteworthy case, personally intervened to save a Rajput princess from immolating herself on the bier of her husband. Similar efforts continued to be made in the succeeding reigns. According to the European traveler Pelsaert, governors did their best to dissuade widows from immolating themselves, but by Jahangir's orders were not allowed to withhold their sanction if the woman persisted. Tavernier, writing in the reign of Shah Jahan, observed that widows with children were not allowed in any circumstances to burn, and that in other cases governors did not readily give permission, but could be bribed to do so. Aurangzeb was most forthright in his efforts to stop sati. According to Manucci, on his return from Kashmir in December, 1663, he "issued an order that in all lands under Mughal control, never again should the officials allow a woman to be burnt." Manucci adds that "This order endures to this day." This order, though not mentioned in the formal histories, is recorded in the official guidebooks of the reign. Although the possibility of an evasion of government orders through payment of bribes existed, later European travellers record that sati was not much practiced by the end of Aurangzeb's reign. As Ovington says in his Voyage to Surat: "Since the Mahometans became Masters of the Indies, this execrable custom is much abated, and almost laid aside, by the orders which nabobs receive for suppressing and extinguishing it in all their provinces. And now it i] very rare, except it be some Rajah's wives, that the Indian women burn at all."

Any generalization about Indian history is dangerous, but the impression one gains from looking at social conditions during the Mughal period is of a society moving towards an integration of its manifold political regions, social systems, and cultural inheritances. The greatness of the Mughals consisted in part at least in the fact that the influence of their court and government permeated society, giving it a new measure of harmony. The common people suffered from poverty, disease, and the oppression of the powerful; court life was marked by intrigue and cruelty as well as by refinement of taste and elegant manners. Yet the rulers and their officials had moral standards which gave coherence to the administration and which they shared to some extent with most of their subjects. Undeniably, there were ugly scars on the face of Mughal society, but the sixteenth and seventeenth centuries had a quality of life that lent them a peculiar charm. The clearest reflection of this is seen in the creative arts of the period.

Bibliography

Adikaram, E. W.: *Early History of Buddhism in Ceylon,* D. S. Puswella, Migoda, 1946.

Agrawala, V. S.: *Shiva Mahadeva: The Great God,* Veda Academy, Varanasi, 1966.

Ahmad, Imtiaz: *State and Foreign Policy: India's Role in South Asia,* Vikas, New Delhi, 1993.

Ahmad, Jamil-ud-din: *Some Recent Speeches and Writings of Mr. Jinnah,* Lahore, Ashraf, 1952.

Aiyar, R. Krishnaswami: *Outlines of Vedaanta,* Chetana, Bombay, 1978.

Archer, W. G.: *The Kama Sutra,* Unwin Hyman, London, 1990.

Ashton, S.R. : *British Policy Towards the Indian States, 1905-1939,* London, Curzon, 1982.

Aurobindo, Sri: *Vyasa and Valmiki,* Acharya Press, Pondicherry, 1956.

Avalon, Arthur and Ellen: *Hymns to the Goddess,* Ganesh and Co., Madras, 1964.

Aziz, Ashraf: *Light of the Universe: Essays on Hindustani Film Music,* Three Essays Collective, New Delhi, 2003.

Bagchi, P. C.: *Studies in Dharmashastra,* University of Calcutta Press, Calcutta, 1939.

Bahadur, K.P.: *The Wisdom of Vedaanta,* Sterling Publishers Private Limited, New Delhi, 1996.

Banerjea, J. N.: *Pauranic and Vedanta Religion,* University of Calcutta, Calcutta, 1996.

Bankimchandra, C.: *Essentials of Dharma,* Sanskrit Book Depot, Calcutta 1979.

Basu, Manoranjan: *Dharmashastra: A General Study,* Shrimati Mira Basu, Calcutta, 1976.

Beaumont, Roger : *Sword of the Raj: The British Army in India, 1747-1947*, Indianapolis, Bobbs-Merrill, 1977.

Benjamin, Joseph : *Scheduled Castes in Indian Politics and Society*, New Delhi, Ess Ess Publications, 1989.

Bhattacharyya, B.: *Nispannayogavali of Mahapandita Abhyakara Gupta*, Oriental Institute, Baroda, 1949.

Borchert, Bruno: *Mysticism: Its History and Challenge*, Samuel Wiser, York Beach, 1994.

Bose, D. N.: *Dharmashastra: Their Philosophy and Occult Secrets*, Kali Press, Calcutta, 1965.

Bowle, John: *The Imperial Achievement: The Rise and Transformation of the British Empire*, Little, Brown, 1974.

Brockington, J. L.: *Righteous Rama: The Evolution of an Epic*, Oxford, London, 1984.

Bromley, D.: *Krishna Consciousness in the West*, Bucknell University Press, Lewisburg, 1989.

Brooks, E.: *The Original Analects: Sayings of Confucius and His Successors*. Columbia University Press, New York, 1988.

Bruhn, Klaus: *The Jina-Images of Deogarh*, MacMillan, Leiden, 1969.

Burke, Mary Louise: *Swami Vivekananda in America: New Discoveries*, Advaita Ashrama, Calcutta, 1966.

Chaudhary, M.: *Partition and the Curse of Rehabilitation*, Calcutta, Bengal Rehabilitation Organization, 1964.

Chaudhuri, Nirad: *Thy Hand, Great Anarch! India: 1921-1952*, London, Chatto & Windus, 1987.

Coomeraswamy, Ananda K.: *Buddha and the Gospel of Buddhism*, MacMillan, London, 1928.

Crawford, Cromwell S.: *Ram Mohan Roy: His Era and Ethics*, Acharya Press, New Delhi, 1984.

Dalton, Dennis : *Gandhi's Power : Nonviolence in Action*, New Delhi, OUP, 2001.

Danielou, Alain: *The Complete Kama Sutra*, Park Street Press, Rochester, 2000.

Dasgupta, Shahana: *Rani Lakshmibai: The Indian Heroine*, Rupa & Company, Calcutta, 2002.

Datta, V.N.: *Sati: Widow Burning in India*, Manohar, New Delhi, 1990.

David, M. D.: *John Wilson and his Institutions*, Mumbai, 1957.

De Bary: *Self and Society in Ming Thought*, Columbia University Press, New York, 1970.

De, Sushil Kumar: *Ancient Indian Erotics and Erotic Literature*, Firma K. L. Mukhopadhyay, Calcutta, 1959.

Deak, Istvan: *The Lawful Revolution: Louis Kossuth and the Hungarians 1848-1849*, Columbia University Press, 1979.

Dhar, Niranjan: *Vedanta and Bengal Renaissance*, Minerva Associates, Calcutta, 1977.

Dikshit, D.P. *Political History of the Chalukyas of Badami*. New Delhi: Abhinav, 1980.

Donat, K.: *Meditate the Tantric Yoga Way*, George Allen and Unwin, London, 1973.

Doniger, W.: *The Rig Veda: An Anthology*, Penguin, New York, 1981.

Duboi, Abbe: *Hindu Manners, Customs and Ceremonies*, Fifth Indian Impression, CUP, 1985.

Dwivedi, M.: *The Principal Upanishads*, Adyar Library, Madras, 1931.

Eaton, Richard M.: *Sufis of Bijapur, 1300-1700: Social Roles of Sufis in Medieval India*, Princeton University Press, Princeton, 1978.

Edwardes, Michael: *Battles of the Indian Mutiny*, London; B. T. Batsford Ltd., 1963.

Erickson, Erik H.: *Gandhi's Truth: On the Origins of Militant Nonviolence*, Norton, New York, 1970.

Farquhar, J.N.: *Modern Religious Movements in India*, Munshiram, New Delhi, 1967.

Fay, Peter Ward: *The Opium War, 1840-42*, University of North Carolina Press, 1975.

Fisher, Michael H.: *The Politics of British Annexation of India - 1757-1857*, Oxford, 1996.

Frauwallner, E..: *History of Indian Philosophy*, Motilal, Delhi, 1973.

Gambhirananda, S.: *Brahma Sutra Shamkar Bhasya*, Adavita Ashrama, Calcutta, 1977.

Gambhirananda, Swami: *Brahma Sutra Shamkar Bhasya*, Adavita Ashrama, Calcutta, 1977.

Gandhi, M. K.: *The Story of My Experiment With Trust*, Washington, Public Affairs Press, 1948.

Garbe, R.: *The Philosophy of Ancient India*, Chicago University Press, Chicago, 1899.

Goradia, Nayana: *Lord Curzon: The Last of the British Moghuls*, New Delhi, Oxford University Press, 1993.

Goudriaan, T.: *Ritual and Speculation in Early Tantrism*, State University of New York Press, New York, 1992.

Gough, A.E.: *The Philosophy of the Upanisads and Ancient Indian Metaphysics*, MacMillan, London, 1882.

Grant, G. P.: *Philosophy in the Mass Age*, Copp Clark, Toronto, 1959.

Grisenold, H.D.: *Insights into Modern Hinduism*, Oxford, New York, 1934.

Growse, F. S.: *The Ramayana of Tulasidasa*, Motilal Banarsidass, Delhi, 1995.

Gurumurthy, S. : *Hindu Heritage, Assimilative, Not Divisive*, Vigil, Madras 1993.

Haich, E.: *Sexual Energy and Yoga*, Aurora Press, New York, 1982.

Hasan, Murhirul: *Legacy of a Divided Nation: India's Muslims Since Independence*, New Delhi, Oxford, 1997.

Hasan, Mushirul: *India's Partition: Process, Strategy and Mobilization*, New Delhi, Oxford UP, 1993.

Heifetz, Hank: *The Origin of the Young God: Kalidasa's Kumara-sambhava*, University of California Press, Berkeley, 1985.

Heimann, Betty: *Facets of Indian Thought*, Geroge Allen & Unwin, London, 1964.

Heinsath, Charles: *Indian Nationalism and Hindu Social Reform*, Princeton University Press, Princeton, 1964.

Heschel, J.: *God in Search of Man: A Philosophy of Judaism*, Noonday Press, New York, 1997.

Hirschman, Edwin: *White Mutiny: The Ilbert Bill Crisis in India and the Genesis of the Indian National Congress*, New Delhi, Heritage, 1980.

Hixon, L.: *Mother of the Universe: Visions of the Goddess, Tantric Hymns of Enlightenment*, Quest Books, Wheaton, 1994.

Hopkins, J.: *Kalachakra Tantra Rite of Initiation*, Wisdom Publications, Boston, 1982.

Hopkirk, Peter: *The Great Game: The Struggle for Empire in Central Asia*, Kodansha, 1992.

Hume, R.E.: *The Thirteen Principle Upanishads*, Oxford University Press, London, 1971.

Hutchins, Francis: *Spontaneous Revolution: The Quit India Movement*, New Delhi, Manohar, 1971.

Irene, S.: *Vedic Heritage Teaching Program*. Arsha Vidya Gurukulam, Coimbatore, 1994.

Iyar, K.: *Vedanta: The Science of Reality*, Ganesh and Co., Mardas, 1930.

Iyengar, B.K.S.: *Light on the Yoga Sutras of Patanjali*, Aquarian Press, London 1993.

Jacob, K.: *Religion and Ethics in Advaita*, C.M.S. Press, Kottayam, 1982.

Jafar, Malik Muhammad: *Jinnah as a Parliamentarian*, Lahore, Afzar Publications, 1977.

Jain, Kailash Chand, *Lord Mahavira and His Times*, Saraswati Press, Delhi, 1974.

James, Lawrence: *The Rise and Fall of the British Empire*, St. Martin's, 1997.

James, Robert Rhodes: *The British Revolution, 1880-1939*, New York, Knopf, 1976.

Jean, M.: *Tantrik Yoga*, The Aquarian Press, Wellingborough, 1970.

John, B.: *Mantras: Sacred Words of Power*, George Allen and Unwin, London, 1977.

John, Elsner: *Pilgrimage: Past and Present in the World Religions*, Harvard University Press, Cambridge, 1995.

John, K.: *The Origin and Development of the State Cult of Confucius*, Paragon Book, New York, 1966.

Karmarkar, D.: *Sankara's Advaita*, Karnatak University, Dharwar, 1976.

Kaushik, Asha : *Globalization, Democracy and Culture : Situating Gandhian Alternatives*, Jaipur, Pointer, 2002.

Kaviraj, G.: *Aspects of Indian Thought*, University of Burdwan, Calcutta, 1966.

Kavlekar, K.K. : *Non-Brahmin Movement in Southern India, 1873-1949*, Kolhapur, Shivaji University, 19790

Keith, A.B. : *Rigveda Brahmanas*, Harvard University Press, Cambridge, 1920.

Keith, Arthur Berriedale: *The Religion and Philosophy of the Veda and Upanishads*, MacMillan, Delhi, 1925.

Kishwar, Madhu : *Religion at the Service of Nationalism, and Other Essays*, OUP, Delhi, 1998.

Klaus, K.: *A Survey of Hinduism*, State University of New York Press, Albany, 1989.

Knipe, M.: *Hinduism: Experiments in the Sacred*, Harper, San Francisco, 1991.

Knott, K.: *Hinduism, A Very Short Introduction*, Oxford University Press, New York, 1998.

Kosambi, D. D. : *The Culture and Civilisation of Ancient India in Historical Outline*, London, Routledge and Kegan Paul, 1956.

Kottackal, Jacob: *Religion and Ethics in Advaita*, C.M.S. Press, Kottayam, 1982.

Kuiper, F.B.J. : *Aryans in the Rigveda*, Rodopi, Amsterdam, 1991.

Kuppuswamy, Sastri S.: *Compromises in the History of Advaitic Thought*, Kalyani Press, Madras, 1940.

Louis, Fischer: *Essential Gandhi: An Anthology of His Writings*, Vintage, New York, 1983.

Low, D. A. and Brasted, Howard: *Freedom, Trauma, Continuities: Northern India and Independence*, New Delhi, Sage Publications, 1998.

Maheshwari, Shriram: *Rural Development in India: A Public Policy Approach*, New Delhi, Sage, 1995.

Makhan, L.: *The Ramayana of Valmiki*, Munshiram Manoharlal, New Delhi, 1978.

Mathew, Arnold: *Culture and Anarchy*, The University Press, Cambridge, 1935.

Mayer, A. : *Caste in an Indian Village: Change and Continuity 1954-1992*, Delhi, OUP, 1996.

Mazumder, Sukhendu : *Politico-Economic Ideas of Mahatma Gandhi: Their Relevance in the Present Day*, New Delhi, Concept Pub., 2004.

Mearns, David J.: *Shiva's Other Children: Religion and Social Identity amongst Overseas Indians*, Sage, Walnut Creek, 1995.

Mearns, J.: *Shiva's Other Children: Religion and Social Identity amongst Overseas Indians*, Sage, Walnut Creek, 1995.

Mehra, Parshotam: *A Dictionary of Modern Indian History, 1707-1947*, New Delhi, Oxford University Press, 1985.

Metcalf, Thomas R.: *The Aftermath of the Revolt: India, 1857-1870*, Princeton, Princeton University, 1964.

Mohan, K.: *The Mahabharata*, Munshiram Manoharlal, Delhi 1997.

Mookerjee, Ajit: *Kali The Feminine Force*, Thames and Hudson, London, 1988.

Mookerji, Satkari: *Modern Polity and Vedanta*, Sanskrit College, Calcutta, 1972.

Moon, Penderel: *The British Conquest and Dominion of India*, London, Duckworth, 1989.

Morris-Jones, W.H.: *The Government and Politics of India*, London, Hutchinson, 1971.

Nanda, B. R. : *Gandhi and His Critics*, Oxford University Press, Delhi, 1993.

Neale, Walter C.: *Economic Change in Rural India: Land Tenure and Reform in the United Provinces, 1800-1955*, New Haven, 1962.

Nevile, P.: *Lahore: A Sentimental Journey*, New Delhi, Penguin, 1993.

Oddie, G.A. : *Hindu and Christian in South-East India*, London, Curzon Press, 1991.

Pathak, Dr S.P.: *Jhansi during the British Rule*, Ramanand Vidya Bhawan, Delhi, 1987.

Preston, Diana: *The Boxer Rebellion*, Berkley Books, 2000.

Raimundo Panikkar: *The Vedic Experience: Mantramanjari*, Longman Todd, London, 1977.

Raja, C. Kunhan : *The Taittiriya Sarvanukramani of Yaska*, Madras, 1931.

Ramamurti, A.: *Advaitic Mysticism of Sankara*, Visvabharati, Santiniketan, 1974.

Ranajit Guha: *A Construction of Humanism in Colonial India*, CASA, Amsterdam, 1993.

Renou, Louis: *The Nature of Dharmashastra*, Walker and Co., New York, 1997.

Robson, Brian: *Sir Hugh Rose and the Central India Campaign*, Sutton Publishing Ltd for the Army Records Society, UK, 2000.

Satyapal Verma: *Role of Reason in Sankara Vedanta*, Parimal Publication, Delhi, 1992.

Savarkar, Vinayak Damodar : *The Indian War of Independence* 1857 Rajdhani Granthagar, Delhi, 1988.

Scheftelowitz, Isidor : *Die Kasmirische Rezension von Katyayanas Sarvanukramani,* Zeitschrift fur Indologie und Iranistik, 1922.

Shukla, D. N.: *Vastu-Shastra,* Motilal Banarsidass, Delhi, 1966.

Singh, Birendra Kumar: *Early Chalukyas of Vatapi, circa A.D. 500 to 757,* Delhi, Eastern Book Linkers, 1991.

Smith, Col. J. T. : *Silver and the India Exchanges,* Effingham Wilson, London, 1876.

Strauss, L.: *Political Philosophy,* The Bobbs Merrill Co., New York, 1975.

Swami Vishnu Tirtha: *Devatma Shakti,* Swami Shivom Tirth, Rishikesh, 1962.

Talageri, Shrikant : *Aryan Invasion Theory and Indian Nationalism,* Voice of India, Delhi, 1993.

Tejomayananda, Swami: *Hindu Culture: An Introduction,* Chinmaya Publications, Piercy, 1993.

Thapar, Romila : *Ashoka and the Decline of the Mauryas,* London, Oxford University Press, 1961.

Thompson, Edward: *The Making of the Indian Princes,* Oxford University Press, London, 1943.

Trautmann, Thomas R.: *Kautilya and the Arthasastra: A Statistical Study,* Leiden, Brill, 1971.

Trimingham, J.: *Sufi Orders in Islam,* Oxford University Press, New York, 1998.

Utpat, V.N.: *Riddles of Buddha and Ambedkar,* Itihas Patrika Prakashan, Thane 1988.

Vable, D.: *The Arya Samaj. Hindu without Hinduism.* Vikas Publ., Delhi, 1983.

Vedalankar, Pandit Nardev : *Basic Teachings of Hinduism,* Veda Niketan, Durban, 1978.

Visvantha, K.: *Essentials of Hinduism,* Narosa Pub. House, New Delhi, 1989.

Wendy Doniger: *Siva: The Erotic Ascetic,* Oxford University Press, Delhi, 1998.

Zaidi, A. Moin: *Evolution of Muslim political Thought in India,* New Delhi: S. Chand, 1975.

Index

R

S

T

U

V

W

□□□

Anmol
59315

12.8.11
5*5